DEDICATION

At my age, it might be more appropriate to title this page
DEADICKATION.

In order of their appearance, here are the people
to whom I owe so much:

Marie, my super mother, who hung around until she was
ninety-nine, dispensing a bottomless supply of love,
generosity, and laughter.

John, aka Boleslaw Wladyslaw Gawrychowski,
my amazing father who left the room way too early,
but before he left, he changed his name to John Gary
to spare all from an impossible spelling exercise.
He planted highly valuable seeds, seeds that took me
way too many years to cultivate and grow.

Dylan, my son, who puts the capital C in Class, Character,
and Creativity and does so much more.

Elsa, my wife, best friend, and partner, without whom
this would have been a much shorter book.

Amanda, my daughter, whose caring and adventurous
spirit makes loving her so much very easy.

In my heart, soul, and mind, I know my life has been
immeasurably enriched by these people.

Thanks Gang

Table of Contents

Prologue

I'm on lap eighty-seven of this race called LIFE, and given the life I've led, I should have been in the pits long ago, but I'm still on the track.

The fuel pump still seems to be working; the lights aren't as strong; I don't get the mileage I used to; the valves are leaking; and the suspension is off-warranty. There probably aren't too many laps left and I want my pit crew to be ready. But the race of LIFE is one in which you are not eager to get the checkered flag.

I started writing this for my family because I wanted them to know more about me; although, it's possible they already know too much.

I've always gravitated to the left and identified far more with the fringe element than the establishment. I make no apologies for that. I feel genuine compassion for the less fortunate and rage at those who would deny them their rights. I fear the world, through greed and the lust for power, is in a very critical downward spiral, and if we don't realize that, come to our senses, and take strong and immediate remedial action, we'll all lose...and the actuarial charts on life span will be written in shorthand. As you read this dissertation on my life, you may think I was trying to reach the podium in a Prince of Clowns contest or simply trying to share how much trouble my big mouth could get me in.

However, by and large, life has been extremely good to me, often despite me. But, of course, life wouldn't be life without screwing some things up, and I've done more than my share of that. The screw-ups aren't much fun while they're happening, but they usually make for a good story when they've been over for a while. I hope that's the case here.

But someday, I may be lying in a coffin in a smelly, lily-saturated room, wishing I could really read the minds of the "mourners." Some will probably fight to stay awake or try to keep the smiles off their faces, while others will be genuinely pissed at the intrusion into their busy schedules.

It'll be tough for me to be in this position and have so little to say about what's going on. I would like to read the scripts of the bereaved speaking at my memorial if they actually have one. If so, the service should be held in the morning and be spelled "mourning," just for laughs.

I don't know where they'd have it, but I'm sure my family knows that reverence is not the emotion we're looking for.

I think if we're honest with ourselves, we all seek some kind of identity...the way we'd like to be remembered. For some it may be for their business acumen; others for their artistic ability in music or art; still others for their athletic prowess, although, personally, I prefer sports that require the balls of the competitors, like skiing and motorcycle racing, to the sports using manufactured balls, like baseball. But for me, I'd like to be remembered for my humor. I'd like people to think, or even dare to say, "He was a funny guy." I'd rather be a success at the Comedy Store than at Yankee Stadium or Carnegie Hall. After reading this, I hope you'll agree.

I may be getting ahead of myself here, but I wanted to start at the end with a few simple requests so that my family will be prepared to honor the deceased's last wishes.

SOMEBODY TELL ME A JOKE. I SURE COULD USE A LAUGH.

That's the sign I want on my coffin should the family choose to put me on display in all my rigor mortis glory. But please don't feel sorry for me. There are some advantages to that condition. First, I'll get all the rest I need. No more fighting for those six to eight hours that the medical profession says are so important to good health. Second, I will no longer have to get up to pee a few times in the middle of the night.

Prologue

The next consideration for the event is venue. Definitely not a church. I think it might be slightly hypocritical. I'm not agnostic. In fact, I feel I am spiritual. It's between God and me. I just can't abide by all those religious clubs and their rules. This is undoubtedly because of being brought up a Catholic, which I feel makes me an expert on the subject. Maybe a comedy club, or one of the small screens at a movie theatre. That way mourners could appease their grief with popcorn.

My Attire: Please don't drag out the tie and jacket. I know they could stand some use but that's not me. I originally thought maybe one of the cool leather jackets my wife, Elsa, gave me, but I'd rather they be given to someone who is cold. And leather may be overdressing for a crematorium. Perhaps it would be more appropriate to have one of the traditional black T-shirts. I always wore black as camouflage for being overweight, but I assume embalming is a genuine thinning process, so I guess any color is OK. I know most of my T-shirts are old enough to vote but try and pick one of the later models.

The Service: Keep it light, not necessarily truthful, but light. More like a roast than a funeral. If you want music, see if you can book Robert Earl Keen to do an acoustic version of *The Road Goes On Forever And The Party Never Ends*. If anyone sings *Amazing Grace,* it better be Grace.

As a fond farewell to my Catholic roots, you might consider taking up a collection and giving the loot to a charity that does good work for those who need it. I think selling commemorative T-shirts might be going a bit too far, but they could be hot items among those grateful for my disappearing act.

The Guest List: Please don't invite the ones that are so important and insanely busy that they spend the entire time impatiently looking at their watches or viewing porn on their iPhones instead of grieving over my passing.

The Ashes: If it's not asking too much, I'd like some placed in the three places that meant the most to me...Malibu, Park City, and New York or Brooklyn (where it all started). In Malibu, on the sand or the rocks on the beach somewhere along Malibu Road. In Park City, I'd like my remains scattered to the wind at the top of the Sterling chair and maybe some in Round Valley. New York poses a greater problem and I guess it could be Prospect Park or a sewer. If all that is too much of a pain in the ass, just donate them to our Dyson vacuum cleaner.

Wait a minute. I'm getting way ahead of myself here. Let's start at the beginning.

ONE
Off And Running...
In The Wrong Direction

"Oh shit! I was afraid this would happen," I muttered as I took the letter from Villanova out of the mailbox and read it. Like everything else in my life at that point, I'd given it little thought, but now I was holding reality in my hand, and it was worse than I had imagined. Four Fs and two Ds don't exactly get you a scholarship to grad school. Later in life, I would laughingly explain to friends that I didn't understand how they could give me these grades when I had passed all my classes. Then one of my classmates informed me that I was also expected to drop in. I guess Villanova, where I had recently completed my junior year in the business school, felt it had given me all the learning I could absorb, and I was free to pursue other options with my life. The worst part of it all was telling my mother that the first person in the family, for whom she had sacrificed so much, would not be getting a college degree. It was the hardest thing I'd ever had to do.

I should've seen the writing on the wall. Early in my freshman year, I was told to meet with the Dean of Admissions. I assumed it would be an invitation to speak at a St. Mary's High School assembly because Villanova was proving to be a popular choice among its seniors, and what could be a stronger recommendation than an actual graduate extolling Villanova's virtues (poor choice of a word) to St. Mary's seniors? Wrong! He told me that if he'd had the results of my New York State Regents exams, given to all high school seniors, I wouldn't have been

allowed into Villanova. And, from that day on, I was on academic probation. Turns out he may have been psychic.

Villanova is a Catholic college that supposedly outlawed drinking.
That was a laugh! I wondered what the results would be if the entire
school was given a breathalyzer test on a Friday night. They'd have to
change the rule or have a plethora of empty dorm rooms. Late one night
at the end of my freshman year, when a couple of us had obviously made
Jose Cuervo a happy man, a few priests were being dropped off by what
we presumed were donors, and they came upon our choral group shout-
ing off key after a rather wet evening. We were instructed to see the
Dean of Men first thing the next morning. Nice to be getting to know all
the deans. The Dean of Men thought that our meeting was at 9:00 a.m.,
but I assumed it was as soon as I regained consciousness. When I finally arrived, after a brief conversation, he told me, "Gary, there are three
kinds of people who should not drink. The Irish, the compulsive, and the
creative."

"BINGO!" I responded with a smile.

He saw no humor in that and bellowed, "Gary, you are not fit to live
with Christian gentlemen!"

"Do you have any idea where I could find some?" I laughed.

That was my second mistake. He smiled ironically. "You may look for
them anywhere, except on campus. You are banned from living on campus in the future, and you are now also on behavioral probation!"

So, my college career was off to a great start. Beginning in my sophomore year, I would have classes to attend, but nowhere to sleep other than in class. But one night during the summer, I ran into another
Villanova attendee named Bob Morrow at the Dome, my favorite home-
town bar in Manhasset on Long Island. When we started talking, I laughingly explained my situation, and he immediately remedied it.

He and a few other savvy guys had rented a mansion on a ten-acre
estate in neighboring Bryn Mawr from some old trust funder guy whose
parents had been highly successful real estate developers. He had

decided that the family had all worked very hard and that it was time for someone to take a break, so he retired from a job he never had. But being an alcoholic can consume a lot of money, so he rented his big house to us and became a roommate.

The place, like the owner, had seen its best years, and it was a strong candidate to be featured in a monthly issue of Architectural Disgust. We operated the household as a co-op and shared chores. Overall, it was cheaper than living on campus. It was also more dangerous for me. With absolutely no responsible supervision, I immediately assumed the role of an absentee student. I was at the mansion reading Hemingway when my classmates were solving accounting problems. So, I got out of college in three years. I make jokes about it to cover my embarrassment, but it's not funny at all. At the time, I actually felt worse for my mother than I did for myself. She deserved better.

Naturally, after my expulsion, I sought solace on a bar stool at the Dome. Manhasset, at the time, was a wannabe town, and the Dome was a respite for those who didn't wannabe. It was a joint, my kind of place. Also, I had started enjoying a drink or two—or more—in high school and was still trying to perfect the craft.

The Dome's habitues included attorneys, businessmen, workers, and some of us college-aged kids. You might see an alcoholic attorney in deep conversation with Echo the garbage man or a college athlete getting his ass kicked on the bowling machine by Al the mailman. The only qualifications for appearing in the nightly sitcoms were a good vocabulary, a cutting sense of humor, and a cynical view of the world. For the major players, every night was open call where many had recurring starring roles while others simply had walk-on parts. We college guys were the Junior League.

Presiding over it all was Ed Bullis, aka The Bull. He owned the place and was the ringmaster. He had a good sense of humor and appreciated the lunacy taking place on the other side of the bar, but he was a responsible adult and he put limits on it.

JUST ANOTHER DICK

Among the stars of the show were Joe Sylvester, who graduated from Notre Dame cum laude in medicine and promptly opened an auto body repair shop on the premise that he was still curing ills, but the patients couldn't talk. One night, he was seen on a pay phone asking the operator if she could change a twenty.

There was Elliott Walter, with a vocabulary that would make Daniel Webster feel at home. After a brilliant college career, Elliot got a job sweeping streets so he could bid his father a cheerful "Good morning" as Dad walked to the train to fulfill his duties as the president of Macy's.

There was Duncan Smith, whom someone had named Drunken Smith. I think he preferred Smitty. One night, or early morning, Smitty and I shared a ride with police officers to a meeting at the local station house.

One guy you didn't see around there anymore was Jeff, who very stupidly brought an underage girl into the Dome one night. We all respected The Bull and the last thing we wanted was for him to lose his ABC license, forcing us to disgrace ourselves elsewhere, so we collectively ratted Jeff out to him. The Bull asked him if he knew his date was too young to drink legally, and Jeff replied, "I don't ask my dates to show me their birth certificates before we go out." The Bull kicked them both out and told Jeff that if he ever wanted to drink there again, he should show up at 2:00 p.m. on Saturday for his trial.

On Saturday, The Bull served as judge, and to stress the importance of the trial, he slapped a white wig on his head. The trial opened with Elliot, as prosecutor, asking, "Weren't you at all suspicious when she kept going to the ladies' room to change her diaper?"

Meanwhile, The Bull provided the jury with free beer, but because he didn't want the trial to drag on for days, he eventually cut us off. Jeff was found guilty and fined fifteen dollars, which he had to spend there before he could get a drink himself. Beer at the time was fifteen cents a glass and Jeff wanted to pay off his fine quickly, so he ordered a round on the house. Not one person accepted it. The lesson: Don't fuck with The Bull.

So, here I was at the Dome for the summer, between my junior year and eternity. Let's say my mood wasn't too positive (given my latest academic recognition) and one night, my dazzling repartee finally really pissed The Bull off. He'd had enough of me for a while, so he reacted by banishing me from the bar for the entire summer. In reality, he knew my situation and I think he was disappointed in me. He saw my potential and felt I was on a fast track to nowhere. He was actually trying to help me. To me, it was like refusing a convicted killer a parole.

So, two days later, I was hitchhiking on the New Jersey Turnpike with Dick Dalrymple en route to Atlantic City. I sometimes called him Damon D (as in Dalrymple) because his wise remarks reminded me of Damon Runyon, the hilarious, wisecracking journalist and mid-century writer who practically invented slang and gave his characters unusual names like Nathan Detroit, a guy named Nathan who practiced his subterfuge in Detroit. Rymple fed me more good lines than The Bull served me beers (almost).

Other than our destination, we had no further plans, so when we got there, we stopped in at a bar called Eddie's Shamrock Inn, owned by a Villanova friend's father, to get a bit of advice on the town. I left there with a job as a bartender in a state where I was not old enough to legally drink. Rymple eventually got a job as a night clerk in a shabby hotel with an elegant name, the Richfield Boscobel, so our accommodations were handled.

There's an old song, *On The Boardwalk In Atlantic City,* that extols the beauty of this "enchanting, romantic city." Actually, Atlantic City was a dump. They should have rented it out for wars because everything there was already broken. The sand looked old and gray; the ocean bored and listless, like if it knew of a better place, it would go there. Eddie's made the Dome look like the Four Seasons. There was a large round bar with the primary illumination coming from neon beer signs and the occasional burst of sun through the dirty windows. But it attracted a good-sized crowd for shots and beers. One time, a woman came in and asked for a Manhattan. From the response she got, you'd think mixing a Manhattan required the skills of a graduate physicist. So, it made learning my bartending skills fast and easy: pour the shot, put the glass under the beer tap and fill it.

To give you an idea of the bar's elegant patrons, the owner decided to bring in a band to play behind the bar over Labor Day Weekend. Business was brisk and all the bartenders worked long hours. When it was over, we split all the tips. We each got $1.50.

Since I worked mostly days, I found an additional way to further enrich myself. The Boardwalk was still home to the Steel Pier where this dirty, rickety old wooden structure pulled the tourists in to see horses "dive" into the filthy ocean. And there was no shortage of characters, like the guy who rode his bicycle around the Boardwalk in a clown's suit, juggling as he rode. I named him Dropsy. I think he wanted to drop me.

The Boardwalk was also littered with an endless variety of hot dog stands, arcade games, and carny booths. I got a nighttime job as a shill at a carny booth. A shill is perhaps the lowest form of predator in the entire marketing chain. The one I worked at sold Power Paks, little plastic things that went on your carburetor to give you "faster starting, smoother idling, more miles per gallon." They cost two bucks each. My job was to stand in the crowd during the pitch and at a certain point, when the pitchman said, "I don't know how fast you drive. That's between you, the speed cop, and the undertaker," I would pop up to buy one and all the mooches would follow suit. Not exactly great training for future fame and fortune in business.

One day, I got an unexpected but pleasurable jolt when Carol, someone you'll read more about in upcoming pages, walked into the bar. We'd had an on-again-off-again relationship for about five years starting in high school. I didn't even know she knew where I was, but I was stoked to see her. Yet, of course, it didn't last. She watched me in action behind the bar, and after a while, she started to cry, got up, and left. I really couldn't blame her. Here was the guy she was supposed to be in love with. I got kicked out of college and was tending a bar in a dump for a bunch of misfits and seeming to enjoy it, all without any future.

Eddie's closed for the winter the day after Labor Day, and that's when Rymple and I headed home. Our first stop once we returned was the Dome. I entered with trepidation and took a stool. The Bull welcomed me, knowing how I'd spent the summer.

"Is the summer over?" I fearfully asked.

He smiled at my signature cheekiness. "Welcome back," he said. "First one's on me. What'll you have?"

"A rainbow pousse café," I answered. That's the world's most difficult drink to make. Few bartenders, and only in super upscale restaurants, can do it, and it's very expensive. It consists of five liqueurs of varying density carefully poured into a glass to form the look of a rainbow.

The Bull's response, "Goddam it. You're still an asshole. You're getting a beer." And that's when I knew I was back among the living.

TWO
Hello World!

How did I wind up there? Let's look at my academic beginnings at St. Mary's Elementary School. It's fair to say I was not a Rhodes Scholar right out of the box, and I imagine there were days the nuns wished I'd hit the road.

My first problem was that I was left-handed, a major no-no according to the nuns.

They called it "malvado," meaning "evil" in Spanish, and they set out to rid us of that curse. There was fear at the time that trying to change from left to right could cause stuttering, but that did not seem to be their primary concern.

Another problem for us lefties was writing. In those days, before ballpoints, you wrote with ink, and the inkwell was in the upper right-hand side of the desk, so when we filled our pens and began to write from left to right on the page, our hands blurred all the ink.

In second grade, I was one of the few in my class who had not yet mastered the art of reading. I guess I felt that enough kids knew how, so I figured I didn't need to. But after a meeting with my teacher, Mom decided to change that and sat me down every night to teach me to read. As a result, I won a class-wide oratorical contest in the fourth grade, narrowly beating out Mary Lou Roach, who I assume has since taken her life from the sheer humiliation. The prize should have been given to my mother.

When I was about eight or nine, all the kids went to the movies on Saturday afternoon to see a mix of cartoons, a serial, and a feature about our nation's invincibility in WWII that was then in progress—if progress is the proper word for a war. One Saturday after the movie, I saw my ride, i.e., my mother, parked right across the street and I ran to meet her. I did not see the car coming. The driver tried mightily to stop but ran into me instead. Fortunately, he was going slow enough that he only knocked me down. I didn't break anything, but it was close. When I emerged from my prone position under the car, I had dusty tire marks on my forehead and road rash all over. And Mom got to see it all. Instead of the hospital, we went to a soda fountain where she medicated me with an ice cream sundae.

When I went to school on Monday, as we were walking in, the Mother Superior took one look at me, and in her most sarcastic, gravelly voice said, "Whatever happened to you?"

I replied, "I was run over by a car."

"That's dumb," she answered.

So much for the gift of charity. I hope she was doing better on faith and hope.

As a kid, I was never that great at sports. I usually displayed my incompetence at baseball and basketball; although, I was okay at football, where you can get lost in the crowd. Later in life, I did get respectable at the sports I liked, such as skiing and water skiing, sailing on a twin-hull Hobie, and maybe best of all, motorcycling. All speed-oriented, single-person sports, no teams, and with maybe an element of danger.

One sport I did get fairly good at in sixth grade was the sling shot. Unfortunately, my only targets were streetlights. However, one of our more security-minded neighbors objected to my removing lighting from the area and leaving broken glass on the street. She shared that thought with the police. Mom, Dad, and I got an invitation to spend a joyous evening in court chatting about it. Fortunately, the judge dismissed it as a childish prank and gave me a strict admonition to take up another sport. That was like a love song compared to Dad's war chant when we left.

Given my lack of success at sports, I decided my skills could best be maximized in the entrepreneurial arena. That career started when I was ten years old. My buddy Duke and I decided to start a beverage business where we'd concoct some cool drinks, throw them into my baby carriage, and go sell them to the construction workers at a new development near us. What they really wanted was beer. So, ever attentive to the desires of our clientele, we'd steal some from Duke's father (who bought beer by the case) and try to satisfy the needs of our clientele. We found that the return on investment on stolen goods was far greater than on purchased or manufactured ones. Fortunately, Duke's father didn't inventory his beer, or he might have turned himself into a rehabilitation center.

My next limited-future position was as a pin boy at a bowling alley. This was before automation and the pin boy's job was to put up all the pins our customers knocked down. This was achieved by pressing a pedal; ten pins would pop up to designate the correct positions for the remaining pins and you'd place them on the pop-up pins, thus the name "pin boy." However, sometimes I'd skip that step with the pedal and just put the pins up. One night, a bowler suspected an inconsistency in the pin lineup and asked me to step on the pedal. I did and the pins fell down. "STRIKE," I yelled...and I was then free to seek other employment.

All in all, despite a couple of setbacks, it was an idyllic childhood, but life changed dramatically for me when I was nine. Dad, who had suffered from rheumatic fever as a child, had a massive heart attack at the age of thirty-eight. But he was a tough son-of-a- bitch, and he tried to keep working. My mother would drive him to work in New York City every day.

His father died when he was fifteen, so he had to quit high school and go to work to help support the family. He had risen from stockboy at W&J Sloane, an upscale furniture company, to General Manager of a ten-story furniture manufacturing and warehouse facility. Despite tremendous and painful effort on his part, he had to quit at age forty. When he did, to show the respect they had for him, his employees chipped in and bought him a television, the second one in our entire neighborhood.

Our dining room became his hospital room, with hospital bed and oxygen tank. We also had a supply of morphine to lessen his constant pain, and that's where I failed him. I was only nine and I was afraid of hurting him with the needle, and that must have hurt him more. Mom had to get a job. Women in those days didn't work, so she had the unfavorable distinction of being the only woman in the neighborhood with a job.

Before television, we spent our Friday nights listening to the radio, my favorite show was *It Pays To Be Ignorant*. I even remember one of the jokes. When a contestant was asked what his job was, he replied, "I'm an airplane mechanic in a clothing store. I take care of the hangars."

So, after Dad's heart attack, my life was an incredibly different situation from any of the other kids in the neighborhood, and Mom felt sorry for me. To compensate, after our evening stick ball games, she would take us all to the local pharmacy and try to medicate me with ice cream, and I wound up wearing those tasty flavors all over my growing body.

Without Dad's income, money was tight, and we had an extra bedroom, so Mom decided to rent it out. Our first tenant was Phil, a recently divorced, ruddy guy in his early fifties, who still wanted to call Manhasset home. He was a good man with one major flaw. He fished. But he wasn't one of those plebians who stands on a pier and listlessly hangs his rod over the side waiting for a miracle. No, Phil was a surf fisherman, one of the hardy souls who dress in chest-high waders, a hooded poncho, and a searchlight on his head and stand in the freezing waters of the Atlantic Ocean for hours on end in the middle of the night, casting some poor dead eel on the end of his line out into the ocean, hoping for a blue fish or striped bass to chomp down on it so he could have it for dinner.

I had never fished, but it seemed like it beat baseball. Meanwhile, my mother and Phil contrived a plan where, due to Dad's illness, Phil would become my surrogate father. He invited me to go with him to Montauk Point, a vacant lighthouse on the ocean at the very end of Long Island, for a weekend of fishing. Despite my reticence to jump into one more sport that I might suck at, I was stoked for a new adventure. Friday afternoon, we hopped into Phil's new Cadillac and set off. The suburbs morphed into farmlands, became sand dunes, and three hours later we arrived in Montauk.

I couldn't wait to get to the motel, have my own room, and watch unsupervised television until the morning light seeped through the windows.

"Where's the motel," I naively asked?

"You're riding in it," he proudly responded.

"Shit," I said to myself. "The Cadillac Motel."

We stopped in a restaurant for dinner, and I ordered a burger and fries. I could see the look of disappointment on Phil's face when I didn't go for the seafood special.

When we finished dinner, we headed for the Montauk lighthouse, that erstwhile beacon of safety for seafaring men of another age. We parked the Cadillac Motel in the lot and the fun began. Phil dressed up in his surf fishing attire and me in my sneakers, shorts, and a T-shirt. Phil foraged in the trunk until he found a junior fishing rod, which he presented to me with a bit of ceremony, kind of like a mafia boss formally inducting a junior hoodlum into La Costa Nostra for making his bones by fatally stabbing an elderly widow in the back.

Phil gave me a quick introductory course in rodmanship and explained that we'd be using lures instead of eels because the bait shop was closed.

Now it was SHOWTIME! We waded into the water and the fun began. Fun, that is, *if* you enjoyed standing in freezing water at night in shorts and getting knocked over by maverick waves, endlessly casting the feathered lures out, fruitlessly trying to attract fish that apparently had no desire to have feathers for dinner.

Around midnight, I decided I'd try to beat hypothermia and asked to be excused to retire to the Cadillac Motel. Phill assented, but I could see the disappointment on his face. I went to sleep knowing I wasn't pleasing my new surrogate dad and hoping I wouldn't jump up and hit my head on the steering wheel.

That lasted until around four in the morning when "Dad" woke me up to go fishing again.

"You must be shitting me," I cried.

Hello World!

He wasn't, but we had that father-son "be a man" conversation. "Come on, sleepy head," he goaded, "get up and get your stuff on," as in my soaked sneakers, shorts, and T-shirt. "Those fish are waiting." From the results thus far, I assumed those fish had great patience.

Morning finally came without a single blue fish showing up, but I did see a beach buggy gliding along the sand with its top filled with blues, so at least I knew the species was not extinct. After breakfast, we headed for the bait shop to get some eels. I regarded them as close cousins to my greatest fear, snakes.

The bait shop, with apologies to Otis Redding, was on the dock of the bay and Phil bought a bunch of eels...live eels.

"But they're alive," I protested.

"Not for long," he retorted.

I stupidly and naively said, "How can you fish with a live eel?"

"You can't. You kill 'em first."

"You're going to kill the eels?"

"WE'RE going to kill them." He saw the expression on my face and said, "It'll make a man out of you."

I seriously doubted killing an unarmed eel was the rite of passage to manhood. I really didn't want to kill any eels, but I did want to be a man, and I felt that, given Phil's attitude, if I didn't give it a shot, I might wind up as bait myself.

The procedure to kill an eel was to pick up this slimy, snake-like sea urchin and, with all your might, slam it down on the wooden dock like a dirty rope, repeating the process over and over until the eel was mercifully dead and fit for bait.

Afterward, there was no ceremony to welcome me into the Men's Club.

After breakfast on Sunday, the trip back to Manhasset was very quiet. I hoped I had proven to be an incurable wimp, but Phil was not finished with his surrogate father role. This was just the start of an endless summer of fishing, which, when ended, corresponded to the end of my fishing career.

So, I transferred my business skills to caddying at a local golf course. This was well before the emergence of golf carts. Each caddy would carry two bags for eighteen holes and get three dollars a bag. Once, at age twelve or thirteen, when the caddy master was out of caddies, I got to carry four bags while the foursome of golfers each labored under the weight of one club. I should have gotten rich out of sympathy, but I still only got twelve dollars.

Another impediment to riches was the card games for money, which went on in the bullpen while the caddies waited to get a "loop." I was the youngest and most naïve of the bunch. These guys had all been around the block a few times. Unfortunately, one of my professional brethren would sometimes bring a deck of cards featuring nudes on the back of each. So, after two loops and thirty-six holes, I might walk home broke because I fell in love with the three of clubs.

Since caddying was seasonal, I preferred a job with year-round stability, so I became a newspaper boy, delivering Newsday, a relatively new Long Island daily, on my bike every day to those people kind enough to subscribe and naive enough to think they would actually get the paper every day.

Eighth grade finally came to a merciful close, and I couldn't wait for high school.

THREE
High School...Not Such A High

Maybe one of the good things about your very early years is you don't remember much. But when you get into high school, you remember everything, especially the stuff you'd like to forget. High school is a coming of age. It's when guys think we are totally adult and blazingly cool. Others feel we are barely out of pre-pubescence and have reached what will possibly be the most disgusting and annoying stage of our lives. It's a time of discovery and the very early stages of independence. And it's the golden opportunity to make more mistakes than a mathematically challenged accountant.

St. Mary's High was a distant second choice for me. I wanted to escape the religious fanaticism and go to Manhasset High, but I was overruled by Mom and Dad, perhaps because I was given a scholarship. It was embarrassing. I think it was more out of sympathy than scholastic excellence; the school administrators feeling sorry because of the strain my father's illness put on our finances. I think I deserved that as much as Donald Trump deserved to be President.

Nevertheless, there were two major improvements when I entered St. Mary's High. First, we were going to be taught by "brothers" instead of nuns. They were mostly young, seemingly good guys, and they were probably better suited to deal with male teenagers than the nuns. However, I thought they might have set the bar too low when they chose the brotherhood over becoming a priest. The girls were segregated and still had nuns.

The second benefit was that there was no athletic field on which to flaunt my incompetence, but I still had to deal with basketball. So, during sophomore year, I found a solution. I joined a gang. A better name than gang might have been group. We called ourselves the *Flying Aces* that some non-members translated to the *Flying Asses* or *Heck's Angels*.

We tried to pattern ourselves after the Amboy Dukes, a famous gang enshrined in literature at the time. That might have been translated to the Amboy Dicks. We instilled fear in nobody.

I figured high school probably was where the real money was, so I became active in the business arena but was a bit stagnant in the academic field. I had to quit my newspaper route because nobody with any cool could be seen riding a bicycle. But at fourteen, you became eligible to get employment papers and I jumped on it.

I landed a job as a dishwasher at a popular restaurant. I never could understand why people waited an hour in line to get in and then seemed to take about three bites of their meal, pay the check and leave. Initially, not believing in wasting food, I'd try and finish the meal for them. That didn't last long before I realized that if I kept it up, I'd look like the Graf Zeppelin.

Once again, as upward mobility seemed to be calling, I jumped ship at the restaurant and went to work as a stock boy and gift wrapper at Lane Bryant, a small store specializing in large women. My mentor was Gene, a tall, strong African American who taught me the ropes and had my back when I screwed up.

Manhasset was a cloistered community, as in white Christians, except for the Valley, the poor section where the Black people lived. Back then, there were NO people of color attending St. Mary's, but the Valley might have been good missionary territory. That was my first experience in being color blind. I never understood how Christians, strong believers in a perfect God, could reconcile that one race was superior to another. Did God create man on a racist basis or are we all truly equal regardless of skin color?

High School...Not Such A High

St. Mary's served Manhasset and a few neighboring towns as well as parts of Queens that were considered ghettos by the upscale Manhassetites. But they soon became the sartorial leaders because they dressed tough, gang-like, a look I immediately adopted.

I was super excited by the social aspects of high school, but I also did want to learn another language. Unfortunately, for the first three years, the only "choice" was Latin. So, the only opportunity for a conversation would have been with a two-thousand-year-old priest.

I did have an unusual social life. When I was fifteen, my Uncle Art was dating Liz, the secretary to the Schuberts, owners of virtually all Broadway theatres. They'd give me tickets to hot Broadway shows so, after school, a friend and I would take the train to New York, have a couple drinks and dinner at the Biltmore, where the waiters obviously had difficulty judging age, see a blockbuster play, and then take the train home. Very urban.

Junior year was an influential milestone. Her name was Carol. She was so beautiful that, in my mind, I thought she hung the moon. In those early days, to me, looks seemed far more important than intelligence, humor, or integrity, but she had plenty of each. I couldn't believe it when she became my girlfriend. She was a freshman when we met, so perhaps she hadn't seen the array of talent available to her. It may have been puppy love but, to me, it was a big-ass Bernese Mountain dog, and it lived on and off for five or six years.

Carol was a dutiful, obedient Catholic who respected authority. She would sometimes babysit, and I thought that would be party time. Put the kids to bed and make out all night. But her mom issued orders that I was not to be in the house and Carol obeyed them, possibly missing out on becoming the only mother in her class.

The summer between junior and senior years was pretty cool. I had a job, a girlfriend, and some free time, much of which was spent at Jones Beach, a highly popular spot on the ocean. It was so much better when we could go there with our girlfriends instead of our parents. I think parenting must be the most thankless job in the world. No appreciation.

Meanwhile, my mother, still the only working woman in the neighborhood, left the dress shop where she worked and got a job as a salesperson at my father's alma mater, W&J Sloane, which had opened a retail store in Manhasset. It wasn't just sympathy, like my scholarship, she was a damn good salesperson, honest and knowledgeable.

Unfortunately, Dad's health was deteriorating, and what he had was never going to get better, only worse. I guess I had gotten used to it and thought it would go on forever, but early in the morning of November 22, 1952, it all changed. My mother woke me up at 5:30 a.m. "Richard, come with me. Quick. I think your father's gone." We raced downstairs and found him sitting up in his hospital bed with his head on his chest, dribble coming from his mouth, and he had turned blue. Dad had passed. He was forty-seven; I was fifteen. His death was merciful, at least for him. He was a strong, self-made man with a potentially brilliant future, lying in a hospital bed for almost nine years, breathing through an oxygen mask, waiting for the next shot of morphine to deaden the pain, with no future other than death. Despite his short life, I didn't realize it at the time, but he had made his mark on me, for which I am extremely grateful.

Nevertheless, at fifteen, life moves on, and ten days after the funeral, I turned sixteen and got my learner's permit to drive—legally, for a change. I already knew how and, fortunately, my mother saw little difference between a permit and a license, so I frequently got behind the wheel after school.

Every day, if I wasn't at work stocking shelves, I'd walk over to Sloane's, pick up the car, and take off on an endless cruise up and down the town's main street, checking out the cool girls who were patrolling the sidewalks on their way to nowhere and fully aware of the guys in the cars. In addition, I had become an auto racing fan and practiced my skills wherever and whenever possible.

Mom got off work at 5:30 p.m., but since I was frequently not there to pick her up, she would join a couple of the other salespeople and the manager for drinks at a nearby Chinese restaurant. As soon as my hectic schedule allowed, I would join them for the festivities, have a few drinks with her and the boys, and head home with a brain totally sated and in no need of further education, a fact soon reflected on my report cards.

Truth be told, I had, despite my self-awarded perception of worldliness, led a sheltered life. Just as I'd never been exposed to minorities, I knew nothing of gay people, other than the cruel epithets directed at them in those days. Other than Mom, virtually all the salespeople and the manager at W&J Sloane were gay. They loved my mother and she them. They were her social life and we had weekend parties at the house. I didn't know I wasn't supposed to like these guys, but I did. They were smart and fun to be with, and I got to drink on school nights. I'm happy for these experiences, because later in life, I have had no prejudices regarding gay people. I strongly support gay causes and despise those who would look down on them. There is no difference between gay and straight people, other than gay people traditionally have far better taste and generally a better sense of humor. Once again, I do not believe that when God created man, he did it with a caste system. Thank you, Mom, for that gift too.

Then came senior year. There were a couple of highlights. We found a whole new use for cars. They became mere transportation that got us to the beach where we could park at night and neck with our girlfriends. We referred to it as watching submarine races. There were also parties, but most of the focus was on college admission. Except for me. College wasn't a top discussion item at our house since no one had ever been to one.

I had no thoughts or preferences on the subject and did no investigation. Kind of sad when you think that's where you'll spend the next four formative years of your young life and get the educational grounding for the rest of your life.

I was having a conversation about it with one of my best friends, Jimmy Stewart, aka Stoogie, and he said, "I'm going to apply for the engineering school at Villanova."

"Where's that?" I asked.

"Jesus, Dick, it's a college outside of Philadelphia with a great engineering school."

"What is it that engineers do for a living?"

"You must be kidding. They build bridges, tunnels, buildings, all kinds of shit."

"Okay, I'll go along with the gag." And I did. We both applied and both were rejected, which was fortunate as I had about as much interest in building tunnels as I did in fishing. We both re-applied to the Commerce & Finance (business) school there and were fortunately accepted, as it was the only school to which I applied. I later learned that in recognition of its ease of entrance and highly manageable academic standards, C & F was referred to as the Comic & Frolic School.

There was a luncheonette called Jim and Joe's right across the street from St. Mary's. It soon became GHQ for the less academically inclined. For a few of us, it became our home room. This fallacy was powerfully demonstrated one day when our homeroom teacher, Brother Kieran, unexpectedly dropped in when we were supposed to be drinking in knowledge at the actual school instead of cokes at Jim and Joe's. He escorted us across the street to his real classroom where, in round one, we spent the entire afternoon writing and re-writing the same sentence, the subject of which had to do with responsibility. He then told us to return at seven for round two.

Unfortunately, this episode had been preceded by a visit from my mother to the school Principal, Brother Nicholas, at which time she expressed concern about my discipline, or lack of same. She felt that without a father's restraining influence, I might be getting a bit too wild. She advised him that if I needed discipline, she would go along with it. That was like telling a professional thief the bank's alarm was broken. This message was apparently transmitted to Brother Kieran.

I arrived at seven and met Brother Kieran. He was a handsome man in his thirties, a little over six feet tall, dark hair, a good build, a sense of humor, and as I soon learned, a vastly exaggerated sense of discipline. He led me into the faculty room where he closed the door, pulled down the shades and said, "I don't want the neighbors to see this." With that, he pulled out an old-fashioned barber's strop, a piece of leather about a yard long and a couple of inches wide that barbers used to sharpen their razors. He doubled it over and said, "Hold out your right hand. When you get tired, switch hands." I did and he wound up and brought it down on my hand with great force. And great pain. I soon changed hands, repeatedly. He probably gave me about twenty good shots, but I wasn't counting. When he was done, he told me to go wash up. When I pushed the soap dispenser with my hand, it shot back from pain. Both hands eventually turned black and blue and swelled up, but I wasn't about to share the experience with my mother. However, on one of her regular visits to Brother Nicholas, he brought up the subject and she was shocked to hear it. "He didn't tell you?" he questioned.

"No," she quietly admitted.

"Well then, he took his punishment like a man." To quote Beretta, "If you can't do the time, don't do the crime." But why pay twice for the same crime?

At the time, New York State had equivalency exams for all seniors at the end of the academic year called Regents Exams. Great effort went into the preparation for them, but my attitude was that I had already been accepted to college, so why sweat it? This philosophy was quite evident in my scores.

Had my father still been alive, I would have the scars to show for my conduct, but Mom was easy going and still compensating for Dad's passing, so I continued to get away with murder. However, her humiliations were not to go quietly into the night. Graduation night was going to be a big deal, with a party after the ceremony at our house for family and friends. Uncle Art would be in attendance. His marriage to Liz, now his ex-wife and formerly my ticket broker at Schuberts, had ended in a flurry of booze-filled invective and he was now toting his new girlfriend, who I laughingly referred to as Aunt Dana, a Southern belle who had probably been attractive in an earlier iteration before the hard laps piled on. My first meeting with Aunt Dana was at the graduation. He introduced me and, instead of a friendly handshake, she kissed me and stuck her tongue down my throat.

"I'm going to love Aunt Dana," I thought.

Naturally, I had been too busy with party preparations to remember to give my mother the tickets to the ceremony, so she was frantically roaming the halls of St. Mary's to find the classroom where she could get the tickets from me.

We were having what was probably our one-hundredth and last practice before the actual ceremony. As Mom was about to arrive at the classroom, she could hear Brother Hugh giving final instructions.

"If you have won a scholarship, stand when your name is called. If you have won multiple scholarships, stand each time your name is called."

And then she heard my reply and his retort.

From me, "You mean I'm going to be on my feet all night?"

From him, "Gary, if you had applied yourself and done your job as you could have instead of jerking around all year, you would be on your feet all night, but not to worry, that's not your problem tonight."

Poor Marie! Those were the last words she heard before her son's high school career came to a merciful end.

FOUR
Now What?

Fall of 1957 came and my buddies all headed to their senior year of college, but not me. Here I was with my whole life in front of me. I had a choice to make. What direction did I want to choose? Wall Street? Sales? Entertainment? I decided what the country needed most was prompt mail delivery, so I revived my career with the Post Office that had begun on Christmas vacations in college. But given my education, I was elevated to Window Clerk, a savage responsibility where I was tasked with getting packages to national and worldwide locations and answering a lot of stupid questions in the process. It was there I learned that honesty does not always pay, and sarcasm pays less.

When a woman pointedly asked what the best way was to get a package to Flushing, less than ten miles away, quickly, safely, and securely, I recommended she take it herself.

In those days, air mail, especially the overseas variety, was very expensive, so most international senders preferred the slower seagoing method. One day, a woman showed up with a carefully wrapped package headed for Southampton, England via boat. She informed me she didn't want the package buried on some tramp steamer and advised me the Queen Mary was leaving New York for Southampton on Friday and that she would like her package on that ship.

"No problem," I replied. "Any particular stateroom you prefer?"

It turns out both women shared their experience with the Postmaster. His reaction was to take me off the window and give me a mail route to carry. As punishment, he assigned me to what he thought was the least desirable route. Spinney Hill, home to the town's African American population. But to me, it was great because the homes were smaller and closer together, so there was less walking.

To handle my transportation, I needed a car. Given that I was making two bucks an hour, money was obviously no problem. I was an avid auto racing freak. Sports cars, as they were then called, were a relatively new phenomenon in the country. They were small, fast, super handling, and immensely fun to drive. Far more appealing than a Plymouth. I spoke with a friend, Don Stearns, a former race driver. The result? I wound up with a heavily financed 1954 Austin Healey. I was ecstatic, but not for long. After the initial thrill of driving the super cool wheels wore off, I referred to the Healey as my Indy car. It never ran five hundred miles without frequent pit stops. I could afford the payments, but not the repairs, so I traded down to a 1955 Morgan and spent many joyous hours on twisting roads, sliding, double clutching, basically doing a poor imitation of my hero, Juan Manuel Fangio, the Argentine Formula 1 World Champion Mercedes driver. I may not have known who won the world series, but I could tell you the record time Tazio Nuvolari, the incomparable Italian racer, recorded on the Frankfurt to Darmstadt Autobahn. The Morgan had a wooden frame, the only car on the road that was susceptible to termites. The top didn't come down; it came off, and the bonnet over the engine also came off, so I could ride around town like I was emulating those pioneer race drivers like Barney Oldfield. But, unfortunately, like all English cars of the day, it required a lot of attention, and I was not going to put another mechanic's kid through college, so I sold it. It's probably worth a fortune today.

I still had to get to work every day. Ah! How about a motorcycle? I had never even ridden on one, but I figured they can't be that expensive. Never did I dream it would become a life changing experience for me. I again went to my mentor for direction. Don's educated suggestion led to Ghost Motorcycle Sales in Port Washington, a dealer that specialized in high-performance foreign bikes. From the stock on hand, Don recommended a Velocette, an obscure English bike with an impressive competition record. It was a 500cc machine with a knobby tire on back and a bash plate under the engine block, so it was good off road as well as on. In reality, it was too much for a novice, but I figured I could learn. At least I hoped I could, but first I had to buy it.

The Ghost's real name was Sal de Feo. He got the Ghost handle riding his bike through town, standing on the seat with his arms widespread and a white cape flowing from his neck. In business, he was known as a tough negotiator.

"How much do you want for the Velocette, Sal?" I asked.

"Six hundred dollars."

"Wow! That's too much." (Remember, this is 1957.) "I'll give you five hundred.," I countered.

"You can give me five hundred, but you won't get the bike."

"Jesus Sal, it's fucking snowing. You'd have to put out a missing persons alarm to find a customer."

"Yeah, but the snow will melt, and I'll still have the Velocette, and I'll sell it for six hundred. You're a cheap bastard, but I tell you what I'll do. I'll throw in a lesson." So, as the Harley guys would say, I bought my first crotch rocket.

When the snow melted, it was time for the lesson, and I had a lot to learn. Turns out the Ghost may not have had a PhD in education. We went to a local beach that wasn't too busy in the winter and unloaded the Velo. He explained the functions of the various pedals, levers, and handgrips. Then he explained the intricacies of starting the cantankerous beast.

Throughout it all, The Ghost was laughing his ass off at my efforts, like he was at a comedy show and I was the entertainer. Nevertheless, I somehow got the bike started and I was ready. It was time for the most critical part of the lesson: driving it.

"Hop on Sal," I yelled over the roar of the engine.

"Are you fucking dreaming?" was his reply. "Throw me about a million and I'll think about it." Given Sal's love of lucre, that seemed like an accurate request, so I was now alone as he hopped in his truck, waved to me, and drove off.

JUST ANOTHER DICK

Unless your IQ is in single digits, the concept of getting on a two-wheel vehicle that goes over a hundred miles an hour with nothing between you and the pavement is at least intimidating, if not terrifying, and this was before we had to waste all that money on helmets. I soon learned why bikers wore the leathers that so closely identified them with thugs. When you fell, leather felt better coming off than skin. But that lesson was for another day.

Time for the reality check! I revved the engine, shifted into first gear, gave it some gas, and got one of the greatest thrills of my life! The Velo heard me and took off at what felt like breakneck speeds. I don't think "breakneck" is the best word to use, but it does describe the feeling. I was waiting to hear the sound barrier break. When it came time to turn, it's safe to say my style in no way resembled that of the racers who go so fast that when they come to turns, they lean over so far their shoulders are almost touching the ground. But I hoped to get there one day. I never did, but I wouldn't trade the experience for anything.

Perhaps the greatest benefit of my Post Office job was that, in addition to my window work and mail delivery, I was also driving Post Office trucks, so I had a government driver's license. I had gotten comfortable on the bike and constantly tested its performance. The result was I was getting stopped virtually once a week for speeding or some other offense. I would show the cop my government license and he would say something like, "I'm going to let you go. We civil servants can't afford these traffic fines."

I have one more bike story. I, like most of my friends, was an auto racing fanatic and followed it closely, especially the European Formula 1 races. One evening, as I was headed home from an interlude with Mom and the gang from Sloane's, I saw my friend Walt waving to me to pull over. He was with another guy. I looked closer. OH MY GOD, it was Dan Gurney! Dan was a former Manhassetite who you could say had moved on, as he had just signed to drive for Ferrari in Europe. I almost climaxed. He was a few years older, but I'd been following his career trajectory. I would rather have met him than Sophia Loren, the very sexy Italian actress with whom I was in love at the time.

Now What?

I was beside myself (which may have put me in bad company). Walt said he and Dan were going to the Dome and then he was going to take him to the airport for his flight back to Europe, and he asked me to join them. I was ecstatic and a bit high. I took off for the Dome like the green flag had dropped and I was in the Gran Prix of Monaco. Then I came to the horseshoe turn that a road crew had recently sanded, and the bike and I parted company. Over it went, and I followed it into the curb. I wasn't seriously hurt but I had road rash all over my body including my head. I got back on the bike and when I got to the Dome, my clothes were in tatters, and I needed a few bandages. I settled for a few beers, and Walt and I drove my hero to the airport. What a night! The hell with the blood. More to come later.

As fall morphed into winter, I realized that perhaps mail delivery would not be my life's work and I'd better get my ass back to college. Since I was adept at setting the bar low, I enrolled as a day student at CW Post College in Westbury, a short distance from Manhasset. It was a new school with non-existent entrance requirements for day students at the time. My kind of college, and I could still work nights at the Post Office.

Unfortunately, my experience at Villanova set the tone for my short tenure at CW Post. The Velocette was far more reliable than I was about getting to the school. At some point, it became clear that if I didn't have time to get to the school, taking finals would be another waste of my time. At least I was paying this time, so I wasn't causing any additional financial stress to Mom. The single event that finalized that decision was a doozy.

CW Post was located on the former estate of the Post family, noted for infusing children's tummies with Post Toasties and other highly nutritious breakfast cereals. A part of the estate, for some obscure reason, had been devoted to potato storage, a crop for which Long Island was famous. It was perhaps one step lower on the fame spectrum than Atlantic City's Saltwater Taffy. Potatoes are stored in underground garages for longer life.

The garage on campus was then serving as the Music Appreciation "classroom." I had elected to take that course so as not to put too great a strain on my intellect. Unbeknownst to me, the professor, who I felt sorry for having to teach in a potato house, had a strong reputation in the industry. In any event, it was my first class of the day. It was near the end of the semester, and through no fault of the Velocette, on this particular day, like many others, I was arriving late. So, I decided to ride over to the potato house and park on the dirt bank above the entry ramp. Unfortunately, a word used frequently in this tome, since it was a beautiful day, the Professor had decided to move the turntable out in front of the garage, about ten feet below the dirt bank. I roared in on the very loud Velo, put it into a slide and rained dirt down on the turntable. From the look I got, there was no encore this time. It was my last class at CW Post.

Summer came and my buddies returned from their academic labors toting degrees. It's fair to say that did little for my ego. They were on the way to successful futures, and I was licking stamps.

My commute was a bit longer because Mom had sold the Manhasset house, rented an apartment in Port Washington, and built a house in Water Mill, a tiny town between Southampton and Bridgehampton on Eastern Long Island. It was a small but charming place right on Mecox Bay.

I had taken up water skiing, compliments of my friend Joe Krajewski, a local Grecian god with a Polish name and a fabulous boat. Joe had amazing waterskiing skills and Mecox Bay was a perfect spot for it. The water was as calm as glass in the early evening and you felt like you were cutting through butter. Joe taught me everything and even brought a guy up from Cypress Gardens to put in a slalom course. Despite my earlier athletic failings, I got pretty good at waterskiing. I absolutely loved crouching down, leaning over and going through the course on one ski at speed.

Toward the end of the 1958 summer, after my glorious career development experience in Atlantic City, a very cool thing occurred.

Carol, my high school sweetheart, and I, despite my apparent lack of a future, still had a powerful mutual attraction; although, we hadn't been practicing it lately. At the end of the summer, when I returned, she re-entered my life. We rekindled our romance with high energy and this time we felt it was for keeps. She was straight, religious, responsible, and ethical. I could only be charged with being ethical. We were an odd couple but felt we really loved each other, and it seemed to be working.

One evening, we had a summit meeting about our future. We decided we would get married. But first, we had a couple of significant details to work out. She had two more years of college, and I had two tasks of my own: military service (the draft still being in force) and finally getting that college degree. Since it was already August, it was too late to matriculate at any college that might have me. Thus, we decided on option number one: two years of active duty with Uncle Sam. At the time, you didn't have to wait to be drafted, you could volunteer and go when you wanted. I said I'd sign up the very next day and Carol was ecstatic.

After I dropped her off, I immediately went to the Dome where I spent the rest of the night downing free beers and getting the razzing of my life. When I woke up the next morning, I felt the entire cast of Stomp was performing in my head and my mouth tasted like I had ingested a basketful of bad clams. My first cogent thought was," No fucking way am I signing up for the draft today, unless I can immediately go on sick call."

However, I consider myself a man of my word and Carol was the woman of my dreams. So, I left the safety and security of my bed, showered off some of the detritus from the previous evening, avoided terminal vomiting by skipping breakfast and got to the Draft Board Office in Great Neck without getting a DUI.

My internment date was exactly four weeks away and I wanted to start enjoying them. It was a beautiful day; I was in ebullient spirits, proud of myself for keeping my word and moving one big step towards lifelong happiness. I thought perhaps I already deserved a medal.

I decided to stop at Carol's on the way home, share the news, and get the living started. It was early. Her mother got Carol up and my future wife looked terrific as usual, especially for having just gotten out of bed, something I would be sharing with her in the future.

"Let's go to the beach," I joyfully suggested.

She squinted and looked at me with faint disgust.

"Anything wrong?" I asked.

"Just that you never do anything you say you're going to do. Didn't you have something on your agenda for today?"

"Done!" I exalted. "In just twenty-eight days, I will officially be Private Gary, U.S. Army. But right now, we're both pale and the sun's out. I don't want to show up at Fort Dix looking like a ghost, so let's hit it."

Sold! Her look brightened; I got a smile and a secret kiss, and off we went. We hit the beach and stretched out on the blanket in anticipation of a lazy, romantic day. I started to think of all the things we could do in the next four weeks.

"Let's go out to Water Mill the weekend after next, do some beaching and hang out at Mom's place, just the two of us. She'll be away for the weekend."

"I can't the weekend after next."

"How come?"

"Paul is going to be in town, and I promised I'd see him." Paul was my stand-in for some of the times our relationship was on hiatus.

"What? Well, I expect that given the circumstances, you can get out of that."

"I promised him a long time ago."

"Like when we weren't speaking? Jesus Christ!! That was before we got ENGAGED. Why don't you call him and advise him of the new development and see if he still wants to see you? I bet he'll understand. I know I would."

"Dick, I promised. He's been gone and he'll only be back for a few days."

Now the sun wasn't nearly as hot as my temper. "Let's put this in perspective. Last night, we decided to get MARRIED. I got up this morning and signed away two years of my fucking LIFE...and you can't break a date with a guy you won't be seeing anymore anyway? Is that the deal? You can't be serious."

"It's not such a big deal. It won't affect us in any way. It's only a couple of days and then we can be together until I go back to school."

Now What?

"It's a goddamn HUGE deal! You gotta be shitting me. I can't believe this is happening." But I knew it was happening, and while I was saying this, I thought, *Can I possibly get out of the mistake I made this morning? Maybe I can explain I was only kidding…and then I can go to jail instead of Fort Dix. I'm gonna give it one more shot.*

"Carol, I made a huge commitment this morning, *for us.* I'm asking you to make a small one now, *for me.* Nobody in the world would criticize you for it. I'm going away for TWO YEARS in the Army, and I don't have a choice. How about it?"

"Dick, I can't. Please understand."

"Well, I don't. Get your shit. I'm taking you home and you can spend the next two weeks getting ready for Paul."

That was it, the shortest engagement in history, sixteen hours. At least I didn't buy a ring. It's possible I acted hastily. Perhaps she was just doing what she felt was right, but I felt like a total schmuck, emotionally naked, hurt badly, my pride shredded. The hurt battled the anger for center stage.

Now, all these years later, it's just a funny Dear Dick story. Carol was—and still is—a good person. We were simply so wrong for each other that we did each other a favor. It was euthanasia. When I returned from the service, I bumped into her one day. She was very pregnant, and I was very single, so it worked out for both of us.

The four weeks went fast. As a last gesture of insanity, after my pre-induction bash at the Dome, I parked my mother's car perpendicular in a parallel parking space and was awarded an appropriate citation and an invitation to attend the presentation ceremony. However, I was unable to attend as I would be out of town on military business.

FIVE
Private Gary Reporting For Duty

September 20, 1958 was a great day for our nation and its military, a day the nation became stronger and safer. It was the day I entered the Army.

Early that morning, my mother rousted me from my pre-induction celebration and drove me to the draft office in Great Neck (what genius thought up that name?) where we said our farewells, she with a tear in her eye. If I were her, I'd be jumping for joy. Her beloved son was finally going to learn some discipline or get his ass kicked.

My fellow draftees and I were then bused to Whitehall Street, the way station for new recruits in downtown New York, for the first rituals of military service: the physicals and our swearing-in. Many of us were of mixed opinions on that issue. If we failed the physical, we could just go home, but failure could indicate a serious medical issue. However, a hangover did not meet the qualifications for early release. I passed my physical and thought that if you weren't lying on a stretcher, you were now a private in the Army.

We were sworn in, boarded another bus, and were whisked away to that garden spot of New Jersey, Fort Dix, for eight weeks of basic training with the emphasis on basic. I had never killed anyone and was not particularly interested in learning the tricks of the trade.

The first order of business for inductees at Fort Dix (another interesting name but perhaps appropriate in this case) was to be stripped of any shred of individuality we might have brought with us in order to be transformed into a cohesive force of fighting men. To achieve this, we lined up at the "Barber Shop." There were the tough guys, unshaven with long hair, the preppies with that well-coifed Ivy League look and the African Americans with their wild Afros. When we emerged, we all were practically bald and looked like we were leaving a chemotherapy session.

Next were the inoculations. Apparently, you needed a multitude to serve in this man's Army. They lined us up like we were at the DMV, a more desirous choice, and marched us through a line of medics, one on the right side and one on the left, each puncturing our arms and depositing their serum as we passed by.

Next stop? Sartorial splendor! Uniforms! After that, we all looked alike, and we were then assigned to a Company, about forty men, for the duration of our basic training. "Basic training" is an apt description of what was in store for most of us, at least for those of us who had not spent our lives climbing over forty-foot ladders, crawling under machine gun fire, and other niceties. But I must stress, this was peacetime, long before we engaged in endless wars with no winner. I expect the attitudes of the heroes entering the service today are far different, and I respect, admire, and thank them. They are in a war; we were in a sitcom. There was nobody to kill. Our strategic mission should have been using that time to perfect our real purpose: keeping the jeeps clean and cigarette butts off the grass.

Our Company, all forty of us, shared a single room in a barracks. The major domo, the man charged with bending, molding, pushing, prodding, threatening, and stamping us out as ruthless killers was First Sergeant Raymer. He had no first name, at least not for us, but he exercised his license to torment with great acumen, and achieved his goals through a process of exhaustion, humiliation, threats, and DISCIPLINE. Basic training was also known as boot camp, another misnomer as I certainly didn't get a kick out of it but was perfectly willing to get booted out.

Raymer had eight weeks to transform a bunch of wimpy mama's boys into a highly trained fighting unit. The days of walking were over. We now marched everywhere in tight formation, sometimes singing military ditties that were designed to help keep us in step, like:

Jody was there when I left

You're right
Sound off one...two
Cadence count three...four
Sound off one two three four...one two...three four

Snappy lyrics. Took a while to learn, but somehow, it never made the charts. I also didn't understand the concept of everyone having to be in step. It seemed unnecessary if we all got to where we were going at about the same time.

One thing I did like was the extremely graphic and highly descriptive military lingo. For instance, when we were policing an area, i.e., picking up junk from the ground, we'd hear the Sergeant's refrain, "All I want to see is elbows and assholes." Interspersed were homilies like, "You're so stupid, you couldn't find a menstruatin' elephant in a snowbank," and the familiar ode about attractive women, "I'd eat a mile of her shit just to bite it off at the ass."

Reveille was every day at 5:00 a.m. to the sonorous tones of a sergeant bellowing, "Drop your cocks and grab your socks." Up in the middle of the night to march to nowhere at a breakneck pace, with the background noise of the sergeants yelling and screaming threats. To hear them ranting, you'd think the enemy had just breached the gates of Fort Dix.

"Nowhere" was always some godforsaken spot miles from the barracks. We were required to carry our rifles, canteens, and loads of other stuff we wouldn't need. After an hour or so, we'd stop and the sergeant would yell, "Take ten; expect five; get two," followed by, "Light 'em up if ya' got 'em, fuck ya if ya don't." On these pitstops, we'd be sweating like crazy, and I was always surprised the water in my canteen was still cold.

We'd finally arrive at our destination for a day of learning to shoot the guns we were carrying. OOPS! They were weapons, not guns, as the sergeant graphically explained with this ditty; "This is my rifle (pointing to it), and this is my gun (pointing to his crotch). This one's for war and this one's for fun." Next, we'd crawl on our bellies under live machine gun fire forty inches above the ground, definitely not a good time to get up to go to the restroom.

One of the real treats at Uncle Sam's Disneyland was a forty-foot-high "ladder" about eight feet wide. I hate heights, and forty feet up is damn high for me. I'd rather be crawling under the machine gun fire than climbing up this ladder, but I was not consulted on my preferences. I had to go up this thing step-by-step and not look down. At the top, the trick was to swing your leg over the top rung and thread your way down the other side. I didn't quite understand the tactical reason for that exercise, as I'd never seen our troops in war films climbing over forty-foot walls with steps in them.

While there were many things of which I questioned the logic, the one I never questioned was why the building in which our food was prepared and served was called the "mess hall." One meal there and you'd agree.

But the most fevered insanity was reserved for the cleaning of the barracks. They must be immaculate at all times. Beds, or bunks, must be made so tightly and precisely that if you dropped a quarter on the bed, it would bounce up. I never quite understood the tactical thinking behind that one either.

By about midway in our training, we would get a "weekend pass" on a Saturday. The cleanest barracks got to leave at noon instead of three. Short weekend, but Friday nights were supposed to be devoted to cleaning. I suggested to a couple of buddies that we shitcan the cleaning and go over to the Enlisted Men's Club for a couple of pissy 3.2 beers.

They looked at me in horror. "What about the inspection?"

I countered with, "For crissake, these fucking barracks have been cleaned every night since 1942. They ain't gettin' any cleaner. You comin'?"

Toward the end of the eight weeks, we were given a real weekend pass, starting Friday. But, of course, before we left, we were given a briefing by Sergeant Raymer.

"OK, now you assholes are trained fighting men. You don't have to take shit from anyone. Anyone gives you shit, you whack the fuck out of them. Got me? Be proud; be Army. Now get the hell out."

I couldn't wait to get home and beat the shit out of my friends.

One of the final features of basic was the "job fair" where we were given choices of jobs we'd never get and asked to select our favorite, which would be the one we'd perform for the next two years. This is called your MOS (Military Occupational Specialty). Virtually nobody gets what they ask for, but disappointment is low because expectations are even lower. The job they were pushing was paratrooper. It was a three-week training of which it was said the first week the men were separated from the boys; the second week the boys were separated from the idiots; and the third week the idiots jumped. I passed on that job.

Another choice was Heavy Rocket Crewman. This one appealed to me because if it was really heavy, I wouldn't have to carry it; I could ride on it, but then I realized that when we got to our destination, I'd have to wash it.

So, I applied to be a clerk. In blatant disregard for my preference, I was selected to be an MP. Imagine! Me, a cop. I wonder what thinking went into that one. Maybe they were looking for guys who they thought might have the greatest familiarity with police procedures.

Nevertheless, after eight weeks of torture, I emerged as a "man", prepared to defend my country and whip anyone who doubted my intentions.

The only thing missing was an enemy.

I bade a tearless farewell to Sergeant Raymer and his macabre training rituals and hopped on a military plane headed for advanced basic training at Fort Gordon, Georgia. Advanced Basic. Does that term remind you of a jumbo shrimp?

This was my first airplane ride. Perhaps my biggest fear in life up until then was snakes, and the idea of eight weeks in Georgia was horrifying. As we neared the Augusta airport, I looked out the window down at the swamps below. In my mind it was seething with rattlers, but after a bumpy, uncomfortable ride, we arrived safely in Augusta.

On the bus to the base, I kept peering out the window, half expecting to see snakes dancing in the woods as we passed. When I got off the bus, I kind of jumped forward in case one was lurking underneath it. As I landed, I looked up and there on the side of a barracks was a huge sign that read BEWARE OF POISONOUS SNAKES, complete with pictures of four different species.

Welcome to Georgia!

MP training was very different from basic, although there was still a lot of running around with shit on our backs. One change was that the lyrics to the same basic training song changed to:

Though we think that we are tops

We're just a bunch of dirty cops.
Sound off one two, etc.

We were also now learning a trade and it certainly was not singing. We were becoming Military Policeman. A lot of the guys were stoked about this career opportunity, especially the younger ones (I was rapidly aging at age twenty-one). The idea of all that spit, polish, and authority appealed strongly to some, but I always wondered just how much authority a private in the Army could really have, MP or not. Imagine being arrested by a seventeen-year-old. But the choice wasn't mine, so I went along with the joke and tried to be as invisible as possible.

The one job I could not avoid was KP, Kitchen Police, another term for dishwashing and cleaning the kitchen in the mess hall after meals, something we all had to do. Even with my prior restaurant experience, I was not seriously motivated to make the pots and pans sparkle. And I didn't get the "police" as part of the name. You couldn't arrest a dirty plate.

My work apparently didn't impress the mess sergeant. How would you like that to be your title? He finally asked me, "What the fuck did you do in civilian life?"

"I was a race car driver," I lied, hoping that would give me male stature with him.

"Yeah? Well get your ass in gear and get this shithouse cleaned up." No matter how hard I tried, I couldn't please this guy, so I stopped trying and let the military way of thinking take over.

Lunch that day was baked chicken, cooked in enormous tin baking pans. The chicken was coated in breadcrumbs and other shit, and I knew that if I spent the rest of my military career trying to clean those pans, it still wouldn't be good enough for the sergeant. So, I got creative, and simply stacked them together, took them outside and deposited them in the garbage. He never missed them. No arrest, no conviction.

Between bouts of stupidity, we were learning to be policemen. We got to drive jeeps, the official vehicle of MPs, and I must admit that my first time behind the wheel was a blast. We also learned how to clean, shoot, and clean our pistols again and again; how to approach a vehicle that you stopped (always from the rear so nobody could shoot you or, at worst, so you couldn't see him shoot you); the proper way to frisk an arrestee; and many more procedures that I hoped I'd never need.

Between our fourth and fifth weeks of MP training, Christmas came, and we all got two weeks leave. Fearful of our behavior in the company of civilians, our leaders prepared us for leave with a series of films. In one, a young man walked up a snowy path to a gaily decorated house with the Christmas tune, "I'll Be Home For Christmas" playing strongly in the background. He opened the door, entered the home, looked around the festively decorated living room, and the first thing he saw was a coffin with a young soldier in uniform occupying it and a small sign on the coffin that read, "Merry Christmas Mom & Dad, from Jim." The army really knows how to get you in the holiday spirit.

Interestingly, Carol had reappeared in letters to me, and I had responded. Why not give it another shot with a romantic evening while I'm home on leave? She was up for it. I miraculously got two tickets to the original *West Side Story* on Broadway. I figured I'd close the sale with some sexy singer entertaining us at a table at the Copacabana. *West*

Private Gary Reporting For Duty

Side Story was sensational, and I thought *for sure* I was on the road to a successful re-engagement.

Unfortunately, a singer was missing in action at the Copa. Commanding the stage was Señor Wences, a ventriloquist who painted his hand to look like a person and then had, what many thought was hilarious, a conversation with his hand. So much for a romantic evening.

When I returned to Fort Gordon, I had four more weeks of MP training. All I had learned was that Army food was not hard to pass up and I was losing a significant amount of weight. My uniform no longer looked like I was wearing a Halloween costume and it felt good. And, of course, my knowledge of military law was expanding exponentially.

Around the seventh week, we got our orders telling us where we would be stationed for the duration of our service. There were basically three choices: a base somewhere in the U.S., an all-expense-paid trip to Korea for a nine-month stint, or Germany for the remainder of my service, about twenty months. I had fervently hoped for Germany. I saw little difference between Korea and Alabama, but the idea of Europe was highly enticing. And I got it! Europe!!! Very few Americans travelled abroad in those days. It was considered a luxury of the rich. I was totally stoked. And I was going via plane, albeit military, but who cared. Beats the hell out of a military transport ship. I flew back to Fort Dix and boarded a plane for Germany.

SIX
Willkomen In Deutschland

I was assigned to the 101st MP Company of the 4th Armored Division, a unit much respected for its heroic performance in WWII under the command of the legendary General George Patton. Most Armored Divisions have a nickname like "Old Ironsides" or something very combative. The 4th Armored had none, with its veterans saying, "The name's enough." I imagine if you'd had to fight them, you'd probably grudgingly agree.

By 1959, the war had been over for almost fifteen years, but there were still many telltale signs in Germany, including bombed-out buildings and shortages of personal items. But the nation was making incredible strides to once again becoming a world power.

The 4th A.D. was headquartered in Goppingen, about twenty miles from Stuttgart, with Combat Command outposts in Ulm, Crailsheim, Nürnberg, Erlangen, and Schwabisch Gmund.

On arriving in Germany, our first stop was Frankfurt. We were housed at a military installation, a way station from which troops went on to their various destinations. On our first night there, we were given a pass to see the town, but were not authorized to travel more than four blocks from the base. Well, there had probably been hundreds of thousands of GIs like me passing through that center. Those four blocks were so Americanized I might as well have been in Tulsa.

Upon arriving in Goppingen via train, I was sent to a Replacement Depot before joining my unit. Some, like me, were just arriving, and some were going home. It turned out to be a very educational opportunity for me because I got to talk to some of the guys heading home who had been in the 101st MPs, and I received excellent advice from one.

"You want to get ahead in the MPs? Forget it. You won't. The MOS (Military Occupational Specialty) for MPs is frozen. That means you won't get promotions (not a big concern for me). So, screw the promotions, have a good time, and then get the hell out, like me." In English, what that means is if you excel, keep your nose clean and kiss the proper asses until they are puckered, you might make Corporal and get about twenty bucks a month more, but miss all the fun. Tough decision.

He also explained how MPs had it so good. There were two primary jobs: supporting the troops in the field on maneuvers and working with the USAEUR (United States Army in Europe) MPs on town patrol, which is essentially local police work, both in Goppingen and at the Combat Commands. There weren't a lot of maneuvers at that time, except when the entire division went to Grafenwohr, a hellhole near the then Communist-controlled Czech border, to play war games.

On town patrol, you worked eight hours on and twenty-four off. The main task was breaking up bar fights. That didn't appeal to me too much, but the advantages of being a street MP (in a jeep) far outweighed the disadvantages of sitting in an office all day, so I no longer yearned to be a clerk.

Thus, when I arrived at Company Headquarters of the 101st, one of the first things that occurred was my placement interview with the Company Commander, a captain. This determined what my job would be for the next twenty months.

"I see here you're interested in being a clerk?" he questioned. "I just happen to need one."

Oh shit! How do I get out of this?

"Well, sir, I originally thought that would be good for me in later life. But after being selected for MP duty and studying at Fort Gordon, I became highly interested in police work, and I'm now possibly considering it as a career, even a possible re-enlistment." Somehow, I kept a straight face through all this. The rough translation was, "I just want to fuck off for twenty months, enjoy myself, do as little as possible and get the hell out."

"That's great!" he replied enthusiastically. "I'm glad the Army could help you find a career." So, I escaped having to kiss his ass on a regular basis and work eight to five daily.

He was less impressed later when he discussed savings bonds with me. In those days, a Private made one hundred dollars a month including overseas pay. The Army felt anyone spending this kind of money must be profligate. Coincidentally, one of the gradients for COs was the amount of savings they coerced from their troops. The more money saved, the better it looked for them. The recommended amount for each soldier was $6.25 per month which earned you, after three months, a savings bond worth twenty-five dollars at its maturity ten years hence. Not exactly a handsome retirement fund, but a lot of guys did it.

On that first payday, when it got to me, he asked, "Private Gary, would you like to open a savings bond account?"

"No thank you, sir."

"May I ask why not? These bonds give you financial security."

"Well, sir, I spoke with my family's investment advisor who said that even if I saved every penny the Army paid me, I wouldn't have enough to buy a cheap used car when I got out, so his advice was to pass." Please understand, I barely knew what a financial advisor was, but my limited knowledge still put me way in front of the rest of my family who had probably never even heard of an investment advisor because we never had anything to invest. But I thought it sounded good and positioned me as a man of independent means.

Apparently, the Captain disagreed. Later, the new Company Clerk, my apparent successor and a budding buddy, advised me off the record that I was now on the Captain's shit list, so I changed my tune.

At the next payday, he asked, "Gary, I assume I can't interest you in a savings bond."

I told him, "Sir, the hell with the family advisor, I want to save now."

"That's wonderful," he smiled. "I assume you'll want the $6.25 a month bond."

"No sir. I really want to save. I want a seventy-five-dollar bond EVERY month." That's about nine times what the average guy saved. I also told him I wanted it sent to me. So, when I got it, I'd cash it immediately, eschewing all those long-term gains. I was a little short for a couple of months, but I made up for it by creating goodwill with our German hosts by supplying them with the necessities lacking in their lives. More on that later.

The barracks in Germany were a big step up from the flimsy wooden structures in the U.S. that looked like they were an unsuccessful experiment in affordable living. In Germany, the Third Reich, planning on many millennia of world domination, built structures that were designed to last. A major benefit of these dwellings was that the bedrooms accommodated two or four rather than forty occupants. Much better sleeping without the sound of your roommates' farting to accompany you on your nocturnal trip into the arms of Morpheus.

In retrospect, I think the Army was a valuable experience. It brought together young men of all races, creeds, and backgrounds from all parts of the nation, from the deep South to the North and West, from college graduates to high school dropouts, and we all had to learn to live and work together. I believe that if we, as a country, could learn to keep our weapons in the closet, the draft would be a good thing for young men, and if the military could be made to understand that rape is not an acceptable part of the training, it would work better for women too.

When I was in the service, civil rights and segregation were finally becoming national issues. One of the guys in my platoon was from Alabama; damn proud of it and was not at all in favor of integrated schools, and he expressed it rather vociferously to me. I told him, "Man, I don't blame you. I think it would be a crime after all these years of segregation to allow Black people into your classrooms and then find out they're smarter than you." Let's just say he and I were never close after that, which was fine by me.

JUST ANOTHER DICK

The 101st MP company was comprised of four platoons. Each had four squads of ten, led by a sergeant. I was assigned to Sergeant Dupont's squad. He was a tough guy, about five foot eight, slightly rounder than the shape preferred in the military manual, but with a chest-full of ribbons earned the hard way in Korea. He had a good sense of humor, not too much formal education, but lots of street smarts. He had figured out the Army long ago and had a realistic approach to military service. He had survived war; peace should be easy.

The nightly patrols consisted of two MPs in a jeep. On my first night, I got to ride with Dupont. We cruised the town, Goppingen, checked out a few bars, and then a call came in on the radio. "Manhood Bravo One, this is Manhood Bravo. Proceed at once to dependent housing area, Unit 24B. A stabbing has been reported at the unit. Manhood Bravo out."

To explain dependent housing, career military men, Officers, and NCOs (non-commissioned officers, e.g., sergeants), were allowed to bring their families when stationed in Europe as the typical tour of duty was two years and that long a separation did many interesting things to a marriage. In all its military sensitivity, wives were officially referred to as dependents. This was long before Gloria Steinem showed up on the scene with better ideas.

Upon receiving the radio call, Dupont hauled ass to the dependent housing area. I was scared shitless. How could this be happening to me, a kid brought up in the protective environment of a pretentious middle-class town, and now racing to get involved in a stabbing on a military base in a foreign country. Who knew if the perpetrator was still around and still armed and angry?

When we arrived at the housing unit, it quickly became apparent we weren't there to break up a gang fight. Rather, it seemed that a sergeant had been having an animated discussion with his wife after spending the afternoon with Jim Beam. Apparently, she had been performing wifely duties in the kitchen, and at some point in the "discussion," she couldn't find a place to put the knife she was holding, so she tried to store it in his stomach, but her aim was poor, and she only grazed him. By the time we arrived, there were more tears than threats and Dupont exercised great compassion and did absolutely nothing to either party, possibly saving the sergeant from unpleasant military action that could have had a highly deleterious effect on both his career and his income. It also freed us from spending the rest of the night doing paperwork. But I learned a valuable lesson. Don't take this shit too seriously.

Every town in a Combat Command had a bunch of bars in which the GIs hung out. There was not much fraternization between the military and the civilian populations, and the reasons were not a mystery. From the German perspective, forgetting the war that created the situation, you can't blame them for not being ecstatic about a bunch of horny young guys, many away from home for the first time, populating their town and attempting to drink it dry while trying to seduce their daughters. On the GI side, most of us didn't speak German, so what was there to say?

I got a kick out the GIs 'reactions to German girls. We rarely, if ever, saw the "good" German girls. They didn't hang in the GI bars. We had won the war and now we wanted to have a few beers, get laid, and go home. The good German burghers preferred the "get laid" part not be with their daughters.

In any event, some German girls did frequent GI bars, and that got some of the fisticuffs started. Many of these girls in post-war Germany worked long hours in factories for low wages, and in the evening, they wanted some escape from their drab lives. The idea of someone buying them a couple of beers was appealing. And, if they liked the guy and it went further, who cared? In reality, the United States is far more provincial than the European countries. But I think the assumption among the young, naïve soldiers, away from home for the first time, was that the ladies were all non-profit hookers since they didn't ask for or expect financial compensation for their labors. I guess you could call it pro boner work. At a minimum, the guys thought the girls were highly promiscuous, but what about themselves? Doesn't it take two to fuck?

Some of the guys were also far too territorial. If they saw a girl they had been with at some point, even if it was months before, talking to someone else, the trouble started. And then the MPs were called. I was amazed at the double standard. For instance, a guy goes over to a girl and asks, "Hey fraulein, can I buy you a beer?"

If she politely says no, he wanders back to his table muttering, "Fucking whore."

Hmmm! How did she earn those credentials? She had just said "No." Wouldn't that put her closer to "Virgin?" If she had said yes and dropped her pants right there on the barroom floor, would she have been a "Princess?"

Town Patrol involved normal police work, the primary role being to prevent and/or break up the bar fights at the GI joints. This was probably my least favorite part of my new occupation. I had never been a pugilist, preferring to use my mouth as my primary weapon, but when the rare occasion arose that I found myself in a fight, I hardly ever came in better than second in a two-man brawl. So, I didn't look forward to Town Patrol.

A lot of our police work could have been material for a sitcom, but not all of it. One night, I was on patrol in Nürnberg with an eighteen-year-old PFC from Mississippi who outranked me and thought having the power of a Military Policeman in Germany, with the spit 'n polish that went with it, was the achievement of a lifetime goal.

Since he'd been there longer than I, he was driving. Suddenly, the radio crackled, "All Manhood Patrols. Be on the lookout for a military sedan (and he gave the numeric designation of the vehicle). It is stolen. The occupant is believed to be armed and dangerous. If you see this vehicle, attempt to apprehend the driver, but use extreme caution. Manhood Jackson out."

I paid no attention until Bright Eyes, my partner, shouted, "There it is!"

I took one look at the approaching vehicle, saw he was right and said, "I don't think that's it. Looks like the wrong numbers on the bumper.

"No, that's it." He spun the jeep around and we took off in hot pursuit, siren blaring and lights flashing, just so we could maintain our cover and make a stealthy approach.

So, I'm sitting next to a future Dale Earnhardt trying to close the gap. I'm thinking, "Bullshit, I'm not going to get killed over something as stupid as this, while Junior here is getting his rocks off with the possibility of a big collar." But we're gaining on the jerk, who I had hoped was a superior driver in a faster vehicle and could leave us in his dust. He now knows he's being chased. He makes a quick turn onto a dark secondary street.

I take my pistol out because I plan to live. But I looked at it like it was a foreign object, regretting I had paid so little attention during training that I was having trouble loading the damn thing. We weren't allowed to carry it loaded but always had a clip of ammunition with us. I'm feverishly trying to figure out how to load the freakin' pistol while Dale is looking for the checkered flag. I finally got it loaded. Meanwhile, our target turns off the secondary road onto a dirt trail and we are right on his ass, literally it turns out, because after he crashes his vehicle into a post, stopping him, we abruptly smash into his rear, stopping us.

I now have the loaded pistol in hand, hoping just the look of it will scare him. We jump out and hit the sonofabitch from both sides. He knows it's over and gets out. Fortunately, he doesn't shoot us, and, per protocol, I holster my pistol and have him spread his legs and lean up against the vehicle while I search him. Dale covers him with his .45 that I assume is loaded. The guy appears to be unarmed.

I take the next step, which is to cuff him. I slap one cuff on, and he says, "Hit me one more time, I've played this song before." Later, we did find a weapon in the car, but I guess he didn't want to get shot either.

There were several veterans who had fought in WWII and Korea who were still serving at that time, and some of them were having difficulty dealing with their demons, as our returning soldiers are today. We would be called to a gasthaus or other place where one of them was fighting or creating some other kind of disturbance or simply passed out. Frequently, it was a career sergeant with a whole row of stripes on the sleeve of his uniform, each signifying six months in a combat zone, many with Purple Hearts. I would make a big deal of arresting him so our German friends thought we were doing our job, and then I'd drive the guy back to base and get him to his barracks. If he had been arrested by the German police, I would claim jurisdiction, throw the guy in the jeep, and give him a ride back to base.

Can you imagine arresting a career soldier who had fought for his country, risked his life for months or years on end, seen his buddies killed and maimed, been wounded himself in many instances, just because he had too many beers? I couldn't, so my jeep was more of a taxi service than a police vehicle.

I loved TDY, temporary duty, at the Combat Command cities, as did Dupont, and he got us as much of it as he could. It was freedom from a lot of the military bullshit that took place at headquarters. When on TDY, we were billeted with the Division's Headquarters Company, frequently a bunch of fuckups that gave MPs extra work. So, Dupont would make a deal with their CO that, if he left us alone, we'd leave his men alone. This usually worked and our schedules were very light. TDY with Dupont was like a vacation.

This also meant we acted like we were not a part of the military, although it was kind enough to house us. We didn't bother to turn our weapons in each day as was military protocol; we didn't bother cleaning the barracks; and we participated in no way in any of the ongoing Saturday morning inspections. It usually worked until one Saturday morning. A young lieutenant, just arrived from the states with the ink on his ROTC degree still wet, and taking it all very seriously, apparently had not spoken with the captain, his boss, and he included our area in his Saturday morning inspection.

I thought he was going into cardiac arrest when he stormed into our barracks, looked around, and became apoplectic. It was about ten thirty in the morning, and those of us who were not still sleeping or on duty were playing cards on the unmade beds. There was shit all over the place. Weapons and ammunition, overflowing butt cans (the Army didn't supply ashtrays, so we used smelly buckets half-filled with water that we'd drop our finished cigarettes in), plus booze, decaying food, civilian clothes, and uniforms strewn all around. It was worse than a college dorm and this guy was totally unprepared to deal with it. They didn't teach them how to handle that level of insubordination in ROTC school.

"Who's in charge here?" he barked. Nobody responded. "Is there a sergeant here?" he screamed. No answer. He then picked on the smallest guy. "Who is your sergeant, soldier?"

"Sergeant Dupont" was the reply.

"Where the hell is he?"

"He is meeting with the USAEUR MPs about scheduling" came the fast-thinking lie.

"OK, you tell that Dupont I want his ass in my office as soon as he gets back" and he stormed out.

His request was easier said than done. Dupont was off visiting his girlfriend in a town rather far from the base. We didn't see much of him on TDY.

After the lieutenant left, we were all in a state of high anxiety regarding what action he might take. We had a very short meeting and decided I should be the one to call Dupont at his girlfriend's place. I got him on the phone and informed him of the morning's events.

"Fuck him" was Dupont's response.

"I think that's above my pay grade. He's a fucking officer," I retorted.

"Look Dick, just go and explain him the *exsitcheration* (his words)."

Fucking him was starting to sound like a better proposition. "How the hell do I, a private, do that?"

"Never mind. I'll talk to the captain and have him straighten this asshole out."

"You should do that, Dupont. And by the way, I'd like to see the film of it."

"Look, I don't have time for this shit. I got bigger things on my mind. Did Ben get my car running?"

JUST ANOTHER DICK

Dupont gave us all jobs to perform in his absence, virtually all having no relationship to military protocol. Ben was good with mechanics and his job was to keep Dupont's piece of shit car running. Finally, he said, "Meanwhile, start writing up his guys and he'll get the message."

I, too, had an extracurricular job. Dupont wanted advancement. His goal was to be a Military Police Investigator, kind of like a detective instead of a routine, run-of-the-mill beat cop. To do this required, among other things, that he pass an extensive military correspondence course. This meant lots of studying. Dupont may not have been educated, but he was smart enough to know his chances of passing it were about as good as his being invited to participate in an international summit on arms regulation at the Hague. So, due to his conversations with the CO that guaranteed our busy and bogus schedules be respected, we all had a lot of time off. I became his surrogate student. My job, given my illustrious college career, the results of which I had not shared with Dupont, was to study the material, take, and pass the exam in his name so he could become a military PI. I did it and he apparently passed with honors, but Dupont rotated back to the states before the graduation ceremonies, so I don't know how it wound up. Just think. I finally got a degree, but under an alias.

Back on the subject of cars, which we really weren't on, I got one even though we technically were not allowed to have them. Here's what happened. Somehow, a guy in our company had managed to get away with buying a car and he was scheduled to rotate home for discharge. However, before you can leave, you must "clear the base," which means you leave nothing behind. This is another area in which COs were evaluated as to their efficiency. It didn't look good if guys were not able to "clear the base," as it tended to give a poor impression of leadership. Well, this guy had a car that he had to get rid of fast. It was a 1949 Mercedes sedan and I bought it for $125 with the captain's very silent and reluctant blessing. I guess he thought he'd get me another day, another way. He was pissed, but it worked out for all of us. The guy got to go home on time, I had a Mercedes, and the captain escaped the black mark on his resume.

That car allowed me to have my greatest experience in Germany. I had made a good friend of Otto Keim, the German interpreter at the MP station. Otto was a kindred spirit and racing fanatic. We decided to drive the Mercedes to the world-famous one-thousand-kilometer race at the Nürburgring, near Cologne. We camped by the side of the track and were awakened by the roar of high-performance cars screaming by in pre-race practice.

Later, we were on the main section of the track, on the straightaway, standing in front of a restaurant frequented by fans and the racing fraternity. Who do we see going into the restaurant? Dan Gurney! My hero. The Ferrari driver I met in Manhasset the night I got friendly with the curb when my motorcycle decided to lie down for a rest. Who is he with? Phil Hill, who at that time was arguably the very best American driver and a future world champion. I said to Otto, "Let's go say hello. I met him once. He won't remember me but what do we have to lose?"

We walked over to their table; I approached Dan from the rear, tapped him on the shoulder and started to say, "You won't remember me but..."

When he looked up, saw me, he enthusiastically said, "Oh my God, you're still alive!" And then he invited us to join him and Phil for lunch. If you're a real fan, like Otto and I, and have the opportunity to listen to two of the best race drivers in the world talk about how to tame the track in their Ferraris, you're in heaven. And we were.

One incident that demonstrated my successful adaptation to peacetime military thinking came a few months after I arrived in Germany. We all carried laminated ID cards as valid identification, serving as our passport and driver's license. We were required to always have them on our person. One day, while we were in ranks, a sergeant explained that if anyone's ID card was damaged in any way, that person would have to go to Stuttgart to get another one. What a shame! I promptly broke my ID card in half and went to Stuttgart for the day. Very enjoyable. I couldn't understand why everyone didn't do it.

The major event on the social calendar was the annual IG (Inspector General) Inspection. It was most feared by privates. NCOs and officers didn't get inspected.

The announcement of it set off a flurry of activity that lasted for months before the hated event, probably longer than the preparations for an actual military invasion.

The strategic preparation for this event primarily took the form of cleaning. Things like waxing the jeeps for a more lustrous shine to make you more visible to the enemy; scrubbing the barracks that had been scrubbed weekly, if not daily, for over two decades, first by German and now by American soldiers; making sure the condition of your personal equipment far exceeded all expectations; and, of course, "policing" the grounds. This usually involves a squad of men shoulder-to-shoulder marching across an area, leaning over to pick up cigarette butts and other effluvia to the tune of a sergeant in the rear bellowing the now familiar refrain, "I just want to see elbows and assholes." I defy anyone to find a cigarette butt or an abandoned matchstick anywhere on a military base within a week of an IG inspection.

This all culminates on the day of the much anticipated and feared inspection itself, when a high-ranking officer, a colonel, gets to capitalize on his years of military training and test his visual acuity by seeing if your blanket is folded properly. But make no mistake, it is taken very, very seriously. The night before the IG, we would make our beds so tightly you could drop the proverbial quarter on it, and you'd better step back quickly to avoid its upward trajectory. On top of that, all our mess gear and other store-bought field equipment would be meticulously displayed with blinding light reflecting off its shiny exteriors. Then you would sleep on the floor next to your bed so as not to disturb it all.

Well, after scrupulously attending to these duties, a few of us went to Goppingen to relieve the proprietor of our favorite gasthaus of any extra beer that might be lying dormant behind the bar and to catch a late schnitzel dinner. We somewhat over-trained, got back to the barracks, slept on the floor as planned, woke up barely in time for the inspection, and then dressed properly. We were ready! Amid great fanfare, the inspecting colonel strode into the room I shared with PFC Benny Patrick of Lubbock, Texas. He scrutinized it carefully for about ten seconds with a great frown on his face, scowled and then marched out. We passed! That was when I looked over at the windowsill and saw the uneaten half of my smelly schnitzel sandwich rotting away on it. I expect that colonel, earlier in his career, may have been a spotter at Pearl Harbor on December 7, 1941, failing to spot the hordes of Japanese attack planes.

I did get one big chance for revenge. The entire division was in Grafenwohr, the absolute asshole of Germany for six weeks of make-believe war. We were all restricted to base for the duration of the exercises, but that was hardly a punishment, as there was absolutely nothing in Grafenwöhr, no town, only a name.

Our evenings were spent in the mess hall playing cards. We trained there to the point at which we could beat the commies at any card game. The war "games" were far more boring than the card games, and we doubted the entire experience prepared us for anything other than a weekend in Las Vegas.

On maneuvers, the main duty of MPs was traffic control. Some of us, the unlucky ones, would direct traffic, standing in the middle of dirt roads at intersections as convoys of tanks and APCs (Armored Personnel Carriers, the army's version of fortified busses) came roaring by, kicking up so much dirt it was difficult to see. But it was a practice much loved by the laundries who got paid to wash our uniforms.

On one of these "maneuvers," I was on patrol in my jeep, tasked with doing nothing, so I was parked by the side of an intersection chatting with a buddy who was In the middle of the intersection directing traffic and hoping not to get hit, when a jeep came roaring through in complete contradiction of his very clear directions to stop, or "halt," as we liked to say. I got a good look at it as it flew by me. And who was in the front right seat? My old Field First, Sergeant Raymer, the guy who got off busting my balls for my eight weeks of basic training at Fort Dix.

In the military, the person occupying the front right seat of a vehicle is not just a passenger, but also the Vehicle Commander and, as such, is the responsible party for any infractions of the law such as speeding or disobeying the lawful directions of authorized personnel, such as an MP directing traffic. Raymer's driver's disregard for the directions of the MP at the intersection was a clear violation, and while I was generally lax on the enforcement of military law, in this case, because it was good old Sergeant Raymer, I gave chase. And, instead of pulling over, he tried to outrun me. Big mistake. Driving was my passion and I had studied and practiced the art of high-speed driving (if such a thing was possible in a jeep) prior to my military escapade. We went racing through the hills and valleys of Grafenwohr until I was right on his ass, and it was obvious that he couldn't outrun me. He knew it was futile, so he had his driver pull over rather than exacerbate the serious trouble he was already in.

According to protocol, when stopping a vehicle, you approach it from the rear so the occupants can't shoot you without you seeing them trying, and, thus, hopefully giving you the first shot. Because I was approaching from the rear, it was obvious I could not see Raymer's name tag on the front of his fatigues, so when I called out, "Sergeant Raymer." He spun around and I saw the quizzical look on his face. When I approached the jeep, I said, "I recognized you as you blew past the MP at the intersection. You were my Field First in basic." His face decomposed on the spot. Here was career-ending retribution from one of the snot-nosed kids he tried to make a soldier out of. In his mind, he could see all those Sergeant First Class stripes sliding down his sleeve to be replaced by a single stripe, signifying that after almost twenty years of military service, after his court martial, he would now have achieved the rank of PFC, and as he was nearing retirement, his retirement pay would be based on that rank.

But I had gotten what I came for. How many times in life do you get a chance like that? But along with those SFC stripes, he wore the ones he'd earned for a couple of years in combat zones in WWII. I wasn't about to bust him, so I said, rather sternly, "Sergeant, I recognized you as you flew by, and I just wanted to say hello, and tell you how much I enjoyed the drive." Then I smiled. It was absolutely classic to see his expression change. He gave me a totally perplexed, quizzical look like he was thinking, "Are you shitting me, or did I just get lucky?" He did get lucky, practically a promotion when you consider the alternative. Finally, we both laughed and chatted for a few minutes.

Grafenwohr did teach me one important lesson. DON'T GAMBLE! Every night we would gather in the mess hall and play cards for money. One of the favorites was an absolutely inane game called In-Between. No card game has ever set the bar lower for human intelligence. In this game, there was a pot that everyone anteed into on every hand. Then the players were dealt two cards each. Here's where the real skill came into play. You had to decide how much you'd bet that the next card, dealt face up, was In-Between the two you had been dealt. If you won, you took what you'd bet from the pot. If you lost, you paid the pot that amount.

Well, it was payday, and I got my monthly stipend of one hundred dollars including overseas pay (I skipped the seventy-five-dollar bond that month). Bob Morrow, my former roommate, and the reigning heavy-weight champion of the Mansion at Villanova, travelled to Europe on vacation and hooked up with me. He wanted me to take a week's leave to travel with him, but I was broke, so he lent me the money, seventy-five dollars, which was enough to cover my expenses for the week. My goal was to pay it back in one lump sum instead of over the three months to which we had agreed. So, I gave seventy-five dollars to a buddy who wasn't playing and asked him to hold it for me.

As the game went on, I was losing regularly and was soon almost out of money, so I said, "The hell with it," found my buddy, got my money back, and re-joined the game, with the same results. I was almost totally tapped for the whole month on the first of the month. That meant no beer and, more importantly, no way to pay for my uniforms to be cleaned. If nothing else, we had to look sharp, and that cost money.

But my luck started to change, and I began doing quite well. Then the sergeant yelled, "Last hand. Get your asses to bed." There was a huge pot. I had decent cards. I bet the entire pot, a couple of hundred dollars, covering the bet with every cent I had. And, while I fearfully awaited the turn of the next card and my fate, I realized that perhaps gambling was not my forte. Perhaps I didn't have the chops to risk it all on the turn of a card. This lesson served me well in later years when I spent way too much time in Las Vegas, Atlantic City, Reno, and Tahoe on business. But that night I won! I paid Bob and bought my mother a statue of the Infant of Prague, and fortunately remembered the lesson I had learned.

While in Germany, I also learned to mix private business with my military service, albeit illegally. I can say this now that the statute of limitations has run out. In post-war Germany, even fifteen years after hostilities had ended, there were still shortages of some items, namely cigarettes, whiskey, and gasoline. Private Gary to the rescue.

All soldiers stationed in Germany were issued monthly "ration cards" that allowed us to purchase a specific number of cartons of cigarettes at the PX (Post Exchange, or the on-base 7-Eleven-type store where you bought all your essentials). American cigarettes were highly popular with the Germans. NCOs (non-commissioned officers like sergeants) with families were also issued cards permitting them to purchase whiskey. It was not a herculean task to buy some of these cards cheaply from the holders not needing them, purchase cigarettes and whiskey to re-sell to Germans at a nice profit, and augment the miserly one hundred dollars a month I made as a private. Gasoline was another story. It was absurdly expensive all over Europe, in some places costing about five dollars a gallon in 1959, and regardless of price, it was not all that available. That's why European cars were so much more fuel-efficient than American cars. But GIs didn't have any access to the gas. Unless, of course, you were an MP and sometimes, while on patrol near the motor pool, a five-gallon gas can or two would fall off a tank and into your jeep.

I no longer put black marketeer on my resume, but for a while, it certainly helped to supplement my income and keep my Mercedes on the road.

There were also some scary moments. I found a gasthaus I really liked in a small town nearby. No GIs went there, I could practice my German, and there were a couple of attractive waitresses, one that I started seeing. You could hardly call it dating.

I made contact with a couple of young Germans, potential clients, who expressed the need for what I clandestinely sold. After much discussion, we agreed on what, for me, was a windfall that included cigarettes, whiskey, and gasoline. I busted my ass getting enough ration cards and took a few extra laps around the motor pool for enough gas to fill the order. I also borrowed money to make my PX purchases. But I got it all together in time for the delivery. I was a bit apprehensive in that it was only me and there were a few of them.

They were at the gasthaus when I arrived with the goods but said they didn't want to make the transfer there because there were too many eyes. They told me to follow them. Apprehension quickly turned to abject fear as we started driving down dark, deserted roads. I didn't think they'd kill me, but beating the shit out of me and stealing the swagg was a definite possibility in my mind. And I wouldn't have a strong case showing up at the German police station to report the theft of illegal goods.

However, my fears were for naught. We finally pulled to the side of a dark road, did our business, and I drove off a free, healthy, and happy man with a fatter wallet.

Prior to that, while on TDY to Nürnberg, I had teamed up with a headquarters guy for some additional fundraising. Dupont had rotated back to the States and my new Squad Leader, aware of my general attitude toward the military, rightfully hated my guts. He felt I wasn't really all that supportive of the program. This was exacerbated after some justified criticism from him of how I did things when I replied, "You're probably right, Sergeant. After all, this is your life. I'm just killing a couple of years until I can get on with mine."

That kind of ended any relationship we might have had. He also disliked the idea that I had a car, which I took to Nürnberg, while he didn't have one.

One day, I was off-duty and spent it "in the field" with my business partner, another American soldier permanently stationed there. We went out selling our line of products to his prospects, and when I got back to base, I went into the barracks in which we were billeted, and, except for my stuff, it was empty. Not a hat, a club, a stitch of clothing or uniform anywhere.

My squad had moved out and I had no idea where they had gone. I was scared shitless. I feared it had all caught up with me and I was SOL, as well as AWOL. I figured that my fat prick sergeant knew exactly when they were leaving and where they were going. He just chose not to share it with me.

I went to the MP station for information. The desk sergeant, a career NCO, who knew me and liked me, laughed as I walked in. "Man, you are in deep shit."

I didn't quite get the joke.

He continued, "You are at the TOP of that sergeant's shit list with a bullet, you should pardon the expression." He then informed me that good ole Sarge had reported me AWOL before departing back to Goppingen with the rest of the squad in the jeeps. He strongly suggested I follow the leader. Fortunately, I had a car in which to do it.

Here I was, a young guy in the Army, a private, not exactly a rank of privilege, in a foreign country and in big trouble. My wise mouth and smart attitude, not to mention the car, got me into this mess. This was real life, not fucking around at bars and parties. I had no net under me, and it could be a big drop. I felt totally alone. My first move was a practical one: damage control.

I went to my on-base business partner, told him what was going down and that, if contacted, he should say we were just buddies and we'd never left base that day. Fortunately, he really was on leave, so that subterfuge should hold up. Then I got in the Benz for the longest drive of my life. As I headed back to Goppingen, a number of scenarios, none good, played out in my mind, perhaps the clearest being my potential adjustment to prison, not a welcoming place for MPs. I now think of that journey as my trip to maturity. I was in real trouble, and I had to find a way out of it myself, with no help. And then learn from it.

I arrived back in Goppingen late that night and went to the barracks to report in. I didn't know the orderly on duty and he greeted me with, "Hi. How can I help you, Private?

I said, "I'm Private Gary reporting for duty."

He said, "Oh man, I can't help YOU." Then he got this conspiratorial smile and said, "What did you do to that sergeant? He is UP YOUR ASS!" Then he added quietly, "Oh, by the way, you made PFC today (Private First Class, an automatic promotion after nine months) but if I were you, I wouldn't race out and blow my money buying any stripes."

The next morning, when the sergeant saw me, he looked like he'd just been served Thanksgiving dinner, and he was going to enjoy it to the last bite. I was invited into the CO's office to discuss the situation. I told him I was as confused as anyone about the AWOL charge because I never left the base that day. I was not informed of the departure in advance, and as soon as I saw the squad had departed, I reported to the MP station and returned to Goppingen ASAP. They knew I was bullshitting them but couldn't prove it, so I was off the hook and went to buy my stripes. I may have gotten away with it, but in those two days, I earned a PhD in life.

Aside from my appearing in the Army sitcom, there were many other positive highlights of my tour in Germany, the biggest of which was travel. I was determined to see as much as I could, and I tried not to let the military get in the way of my tourism. As I said earlier, being in Europe in 1959 was a big deal, and since the Army was hosting my trip, I wanted to get as much out of it as possible. Every GI was entitled to thirty days leave a year and I intended to take every minute of mine.

In all, I visited fourteen countries. Some of these, like Luxembourg and Lichtenstein, were basically drive-bys, and I didn't spend enough time in them to learn anything other than how to spell the name. And, if you divide the number of days leave I had by the number of countries visited, you can quickly figure that I did not become a learned historian in any of them. But then, that wasn't my mission. I was primarily on a beer run and wine tasting tour coupled with some other hopeful couplings. The latter, in all honesty, were not terribly numerous or noteworthy.

The cities where I spread goodwill on behalf of my countrymen included Paris, London, Copenhagen, Amsterdam, Munich, Vienna, Salzburg, Venice, Rome, Madrid, San Tropez and many more. It was truly the experience of a lifetime, especially for a twenty-one-year-old naive guy from Long Island.

My first extended foray off-base, the first of many, was with Bob Morrow when he was in Europe on his vacation. Bob had rented a car and I got a week's leave. Our destination was Stockholm to find out if those Scandinavian women were as beautiful as reported. First stop Hamburg. The main attraction there was the Reeperbahn, a street you walked down where all the first-floor windows were open and occupied by prostitutes. Let's just say it was a big change from Manhasset. They could probably see us coming from a mile away, but it didn't matter, as we didn't have enough money to indulge our fantasies.

The next morning, we boarded the ferry from Grossenbrude to Copenhagen. Copenhagen was beautiful, but we couldn't wait for the sun to go down. By night, we wound up at Tivoli Gardens, a highly popular spot for both residents and tourists. There was music and dancing and I got to talking with a few different girls. One in particular seemed to be worth every minute I could possibly spend with her. And she seemed to be in love with me. When it came time to leave with her, I found out exactly how much that love would cost me. More than I had, but she was overcome with a spirit of giving for her American allies and chose to work on a complimentary basis, another pro boner job. Moral of the story (as I later learned): pretty girls wearing tight, bright red dresses in Tivoli Gardens are there on business.

Willkomen In Deutschland

One short leave that had a lasting effect on my life was to Garmisch Partenkirchen in Bavaria. Garmisch was also the site of the 1936 Winter Olympics, and as such, it had a famous ski area. It was also the location of an Armed Forces Recreation Center. There were a number of these throughout Europe, semi-day care centers designed to occupy the troops on leave and keep them away from the local population. They included inexpensive lodging ($1.25 per night) and some type of popular activity. Normally, I avoided these like the plague, but I had a few more days of leave coming, and it wasn't far, so two buddies of mine and I thought it might be time to learn to ski. It was my introduction to a fabulous sport that became an integral part of my life from then until today.

Alas, the military sitcom was ending after two enjoyable seasons. Repatriation was near. I had had a truly interesting and mostly enjoyable twenty months in Germany. I was ready to get back, get discharged, and get started on the life to which I had given absolutely no thought. I wasn't so lucky on the return trip. I was assigned to ride the USS Rose, a military troop ship that took nine long days and nights to get from Bremerhaven, Germany to the Brooklyn Navy Yard. I thought I could have rowed it faster.

In those days, military transport ships made prisons look like spas. Unlike the Holland America line, there is no indoor golf, nightly theatrical productions, or swimming pools. There are humungous rooms, not staterooms, although they appeared to be in a sorry state, in which hundreds of enlisted men slept together. The bunks are five high. That's where important decisions are made. Do you want to be on the top bunk directly under the hot pipes that will give you a nice roasting? Or on the bottom bunk where you are a target for the vomit of every seasick GI above you? Tough choices.

Finally, on the last night, we pulled into New York Harbor and anchored off the Brooklyn Navy Yard, the site of disembarkation.

As I walked down the gangplank, I spotted my mother and Uncle Art, who, unbeknownst to me, had come to welcome me home. It was great seeing them, and it made homecoming seem real. My mother asked where I was going and I replied, "Fort Dix."

"Oh, we'll drive you," she offered, in a well-intended but absolute classic display of her complete naivety of military procedures.

"I think the Army has provided transportation and, if I don't take it, they'll arrest me when they find me," I replied with a laugh.

The mustering out process took a few days, and then I got the hell out. Fort Dix is a place you hate to go to but love to leave.

That was then and this is now. We are in a different world, and we have a very different Army. When I think back on my military service, I realize how fortunate I was to be in the Army during the short period of time in the past century that we were not at war. I had a tremendous experience and (mostly) a genuinely good time, and I did a lot of growing up. When I compare that to what faces the members of today's military service, I am in awe of them. They weren't drafted; they volunteered. My experience may have been a sitcom; theirs is a combination drama, action adventure, and horror show. We were trying to keep the jeeps clean; they are trying to stay alive. We should all show the deepest respect and our genuinely heartfelt gratitude to all of them. They are true heroes!

SEVEN
On The Fast Lane To Nowhere

On September 9, 1960, our nation was weakened when I left the Army and rejoined the ranks of civilians, free to once again repeat all the mistakes that preceded my military career.

I had to admit I felt good about my military service. It seemed like it was one of the few obligations I had satisfied thus far in my life. That experience started my maturing process, ever so slowly.

A couple of the guys from the 101st also returned to the States with me on the USS Rose, and we were discharged together. We left the base for the last time, took a bus to New York, had a couple of farewell beers, told a few jokes, and went our separate ways. Mine was to Water Mill to see my mother. From the Port Authority Bus Terminal, I walked over to the Queens Midtown Tunnel, stuck my thumb out, and three rides later, arrived in Water Mill. I thought about keeping my uniform for situations like this.

My last ride left me off at the corner of Montauk Highway and Rose Hill Road where my mother's house was located. As I walked down the road, in uniform and with a duffel bag slung over my shoulder, a convertible passed me and stopped fast. In it were two girls, Sandra Reilly and June Rapp. They were from Manhasset, and I knew them both. Unbelievable!

Sandra had taken over the letter writing when Carol quit and June had been Carol's best friend and the girlfriend of one of my best friends, Lee Jacquette. They had spoken to my mother and wanted to surprise me. It worked! Less than eight hours after my discharge, my first post military romance began. I had always liked June and I liked her even better now that she wasn't going out with Lee.

I had decided that I wanted to stay in Water Mill. I had just spent two years sleeping with too many people, virtually all men despite my valiant efforts otherwise, and I welcomed serenity of Eastern Long Island. I had absolutely no plan for my future and my military severance pay would last about forty-eight hours.

I had led my life like it was an AA meeting: one day at a time. In Germany, I had been too busy having fun or breaking up fights to give my future a single thought. In the far recesses of my mind, I knew I'd get a job. I never defined what kind of job, but people had said that, with my personality, I'd be a good salesman. That's what I went for.

My first gig was a battle for survival selling Kirby vacuum cleaners that went for $275 in 1960. No salary, strictly commission. If you sold, you earned; if you didn't, you starved. To say it was a hard sell is an understatement, but I did sell a bunch before I became disenchanted. I lasted a few months there. The one lesson I really learned was that it's impossible to sell a vacuum cleaner in a dirty house. The dust could be rising from the rug as you walked across it, but still no deal.

Next came the opportunity of a lifetime, selling Dodge cars in the winter in a summer resort—the road to riches. When you saw an aging Dodge drive by, you hopped in a new one and chased it. My classic, or perhaps most shameful, sale came when I saw a photo in the local newspaper of a car that had been t-boned by a passing train at a crossing. The driver was in the hospital. I called him and said, "I guess you'll need some new wheels," and sold him a car when he got out. Subtlety is apparently not my style, and hunger is a strong motivator.

On to American Machine & Foundry (AMF), the company that introduced automatic pin spotting to the world, eliminating one of my former career opportunities, pin boy. The company was on a roll (no pun). I was hired as a sales trainee with a seventy-five-dollar weekly salary. It even included a secretary. God knows what she made. After a few months, I noticed there was no training, so one night, I snuck into the admin office, found my personnel file that clearly defined my job as a senior clerk. Auf Wiedersehen AMF!

My next job was a beauty! Selling magazine drives for the National Catholic Decency In Reading Program. It was a promotion sponsored by the Catholic Digest, where I would sell Catholic elementary schools on a promotion where the kids sold subscriptions to national magazines at a discounted price and the schools made money. How did I get this lucky? Bob Morrow's father ran it, and Bob worked there too. He said the money wasn't bad and you were off when school was out. If you're still with me, you may be thinking that, nevertheless, this was probably not my cup of tea, and you'd be right. My clients were all nuns and, needless to say, our reading materials were quite different. But I did OK the first year, and I learned an interesting fact: poor schools performed much better than wealthy ones.

Best of all, I got the whole summer off. I used it to take up a new sport, go-cart racing. I could afford it, so I bought one and it was a kick, speeding into turns, passing, and unfortunately, being passed. It was thrilling. You could go really fast, and it was relatively safe as the cart's center of gravity was low.

Carting wasn't a full-time hobby, and on weekends, action shifted to the beaches in the Hamptons by day and the very popular local hangout, the Post House, by night. There, my needs were diligently served by Lee, the bartender. We exchanged free drinks for healthy tips. In addition to his bartending skills, he also had a biting sense of humor. One night, a customer asked him if he could make a truly dry martini. His response, "Sir, my martinis are so dry, we took the urinals out of the men's room and put dust pans in."

I also got to be a decent water skier that summer. It was interesting. After my humiliating sports career in baseball and basketball as a youth, I found I could do other things fairly well. The sports I was attracted to were all single participant, not team endeavors, and all seemed to have an element of speed, grace, and danger. But more than the danger, I think the common thread was grace in motion. I found it exhilarating to be out on the end of a water ski rope on one ski, crouching down as the boat turned sharply and hanging on for dear life. Or going over big bumps down a steep ski run. Or leaning way over into a turn on a motorcycle. I later asked a race car driver what he thought the attraction of these various sports was and he said "freedom." Makes sense to me.

But then, summer ended. When schools opened again, I just couldn't keep up the pose any longer. I had stopped living day-to-day and realized I had no future the way I was headed. I had to go back and finish college, but meanwhile I had to make some money to live. At the time, I was renting a house in the seedy section of Manhasset with two friends. The rent was $110 a month and the deal was for two of us to split the rent and the third guy pay the utilities...only he didn't, and in the very cold month of November on Long Island, the gas was turned off; no heat or stove. I compensated by learning to make instant coffee. I filled the steam iron with water, plugged it in, and when it was hot, poured it over the coffee grounds. Very inventive, but hardly a solution for life.

I saw an ad from a New York City employment agency that read like they might be looking for a lifeguard at a health club. I figured that might be the way to kill time, pulling grateful ladies out of the pool before I returned to college, although I had not given the monetary aspects of that decision any thought. It turned out the author of the Help Wanted ad should have been awarded a prize for fiction. The job was a chaser for a financial company and my territory would have been Harlem. Imagine, a nice white boy chasing black deadbeats in Harlem. In 1960, Black people were not really up for supporting white people, given the horrible treatment they'd received for centuries. I passed, and the agent, who was now acting more like a mob tough guy said, "I got one other job, a salesman/announcer at an FM radio station."

"I'm not an announcer," I replied.

"And I'm sure you're way too busy to go on the appointment," he replied in a pissed-off voice.

"Fuck you," I diplomatically replied. "Make the appointment and I'll go." He did and I did, and life changed.

EIGHT
New York New York

The station was WBFM. Ring a bell? Of course not. Never did; never will. In those days, the programming on FM-only stations was about as popular as leprosy, but twice as hard to get. Most had automated, background music formats and you'd need a team of EMTs to keep the audience awake. There were no FM radios in cars then, so falling asleep at the wheel wasn't a problem. In fact, there were hardly any FM radios anywhere.

I had never even heard of FM, which put me in a rather unique position for my interview. Plus, Google didn't exist yet, so no help there. The interview was with the station's General Manager, Stan Gurell. Stan was tall, lean, important looking, impeccably dressed, and with a set of pipes that screamed RADIO ANNOUNCER. When he spoke, the room shook. I liked Stan and the idea of radio time sales as he explained it...and he had to explain it. I figured, what the hell, it was only until I went back to school, but I may have forgotten to mention that in the interview.

From Stan's viewpoint, my sales background was highly appropriate, given my experience selling the impossible to the disinterested. I got the job, which included an eighty-five-dollar-per-week draw against a 33.3% commission and a fifteen-dollar weekly expense account. It was obvious to anyone in sales that when the commission rate is that high, it's a very tough sell. It turned out the station had not really been looking for an announcer. That part of it was to attract more applicants.

FM has two channels, the main and the sub channel. WBFM was owned by Muzak. Their sole reason for purchasing the station was so they could use the sub channel to distribute their musical sleeping aids to the businesses that subscribed to their service. That was their road to riches, but they didn't want to pay any tolls along the way like the main channel, WBFM, losing money.

Most radio stations then were AM/FM combos, meaning both simulcast the same programming. The FCC had not yet decreed that AM/FM stations had to separate and offer a different listening experience to each audience.

I knew nothing about adverting sales. Radio was an intangible, and I was used to selling things that were real, but Stan taught me the basics of radio and, over time, a lot more. He was a great teacher. My job was simple: help him make money for the station.

The WBFM format was an automated blend of totally unfamiliar and forgettable music designed to relax and ameliorate the fears of those sitting in dentists' waiting rooms. But it was cheap to program. Evenings were prime time for FM stations since there were no FMs in cars, as opposed to AMs where morning and afternoon "drive" times were prime.

In the evenings, also to fulfill FCC requirements, Stan hosted a few live-on-tape shows, such as "Curtain Time," a daily one-hour musical presentation of a Broadway show. He also did stock market reports and other offerings. He voiced the commercials as well.

Ratings were the lifeblood of AM stations, but they were a liability to FMs due to its miniscule audience size. Our only recourse was cheaper rates. Or, since hardly anyone was listening, we could program anything we could sell. And there were some beauties.

Radio is an intangible and its products, the commercials, are creative concepts with a sales message. Stan asked me to write the copy for the commercials I sold, and that really turned me on. It was my first involvement in the creative process. Suddenly, I was loving my job. I liked writing the commercials as much as selling them. I just wished there were more. Thus began my unrequited lifelong affair with writing. Not to mention I really dug the fact that I was making money every time a commercial that

I sold aired. I would listen to the station, hear one of my spots and yell, "Yeah. I made a buck just sitting here on my ass."

As Stan got more confident in my ability, he brought me in closer. The shows Stan hosted cost fifteen dollars per sixty-second commercial, and as part of his compensation, he got a talent fee for every spot that aired in any of his shows. Other non-prime spots sold for three dollars, so none ran in his shows. Fifteen dollars was a tough sell when the alternative was three dollars. Since I appreciated what he was doing for me, I wanted to do something for him, and I found a solution. I sold fifteen-dollar spots in Stan's shows and gave four free bonus spots for each one I sold.

One day, Stan told me it was time for me to start cutting my announcing chops. My first project would be the daily stock market wrap-up that ran daily at 7:30 p.m. It was a show that Stan had done. I had a decent voice and I liked to play with it and do imitations, so I thought I could pull it off; although imitations might not be pertinent to a stock market report. I asked Stan how the show was compiled. He said it really wasn't. He suggested I buy the afternoon newspaper, the *New York Post,* and prepare a two-minute report. The stock market show ran well after the market closed, but the *New York Post* hits the newsstands before then, so my information wouldn't be too accurate. I did want to be honest and do it right, so I called my friend Bob Stemmerman, aka Stem from the Dome.

Stem was selling stocks for Merrill Lynch. He told me they prepared a daily report after the market closed that would fit in the time slot, so every day I would call him in late afternoon, and he would dictate the report to me. I would take it down in longhand, a challenge for me given my very poor handwriting, and record it for airing. At the end of each broadcast, I would say, "This report has been prepared through the cooperation of Robert Stemmerman in the Pan Am Building office of Merrill Lynch Pierce Fenner and Smith." Then one day, his superior came to him and asked, "Stemmerman, are you unhappy with Merrill Lynch's advertising program? Isn't it big enough for you? Is there any particular reason you have chosen to expand it on your own without consulting us?" Stem explained the deal and it all worked out. I was flattered that someone in that business actually listened to the station.

Meanwhile, I decided to move to New York City. What was the point of a single guy leaving the most exciting city in the world every day just as it was getting ready for the antics of another night? I found a tiny, one-bedroom, fourth-floor walkup with a pullman kitchen and a fireplace on Nineteenth Street, between First and Second Avenue. Heaven for $115 a month and I didn't need a car, so I dumped what was left of mine.

After work, I'd detour around the corner from work to Sparks Pub on Eighteenth Street between Park Avenue South and Irving Place. That became the meeting place for the nocturnal adoration society of which I was becoming a devout member. It became my New York City Dome, but without the depth of characters.

Sparks was a cool joint frequented by neighborhood locals. (Forgive the oxymoron. Are there any other kind of locals?) and occasionally by some single women.

I didn't have any single friends in the city when I moved there, so I became friendly with some of the single advertising execs I spent my days trying to sell radio spots to. Despite ad agencies' lack of interest in FM, that's where the real money was.

It started with Peter Berla, the Media Director at Carl Ally Advertising. Ally was a new agency that could have been called Carl Attitude because they had that in spades. They did great stuff that an outsider like me truly appreciated.

When Volvos were first imported into the USA, Ally got the account and their debut TV commercial featured an in-car camera shooting a Volvo bouncing through the woods, sliding around turns, going over jumps, with real sound effects but no voice-over until the very end, when the announcer said, "Volvo. Drive it like you hate it."

Peter introduced me to Earl Gandel, a recent import from Los Angeles where he had worked for Volkswagen and who was going to become a lifelong friend. Earl was the Account Executive on Volvo and had a couple of buddies, Bob Grossman, an Account Exec at DDB (Doyle Dane

Bernbach, another highly creative agency), and Baron Bates, an amazingly entertaining guy who worked in PR for Volkswagen in New Jersey. Baron had a buddy he worked with, Tony Weaver. We became kind of a rat pack with headquarters at Sparks.

Tony was an African American, a bit older than us, who had a few fast laps under his belt. He also had a way of expressing himself that was hilarious. Tony was a staunch Greenwich Village devotee who very clearly stated, "Nothing interesting happens above Fourteenth Street." He only came north of Fourteenth for special occasions, like a Tuesday night at Sparks.

The one thing I found missing from my New York life was a motorcycle. City life was great, but I really pined for the feeling I had when my ass was seated on a bike, the fun and freedom. So I convinced myself, an easy sell, that having one would give me a cheap means of transportation, especially to the Hamptons for my weekend outings.

Back to the Ghost I went. Nothing had changed there. He still had the best inventory of performance bikes on the East Coast. I knew what I wanted, a 441cc BSA Victor. The Victor was cleaning up in all the scrambles races around that time. Scrambles were the precursor to motocross, off-road races on dirt with jumps and other features highly appealing to the immature or slightly deranged.

Sal didn't have any 441s in stock at the time, but he had this 500cc single cylinder Matchless G80CS, another English product that was highly competitive at one of the most prestigious motorcycle races in the world, the Isle of Mann. The bike was used, but it was of the current year's manufacture. With great skepticism, knowing Sal, I asked why someone would be selling a bike that was less than a year old if it was so hot. Sal went into a long song and dance about how the guy who bought it loved the bike, but his mother, who lived in Italy, got sick and he had to sell it and go there to take care of her. More of his bullshit, and I let him know it. But Sal didn't care what you said if you had the money that gave you the right to say it. Nevertheless, he was a 24-karat character and his loyal tribe of bikers, including me, loved him, mostly on the days we weren't buying anything.

I bought the Matchless. I hadn't been on a machine for a few years, and to say my style was rusty would have been a compliment. My first task was to get it to its new home, New York City, where it could make friends with the cabs and trucks. My maiden voyage and training ground was the Long Island Expressway, considered one of the most over-crowded thoroughfares in the nation. I made it home somehow and thus, my love/hate relationship for another English vehicle with Lucas Electric began.

As a footnote to that, a year or so later, I was sitting outside having a beer at Pete's Tavern on Irving Place and Seventeenth Street with my bike proudly parked in front, when I noticed a guy paying way too much attention to it. I wasn't worried about him stealing it because I was the only mammal in America that could start it. Nevertheless, his interest in the Matchbox, as it was affectionately referred to by the cognoscenti, was a bit unnerving. I was anticipating a possible confrontation.

Finally, he looked over and asked, "Anybody here own this bike?"

"I do," I suspiciously replied, trying to look as tough as I could.

"Did you get it from the Ghost?"

"I did!" I answered.

"I used to own it," he said with a smile. I jumped up, went over, shook his hand, and asked, "Why did you ever sell it?"

"I loved the machine, but my mother lived in Italy, and..."

I interrupted him with "and she got sick, and you had to sell it and go over and take care of her."

"How'd you know?" he asked.

"Never mind," I said, and thought an apology letter to Sal might be appropriate, but quickly dropped the idea.

I had also gotten friendly with a Nineteenth Street neighbor, Michael Sumner. Mike worked at yet another ad agency and was another bike freak and an aspiring writer. He wanted to do a story on a motorcycle gang, which he eventually did, for Esquire no less. His research took him to Laconia, New Hampshire for the major annual bikers' gala that was the East Coast version of the renowned Sturgis event. In Laconia, he hooked up with a motorcycle club, club being the more acceptable term for gang. He wanted to join, and they welcomed him, provided he was ready for the initiation, which consisted of their presenting him with an earring, the symbol of the club, followed by heating a fork over a fire, bending one of the prongs back, sticking it through his ear lobe, and inserting the earing in the hole. Anything to be one of the guys.

Michael had a BMW, a real gentleman's bike, glaringly different from his buddies' two-wheel Christmas trees, the Harley-Davidsons. I called them "glopulent" because they were so over-decorated it was difficult for the eyes to process. They'd be right at home in Las Vegas. To make the "Beezer," aka BMW, more acceptable to the guys, he put ape hangers, the high handlebars associated with outlaw bikes, and straight-through exhaust pipes on it, so it looked and sounded like something BMW might want to buy back from him and destroy. It was like making a low rider out of a Rolls-Royce.

When the gang came to town, Michael would ride with them, and he often asked me to join them. It was fun riding with these ersatz gangsters who were a phenomenon riding through Manhattan, especially Greenwich Village, where nothing exciting had happened since Jack Kerouac left. Believe me, if you want to attract women, get a Harley.

Bob Grossman, at that time, had a Vespa motor scooter that, next to a Harley, looked like the waspy son of a Mafia enforcer. One day, Bob was at my place when Michael called to say the boys were in town and we should all go for a ride. Bob, a pale-skinned, balding white man in khakis, a polo shirt, and a plaid McGregor windbreaker, came along on his Vespa. As we rode through the streets of Manhattan, we presented a broad visual spectrum...the outlaw Harleys, Michael's wannabe bad boy BMW, my all-business (if racing is your business) Matchless, and Bob's Vespa that, next to the Harleys, looked like a CPA at a rap concert. After our jaunt through the local environs, we adjourned to Max's Kansas City, a seminal white-hot bar and restaurant near my apartment that was the hangout for the Sex Pistols and similar groups and entourages. The Gucci Pucci set from uptown liked to go slumming there on occasion. I guess they thought it would give them some swagger or at least bragging rights, but they were strictly voyeurs. After our ride, our gang-like entourage marched in, sat down, had a few drinks and something to eat, and left. The next morning, as Bob got on the elevator at DDB, one of his fellow passengers, a female co-worker and voyeur who had obviously been at Max's the night before screamed, "Bob Grossman! What kind of a double life do you lead?" I would have considered it a form of hero worship, but Bob was embarrassed.

Many times, on fall weekends, I'd wake up on Saturday without a plan, stuff a map, toothbrush, toothpaste, and some clean underwear in my little canvass Pan Am bag, get on the bike, and take off alone, destination unknown.

Generally, I wound up in Woodstock, got a cheap hotel room and hit the town. It was a cool place with a fabulous heritage thanks to the festival that was born there. It only had one weekend of life, but the reputation lives on. Woodstock had become kind of a hippy paradise. There were interesting people to talk to, and I enjoyed my times there.

I didn't always love the mornings, especially the one when I woke up to a heavy, pounding rainstorm. It wasn't going to stop, and I was over one hundred miles from home. That was a painful and hairy trip. Because of my disdain for helmets, each raindrop at sixty-plus miles per hour felt like a needle sticking into my face, I must admit that after that trip, I bought a helmet for protection. Bike accidents aren't so rare, and bikers don't usually fall off motorcycles; they're knocked off by cars. A doctor friend told me that in their profession, motorcycles were referred to as donor cycles.

Prior to my purchasing the "brain bucket" as helmets were referred to by, *"we the cognoscenti,"* aka the morons who rode without one, I had a problem one Friday afternoon on my way to Southampton. Unfortunately, a couple of laws had been passed prohibiting motorcyclists from creating a new lane in order to pass between cars and mandating all bikers wear helmets. Since I didn't have one yet, my cruising on the Long Island Expressway between cars in my own lane as well as my bare-headed appearance caught the eye of a sharp Nassau County policeman who got closer to his monthly quota by awarding me a citation.

I didn't take it seriously and did nothing until I was informed by mail that there was a warrant out for my arrest. That caught my attention, and I called the Sheriff's Department, assuming we could work it out on the phone and I would send a check. I was the only one under that misapprehension. They would accept nothing less than a court appearance. So, I hopped on the Matchbox and headed for Mineola, the site of the court.

I walked in, identified myself, and was informed I was under arrest. I next got to become familiar with the fingerprinting process and was transported to the court, under surveillance and in the company of the other "felons."

The fun wasn't over. When my turn came, I pleaded ignorance of the law, a defense the judge found wanting and thus imposed a guilty verdict and fine. I didn't have enough money on me to pay the fine, so I countered at a lower number. The judge was shocked and incensed that I was trying to bargain with him, but I explained I'd give him all I had less enough to get me through the tunnel and back to Manhattan. He agreed. I guess it was cheaper than locking me up.

I garaged the bike in an apartment building at Eighteenth Street and Second Avenue. One day, I went to pick it up, and it would not start despite my best ministrations. That's a very frustrating feeling. I'm three floors underground and I can't start the bike. What do I do? Simple! Just push it up the three steep floors to the street and then to the nearest dealer...on Fifty-Second Street and Eleventh Avenue, over three miles away. How do you spell compulsive? You get the picture. I loved my motorcycle and it certainly added to what had become my outsider status, at least to the insiders with normal lives.

In those days, photographers that were doing business with ad agencies would have parties at their studios and invite lots of agency people.

There would also be a slew of models on the invite list, a sure way to get maximum attendance from the agency guys, and possible future business for the ladies. Earl was privy to these and one night asked me to join him. It was the Friday of New Year's weekend and for once I wasn't going skiing. Free booze and pretty girls? Why not! Earl had wheels. It was his Volvo client's new prototype car, the only one in the country and the client had generously loaned it to Earl for the weekend.

At the party, I got particularly interested in one of the highly attractive models, Bonnie, whom I engaged in conversation. I think Bonnie had an active ambition gene, because once it was established that someone in radio couldn't help her career, she kept looking over my shoulder for someone who could until I wished her luck and walked away. She apparently didn't have any because later in the evening she came back.

As the party wound down, Earl and I, accompanied by Bonnie, got in the Volvo and headed for Spark's. We almost got there, but as we were cruising down Second Avenue in sync with the lights, at Thirty-Sixth Street by the entrance to the Queens Midtown Tunnel, some asshole came barreling down Thirty-Sixth, ran the light and T-boned us. It was a serious crash, and we were all quite banged up but not seriously injured. Nevertheless, an ambulance came and took us to the hospital. We were rolled around in wheelchairs as each of us was examined. Earl and I were sitting there waiting our turn when the nurse came rolling by with Bonnie in the wheelchair, looking like she was not quite ready for a Vogue cover shoot. She kind of glared at me and I called out to her, "Hey Bonnie, if you think this was fun, wait until you hear what we have planned for New Year's Eve." That was the last I saw of Bonnie.

Meanwhile, Stan Gurell knew I was an avid (but not accomplished) skier and said if I could sell a ski show, the station would air it. Talk about motivation! I sold two ski shows, each fifteen minutes weekly, one to Peugeot and one to Davos, not the Swiss mecca, just a small ski area in the Catskills near Grossingers.

Creating, producing, and airing a show was a new world for me, and saying I was somewhat unprepared for it might have been an

understatement. The shows were designed to be a combination of interviews with recognized ski world personalities and/or any newsmakers I
could get ahold of, as well as features on ski areas and ski reports.

Wanting to start at the top and not having enough sense not to, my
first interview was with the man who was the god of the ski world at that
time, Stein Eriksen. I was beside myself with excitement, reminiscent of
the Dan Gurney and Phil Hill lunch. I was determined to make it important. I researched his life, career, and pertinent issues in the ski world.

When he showed up, Stein was extremely gracious, and I knew this
would go well. The show was taped in advance, not live, and to make it
better, I decided to review my list of prepared questions with him before
we ran tape. Stein's answers were thoughtful, complete, and compelling. I figured I had enough material for a month of shows. So, I started
the tape, asked the questions and he'd look at me a little oddly and give
simple short, abrupt answers like "yes" and "no." When I thought about it
afterwards, it made sense. Stein, in his mind, had already answered the
question. Why was I asking it again? I learned an important lesson. Go to
tape first and edit out what you don't want. For his part, he may not have
known tape wasn't running the first time and thought I was a complete
moron. But I never made that mistake again.

In those days, ski reports were a highly questionable guide to current
ski conditions at the various areas. They had about as much credibility
as a Donald Trump interview. Each area reported its own conditions as:
excellent, good, fair, or poor. Eastern ski areas, especially in lower eleva-
tions such as the Catskills, were notorious for fictionalized snow reports.
I think many of those resorts geared their snow reports on the number of
room reservations they had. The fewer reservations, the better the snow.
Areas would have to be under nuclear attack to report poor conditions. I
finally offered commercials "on the house" to any ski area that reported
poor snow conditions, and never had to run a single free spot.

One of the great perks of being a ski reporter was free skiing; I never
had to buy a lift ticket. One winter, a group of friends and myself rented
a house near my favorite Vermont ski area, Sugarbush. My cost for a bed

for the season? $125. An entrepreneurial friend of mine had started running bus trips to Sugarbush on the weekends and felt it advantageous to have, in his mind, a ski personality such as myself on the bus, so he gave me free transportation. Between the free lift tickets, free transportation, and cheap accommodations, if I wanted to save money, I had to go skiing.

At the time, there was an annual International Ski Show in New York City where skiers were introduced to all the new equipment, clothing, new ski areas, etc. for the upcoming season. I thought it would be a good place to generate a new audience for my show *Ski Time With Dick Gary,* and I could probably pick up a few interviews there, so I made a trade deal with the promoter, Harry Leonard. I'd do on-air mentions for his show in exchange for a free booth.

In the process, Harry and I became friendly. The next year, he decided, as a promotion, to have a "Mister Ski Show" contest with four candidates vying for the honor, and he asked me to be one of them. Try as I might to be too cool to care, I was flattered and kind of shocked. My photo was included in all the promotional materials and plastered all over the walls of the show along with my competitors. I had never seen myself in that light. It turned out that most others didn't either as the winner of the contest, by popular voting, was a writer for *Mad Magazine.*

WBFM also had a jazz show hosted by Esquire's jazz editor (yes, they had one then), John Lissner (great name for a radio host). I was elected (since there was nobody else) to work the board for John's shows, i.e., spin the records and work the microphones for him and his guests. I met some of the luminaries of jazz in the day, Artie Shaw, Gerry Mulligan, Count Basie, and lots more.

I guess I got so good at spinning that Stan decided to give me my own music show, *Weekend In New York With Dick Gary*. It ran for an hour on Saturday and Sunday evenings and was a simple format: spinning records, talking up what was happening in town, and having an occasional guest. If being a DJ was my hidden talent, it may have been hidden too well. I just never got comfortable with it. I was always a bit intimidated when the mic was open and never got to share my real personality with the audience, which may have been a blessing, as that might have caused the FCC to revoke the station's license.

In those days, media buyers weren't interested in FM stations for a couple of reasons, the dominant one being the diminutive size of the audience irrespective of its supposed quality. They don't sell Coca Cola at Tiffany's. The other, the one they wouldn't mention, was that as soon as they bought one FM station, they'd be inundated with calls from every other station, and that would be a pain in the ass. I didn't care. In the immortal words of the fabled bank robber Willie Sutton who, when asked why he kept robbing banks, replied, "That's where the money is." I haunted the ad agencies, and some agreed to see me.

Also, about that time, FM got lucky. The FCC decreed that AM/FM combinations had to separate their programming. This meant that AMs and FMs, even under the same ownership, had to program their stations differently. This created tremendous new opportunity and interest in FM, and I had a rolodex of many agencies and buyers. Perhaps I no longer needed a subpoena to see prospective clients.

J. Walter Thompson, a major ad agency, was in the vanguard of evaluating FM, especially for Pan Am, then a major international airline. Naturally, if they were to buy time on an FM station, they wanted "added value" in the form of bonus on-air plugs. Stan and I decided to pitch them a fifty-two-week sole sponsorship of *Curtain Time,* Stan's evening Broadway show program. At that time, Pan Am was introducing the 747 aircraft into service, so I said that every morning and evening at 7:47, our announcer would say, "It's 7:47, time to fly Pan Am's deluxe new aircraft, the 747, to anywhere in the world." It worked. They bought a fifty-two-week schedule, and I was one step farther from the bread line.

Stan was very happy and wanted to find a way to thank me as well as create additional revenue for the station, so he created *Curtain Call,* a five-minute show that ran at the end of *Curtain Time,* giving news of the theatre, new shows, etc. The etc. is there because there simply wasn't five minutes of theatre news every day, but I sold it to Blue Cross, another

J. Walter client, for twenty dollars per show. Stan reciprocated by giving me a producer's credit and a production fee per show.

My social life since my discharge was not something you'd be reading about in the society pages of the New York Times. My romance with June had flamed out long ago and Pete's Tavern and the Dome were like visiting Boy's Town.

It turned out that one of the best things about my apartment's location on the fourth floor was that to get there, I had to pass the second floor that was occupied by Dorothy, a highly attractive woman a few years older than I am. Dorothy was a former model, then working as a stylist for photographers. I was mesmerized by her. I was a wet-behind-the-ears young guy from the suburbs and Dorothy was a savvy, experienced New Yorker. She became my part-time muse. Part-time because she had her own life and wasn't any more interested in monogamy than I was.

Dorothy had previously been married to an illustrator and was a fierce devotee of the art world. She took me places I had never been and some I wasn't terribly interested in going back to. But I went anyway to be with this highly attractive, cool, chic, sophisticated lady. One of the photographers she worked with was the venerable, celebrated African American Life Magazine contributor, Gordon Parks. I had met him one evening when he dropped Dorothy off at the apartment. I was a bit jealous because I assumed they were shooting more than pictures. Even while subconsciously not wanting to get serious, I also didn't much like the idea of her seeing someone else. But the fact that she didn't give a shit about the social mores of the time, which definitely did not include black and white sexual fraternization, made her all the more exotic to me.

One Saturday afternoon, Dorothy suggested we go and visit the Time-Life Building where there was a photo exhibit of Gordon Parks' work. At the time, he was one of the most esteemed photographers in the nation and I was fairly interested in seeing what that was all about. What I didn't expect to see in the exhibit was nude photographs of my date, but there they were, right in my face. I guess I hadn't reached a significant enough degree of cool to proudly accept that it was MY girl-friend in those photos, so you other guys can eat your hearts out. It reminded me of the joke where one guy asks another, "Do you have any nude photos of your wife?" The guy, seemingly offended, says he doesn't, and the first guy asks, "Would you like some?" Anyway, I got pissed and proved to the world and myself that I still had some growing up to do. But I think Dorothy enjoyed my naivete and took on the task of sophisticating me.

For all her sophistication, Dorothy wasn't snobbish or a dilettante in any way. Once, in the summer, I asked her if she wanted to go away with me to Montauk for a week on the Matchless and she said, "Sure." She was even OK with the luggage arrangements. She got a fifteen-inch-by-fifteen-inch canvas bag about four inches deep and I told her she could bring as much as she could fit in it. I explained that the Matchless didn't have a trunk and it was only a week.

It was while there, in Montauk, that she told me about a guy she was seeing and expected to marry. Instead of getting pissed, I think that, given my avoidance of responsibility and obvious inability to support another person, I was secretly relieved and pretended to take it in stride. After all, she was still playing away games with me, and I was getting to spend time with someone I really liked and kind of idolized. So maybe after all, I was making some progress on the sophistication trail.

At some point, Dorothy did become engaged to him and she thought we should put our relationship to bed, but not in the way I would have preferred. She had taught me well and I was cool with it. Then, one night, as I was coming home from Sparks with my trophy of the evening, we must have made a bit of noise laughing as we went up the stairs to my place. A few minutes after we got to my apartment, and before the main event started, who knocks on the door? Dorothy! That really pissed my "date" off and she left in the appropriate huff, and Dorothy and I started a whole new relationship. I was becoming very cool, at least according to me!

During our relationship, Dorothy hooked me up with Ed Leach who owned a modeling agency that specialized in "real people" models, the definition of which is people who couldn't make it in the big time but would work for little money. I maintained that tradition by doing a little work for Ed for very little money. I thought it would be fun and exciting. Actually, I found it boring. It seemed to me that all you did was stand around and wait and then the photographer appeared, took a few shots, disappeared again, and then there was more waiting. But I appreciated the money, as little as it was. Plus, I had a real job.

I thought things were going along smoothly at WBFM. Sales were increasing, I was making more than my eighty-five-dollar-a-week draw, and it was a pleasure working with and for Stan. There was more interest in the future of FM stations as their signal, while not as strong as many AMs, was clearer and music sounded better on FM. However, I soon found out how this would affect me.

One day, Stan gave me a heads-up that someone was interested in buying WBFM and that when, and if, it happened, we would all most likely lose our jobs. I had long since dropped the thought of returning to college. I loved radio, so I started looking for sales jobs at other stations.

It soon became evident that the station would be sold to WPIX-TV, then owned by the *New York Daily News*, part of the Chicago Tribune Syndicate, one of the most conservative media companies in the country at the time. They bought WBFM in early 1964 and got a prime signal at 101.9 in the nation's #1 market for only $400,000!

I was sorry to see my relationship with Stan Gurell end, and I will always be thankful to him for all he did for me and the opportunities he opened for me. In radio, I finally found something I loved and really wanted to be good at, a first for me. Now what?

NINE
Up Up And Away

Lynn Christian, an FM pioneer who had achieved notable success running KODA-FM in Houston, was brought in as General Manager of WPIX-FM. Lynn was smart and soft-spoken, had a sense of humor, and was a highly knowledgeable radio guy.

To build a strong, loyal audience, his intention was to move PIX from a pay for play type station where, if you could sell a show, the station would run it, to a tightly formatted station that programmed familiar music by popular, but not rock, artists on a consistent basis, like the AMs did. He dubbed the new format the PIX PENTHOUSE. The name gave the station a strong and unique personality and helped define it to potential advertisers.

Out of curiosity—or courtesy—Lynn interviewed all the WBFM employees as he began the hiring process. I was nervous as hell because I desperately wanted to stay in radio, the only job I ever took seriously. I got all gussied up for my interview, wore my best suit, even got a haircut, and went to the interview with a high degree of nerves, fear, trepidation, and hope My search for a sales job at other stations had produced no luck thus far, After talking with Lynn, I found I really liked him and was excited by his plans for the station, and I absolutely wanted to be a part of it.

After a few anxious days, I got the call from him. I was hired; the sole survivor from WBFM. My title was Account Executive, radio's name for salespeople. The job came with a salary, not a draw, plus commission,

$110 a week, plus ten percent commission, and a real expense account. Progress!

Lynn was an innovator and visionary in many ways. He led the way in treating an FM station like an AM in terms of programming and personnel. He was the first in New York to hire a female salesperson and an African American salesperson. Lynn also broke the color barrier in the radio booth by hiring one of the first African Americans, if not the first ever, to work as a DJ for a non-ethnic station. Ken Harper, who had been an Armed Forces Radio announcer, became the midnight-to-six-in-the-morning DJ. Ken later went on to create *THE WIZ,* a highly successful Black adaptation of *THE WIZARD OF OZ* that first ran on Broadway and then became a film starring Diana Ross.

After taking ownership of the station, there was some work to be done before they could "flip the switch" and put the new format on the air. We kept running the WBFM "elevator music." And when there was a paid program I hosted it, as I was the only survivor of the old station, and thus the only person familiar with WBFM programming. One night, while airing *Curtain Time* for sponsor Pan Am, I came to a commercial break and proudly announced that "Pan Am serves twenty-six international shitties daily." Lynn and Charlie Whitaker, the new program director, were standing outside the studio and looking in when I said this. Fortunately, they laughed at my *faux pas.* They were ready to introduce the new format anyway, so it was almost my last night on the air.

The revised station debuted to some fanfare with free TV spots courtesy of WPIX-TV. It was great having a TV station for promotion, but there were still very few people who owned FM radios, so our audience was limited. But Lynn also had some innovative sales ideas. One was to offer new sponsors a Charter Package: a fifty-two-week, high-frequency plan with category exclusivity. Since I had been selling FM for over a year and knew where "the bodies were buried," I set out to exhume them. I already had some agency contacts, and that gave me an advantage, so I soon became the star salesman; although, that star was quite low in the overall advertising galaxy. I sold most of the Charter Packages. The spots were sixteen dollars each, which meant every time a spot aired, I made $1.36, so I was making well over one hundred dollars in commission a week on the Charter Packages alone. I felt like I was stealing. My dream, in those days, was to make $15,000 a year. I thought of fifteen grand as a killing. Talk about setting the bar low! But I rarely thought of money if I had enough for the essentials. What was most important was escaping boredom, being challenged, and doing something I liked and believed in, a totally new experience for me. OMG! Is this what maturity feels like?

After the kickoff, WPIX-FM slowly gained recognition in the small but growing world of FM. I now had a product I loved and believed in, and maybe now I could come in through the front door after years of sneaking around the back.

Perhaps I was doing too well because I got a bit cocky a little too early. Part of my job was to knock down the walls that kept FM salespeople from getting agency business. The fear that as soon as they let one of us in, they'd have to open the doors to everyone else still prevailed.

I became frustrated at meetings when a potential buyer expressed little or no knowledge of FM in general, much less our station. At one meeting with an ornery guy who acted like I should be paying him for the meeting, I reached the end of my patience, which was separated from my mouth by a thin cord. I asked him, "Do you have an FM radio?"

"No, I don't. Why don't you get one for me?" he snottily countered.

"Who gave you your TV...NBC?" And thus ended the meeting with this guy who had gone from suspect to prospect and now, reject. I resigned the agency and warned my successor that I had paved a rocky road for him.

Another time, I was meeting with the buyer for American Airlines at Doyle Dane Bernbach, a top agency. Of all potential advertisers, American Airlines was the bullseye for the upscale audience that FM stations offered and WPIX-FM was becoming a leader in the pack. But I was getting nowhere with this guy and frustration was setting in. Finally, I asked him if he was familiar with the station, and he replied, "No." I asked him if he had an FM radio and got the same response.

I lost it. I didn't give a damn anymore and said, "You really should have one."

He asked why and I replied, "Because it's your fucking job."

I got up to leave, hoping I would still have a job when I got back to the station, and he said, "Wait a minute, wise guy. Sit down and tell me more about this fucking FM." I got the business and became a trusted source of information for him on the medium. Sometimes I guess it pays to be a New Yorker if you're willing to take the shit along with the shot. But I was very lucky I said it to the right guy.

Most of the media buyers then were single females, and while I was very social with the guys, I was careful not to fraternize with the women. Lunch was fine, but drinks after work was verboten in my mind. It was undoubtedly misplaced arrogance on my part, but I figured if I asked a female buyer out for a drink after work and she agreed, that could lead to dinner, and after dinner, who knows. I didn't think it was a good idea to start dating a buyer and then do my usual disappearing act.

The exception was Gail Roman. Gail worked for an agency with movie clients, in fact, most of the movie clients. Gail was smart, very attractive, super cool, a lot of fun, a good source of business...and married. At one time she had been engaged to the son of the French Ambassador so, in addition to everything else, she also had a lot of class. Given my attire and attitude, she kiddingly referred to me as a carnival barker. I really liked her. We became friends and immensely enjoyed our time together but respected our boundaries. She's married; I'm single. She's a buyer; I'm a seller. Don't screw this one up, Dick. Nevertheless, at one of our relatively infrequent lunches, she told me she and her husband had just split up. I extended my sympathies and asked her out for drinks that night. It turns out she kind of liked me too, and we had a brief romance.

About that time, my friend who ran the weekend ski trips to Sugarbush in Vermont decided to expand his repertoire and organized a trip to Aspen. This was in 1965. I had only skied for a few days in

Up Up And Away

Germany and a lot in Vermont and upstate New York, so I signed up to *Go West Young Man* in the immortal words of Horace Greeley on his advice to Eastern skiers. Huey Maher, a Dome alumnus and one of my best buddies, came with me.

The chartered plane that left JFK at the crack of 2:00 a.m. (EST), shortly before the airport bars closed, landed in Denver about 5:00 a.m. (MST), where we transferred to busses for the six-hour trip to Aspen. Everyone was oohing and aahing at the mountains as we drove past, most of us for the first time. Finally, after a few hours of this, Huey groggily turned to me and said, "Enough of this majesty. Let's just get the fuck there." When we did, it was well worth the trip. Aspen was phenomenal. It was still a cowboy town back then, undiscovered by the rich and famous. Most of the streets weren't even paved. The town itself was at about eight thousand feet and over eleven thousand at the summit of Ajax Mountain. I had never breathed—much less skied—at that altitude. It literally took my breath away.

As Eastern skiers, we couldn't believe the width of the runs and the sensational quality of the snow. Absolute heaven! In those days, there weren't a lot of Eastern skiers trying it in the West. We were used to skiing on ice. I used to say if the driving was good, the skiing was bad, and conversely, if the driving was bad, the skiing was good, at least for an hour or so before the new snow got skied off and became ice.

One Aspen local commented, "Some of you Eastern skiers aren't bad."

I explained, "You don't understand the difference. Here, if you miss a turn, you make the next one. In the East, if you miss a turn, you wait for the toboggan and hope you didn't kill the tree."

Given the altitude and the enthusiasm we had for the mountain, our evenings were generally short, but I did meet a girl from New York, Susan, aka Susu, who stole my heart. That was petty larceny in those days. But when I got back to New York, I had to explain to Gail that I was otherwise occupied.

I must admit, Susu gave me a dose of my own medicine. She was from a social family in Washington, DC. Her parents had passed away, but not before imbuing her with some of their social mores.

I was comic relief for her, a diversion from her norm. She liked the difference in our lifestyles; she thought my motorcycle was cool and enjoyed visiting the other side of the tracks, if having a decent job in the media and an apartment in Manhattan was *the other side of the tracks*. But she got to me, nevertheless.

One Friday afternoon, I went to pick her up. She had wheels and we were going to Southampton for a skeet shooting weekend. I preferred skeet to live creatures as targets. I had never done it, but I assumed Susu was an aficionado. I had a shotgun from my hunting days, borrowed a hand-held skeet thrower and bought a carton of clay pigeons. I schlepped all this shit to her Upper East Side apartment on the bus and, when I was there, she wasn't. No note, no nothing. I didn't know if I was more hurt or more pissed, probably both as I maneuvered all this crap back to my place. She called on Monday and gave me some lame-ass, obviously bullshit excuse. She wanted to see me, so I picked her up on the bike and we went to dinner in Brooklyn at Lundy's, a hugely popular seafood restaurant. When we got back, she asked me up to her apartment. I came to my senses and told her, "No. Let's stop playing games. It was fun for me, and I hope for you, but it's over." I felt like the leftovers after a meal where sometimes you get picked up, swallowed, and appreciated, but sometimes you're just left on the plate because nobody wants you.

Meanwhile, not surprisingly, I hadn't gotten any business from Gail. So, after a few months, I called her and said, "Gail, I'm going to resign your agency and give it to someone else. We should be doing business and it's my fault we aren't. I apologize for that. I really like you and I screwed it up."

She responded, "Don't worry about it. I met a guy and I'm in love. Keep the agency and let's be friends." Gail was one classy lady, and we did exactly as she suggested. And, by the way, she married the guy. But that wasn't the last time her name came up in my life.

I did have one very unpleasant experience on my Eastern skiing forays. I was in Vermont skiing with "the guys." We were on a black diamond run. It was icy. I was doing what I did best, trying to ski at speeds above my ability. Suddenly, I fell, and I slid headfirst off the trail and saw a tree coming at me...or, more accurately, I was coming toward the tree. I had one shot to avoid it. I tried to twist away from it but didn't quite make it. I glanced off the tree with my lower spine and I immediately knew I was hurt.

I lay in the snow in pain as my friends skied over to me. They tried to make me laugh, but that hurt even more. I had to admit I was scared. Did I break my back? Am I paralyzed? I was too afraid to try to move, but shock set in, and I started shaking...which hurt more. A ski patrol guy finally arrived. Alone. Terrific! Could he manage me by himself? I couldn't stand the suspense, so I tried to move my arms and legs. They worked, at least for the time being they did, but would the patrolman be able to get me into the toboggan and down the mountain without slicing my spinal cord or crashing the toboggan on the ice?

He did. They threw the toboggan, with me in it, into the back of a panel truck and took off for the hospital in Montpelier. When we got there, it was into the x-ray room we went. The doctor, who obviously had better things to do on a Sunday afternoon was surly and perfunctory as he read the x-rays. He looked at me like I was one of them candy-assed New Yorkers that had no place on a real man's mountain. He told me there was nothing wrong.

I asked him, "Can I leave?"

He sarcastically replied, "If you can walk."

He gave me a prescription for four Darvon. I had them for dinner.

It was an agonizing drive back to New York the next day. But I was OK, right? So, I went back to work. But when I walked down the street, sometimes the pain would hit me. It was like being blindsided or, in football parlance, clipped. I literally fell on the sidewalk time and again. It was not impressive when I showed up for a client meeting with holes in the knees of my suit. A few days later, I received a letter from Dr. Mengele telling me that he read my x-rays wrong. Turns out I had two broken bones in my back.

Fast forward two years. I was back in Vermont fun racing with my ski club. I missed a gate and fell hard on my shoulder, which resulted in incredible pain. I thought it could be dislocated, so I skied down to First Aid. It was in a large room and the doctor treated patients right there, no privacy. Guess who the doctor was? Right! The x-ray king.

When my turn came, he didn't recognize me, and with the same shit-eating smirk, he examined me and said, "You're fine." But his attitude said, "Just another wimp."

The other people in the room could hear his diagnosis and pick up on his attitude.

So, I replied in a loud voice, "Doctor, the last time you told me I was OK, I had two broken bones in my back."

I get a big laugh from the other patients in the room and the smirk went sliding down his face like Killy falling in the downhill at Chamonix. He suddenly recognized me and registered concern. But whether it was about me or his medical malpractice policy, I couldn't tell. But in this case, the payback was worth the pain.

But, aside from my skiing problems, I still had professional problems. In those days, if you had a low-rated product to sell, you had to have some shtick if you were going to be successful at ad agencies. This was before computers and the empirical information they spew out. They took a lot of the fun and fiction out of selling and replaced them with annoying facts. In truth, I liked most of the people I dealt with, and despite my protestations otherwise (when I was just looking for a laugh), I was fair and honest and tried to build lasting relationships instead of one-shots. But I also wanted the business and sometimes was unorthodox about getting it, but never unethical.

One case was at a major agency that had a tobacco account that was running fifty-two-week schedules annually, great business if you could get it, but not easy for a low-rated station. That was obviously before tobacco was prohibited from advertising on broadcast media and before we knew that cigarettes were cancer carriers.

I was told there was a new buyer on the account, and she was really tough. I set up an appointment with great apprehension, given that our story wasn't exactly compelling. She seemed very stern. Her first question was, "Tell me about your station. Why should I buy you?"

Good question. How do I answer that? Like all the other guys with an earful of bullshit? No! I decided I had nothing to lose, so why not take another tack and kind of go for broke. I answered, "Well, Hillary, we have great plans for the station. First, we're going to try and get our FCC license back."

She broke up laughing. She was smart and had a good sense of humor. My response was probably a breath of fresh air for her after all the crap she heard. And, because of my off-the-wall response, she trusted me. I gave her a good deal and we got the business.

With the FCC decreeing that AM/FM combos must program each separately, owners of combos began to take their FMs seriously and try new things. One of the innovations was an all-female format that debuted on WNEW-FM. Because I had experience and agency contacts and could write my own name without the help of witnesses, I became of interest to the station.

The GM called me for a job interview. Female DJs were new to the medium, all without prior experience, and the format wasn't really getting any traction with an audience. The GM was ready to offer me a sales position. I was interested because it was owned by Metromedia, a big operator that I thought offered great opportunity, especially since the WPIX owners seemed so myopic that Lynn was becoming disenchanted, and I didn't know how much longer he could take it.

The GM asked, "How much are you looking to make?"

I confidently replied, "A minimum of $15,000 a year."

"$15,000!" he repeated. "Are you insane?"

I snapped back, "Have you heard your station recently?"

That ended my career at Metromedia. You may be starting to see the validity in that saying, "I have met the enemy, and it is me." I know. It should be, "It is I."

Soon after that, I got a call from WOR-FM. They, too, were strong operators, with their AM station being dominant in the marketplace. They announced they were going to be the first FM station in America to program rock 'n roll on FM with legendary DJs Murray the K, Scott Muni, and Rosko. They were obviously going to make some big waves. The idea of rock on FM was heresy, like farting in church...but highly interesting to me, the outsider.

The Sales Manager asked, "Do you want to talk?"

"Try and shut me up." I replied. I wanted nothing better. The idea of selling FM's first rock station was beyond cool. But leaving Lynn would be tough.

I really liked the Sales Manager at WOR-FM and we hit it off. Since I knew where the bucks were buried and had some success in turning suspects into prospects...and clients, he thought that I could contribute. Also, I was young, and he felt I was living the lifestyle. He gave me a good offer. Now I had to go back and tell Lynn this rat was abandoning the ship. I felt really shitty because I liked him so much and believed in the station. But it was my career, and the thought of being with the first FM rocker drowned out the misgivings.

When I got back to the station, I went into Lynn's office and spilled the beans. He was surprised and then he surprised me. He said he was putting me up for General Sales Manager, a new position at the station and a huge promotion.

I said, "Come on, Lynn. We're friends. Don't bullshit me."

He countered, "I'm not. I'll show it to you." And sure enough, he dragged out a recent memo (no emails then) he had written to his superiors recommending me for that slot.

I was very appreciative, but knowing the glacial pace at which WPIX moved, I thought I'd be in a rocker rather than working at a one before that happened. "Lynn, I've got to give WOR an answer by the close of business today. That ain't going to happen in this place."

"We'll see about that," he said. And damned if he didn't pull it off. I became the General Sales Manager of a New York radio station at a very young age. It really had nothing to do with my potential management skills. It was all about my sales ability, and the truth was I was happy to be staying with Lynn and somewhat impressed with my luck.

Nothing really changed, except I now had to hire and help the other salespeople, and I still basically had my agency list, but I was now a member of management.

Lynn then introduced me to the concept of having a national sales rep selling the station to out-of-town buyers, like in Chicago, Detroit, LA, etc. where we had no sales coverage. At that time, McGavren-Guild was a prominent national radio rep firm that Lynn had worked with in Texas. Initially, given our ratings against AM stations in the market, there wasn't much for them to sell, but we had nothing to lose.

TEN
Anchors Away

It wasn't all work. One Thursday night in early May, I was anchored to a barstool at some New York City singles joint, surrounded by a throng of bright young professionals with great expectations and supposedly brilliant careers in front of them. They were all networking, looking for the next big opportunity to present itself. Unfortunately, most of them were destined to stay on this conveyor belt to mediocrity until they fell off or got kicked off.

I saw a friend, Jus Fisher, enter the joint. We'd gone skiing a few times with the same group in Vermont and Colorado and we got along well. We exchanged mindless bar chatter for a few minutes and then he hit me with it.

"Hey man, you got any plans for the weekend? You up for an adventure?" I mean, how do you answer a question like that? Say "no" and you lose your membership in the Boys Club. But I was usually up for the unusual. I liked action.

"What do you have in mind, Jus?"

"Sailing. I race a sailboat in the Atlantic class. It's up in Buzzard's Bay on the Cape getting updated and I need to get it to Westport for the season. I'm flying up tomorrow morning. Come with me. It'll be a kick, and I could use the help."

"How big is your boat?"

"Thirty-one feet." That sounded OK and I liked the idea of a weekend on the water, even though it was still quite cold. I didn't really know much about sailing, but the previous summer I'd been on a friend's twenty-nine-footer, and we had a blast port hopping. It slept four, had a galley, a toilet, and a shower.

"When will we be back?"

"Probably Sunday afternoon."

"Sold. I just have to make some adjustments to my work schedule."

"Great! Wings up at 11:00 a.m. out of LaGuardia. I'm going to go see if I can shanghai Billy. Three will be better than two." He sauntered over to put the proposition to Billy O'Brien. I thought the chances were slim, as Billy had the most envious attendance record at that bar of any of us. I was wrong! Billy was on board (no pun) with it.

At 9:00 a.m. sharp on Friday, I show up in Lynn's office. He was my boss, but by that time, also a good friend. He looks at me quizzically as I'm dressed in jeans and a sweater and carrying a sleeping bag.

"Hey Lynn, something personal has come up and I'm going to have to leave a little early today."

"OK! That shouldn't be a problem," he answered. "What time are you going?"

"In about fifteen minutes."

Jus appears to be a very competent guy. Tall, ruggedly handsome, quiet, confident, the kind of guy you'd want to share a foxhole with if you were unfortunate enough to be seeking those accommodations.

Billy, on the other hand, is the guy you'd hire to work the room as a warm-up act in a Catskills showroom. A bit short, wiry hair, ruddy complexion, and funny as hell, but...get out of my foxhole.

We got to the marina at Buzzard's Bay in early afternoon and Jus went ballistic. "There it is. There it is!" he shouted. The boat he indicated looked to me like it was about eight feet long.

"Jus, that little thing can't be it. You said it was thirty-one-feet long."

"Dick," he replied, looking at me like I was stupid, "All day sailers look small. They're fast because they're light. The hull doesn't displace much water because there's no cabin or bunks or galley to take up room and weigh the boat down.

"How about a toilet," I hopefully asked.

"Don't be absurd. They weigh a ton."

"Where do we sleep?"

"In the cockpit." Exactly. "In" implies underneath something, like protection from the weather. Not the case here. The cockpit is an open area.

"What about that place?" I said, eyeballing the miniature cabin-like enclosure in the middle of the boat.

"That's for the sails so they don't get wet." Priorities!

"Where do we buy the beer?" screamed Seaman O'Brien.

For a guy who doesn't like commitments, I sure outdid myself on this one. Three guys, two of whom only add weight to the boat, are now taking an open sailboat into the Atlantic Ocean in early May.

Anyway, we went to town and bought provisions for the voyage. We got enough beer so that if we were boarded by a large band of pirates, we'd have been able to entertain them in style for a couple of days.

As we loaded the stuff aboard, the reality of what we were about to do hit me, and I suddenly became a bit nervous. "Where's the radio, Jus?"

"Nah, don't have one. Our races are all day races. Don't want the weight."

"Got any life preservers," I asked in a wiseass voice, "Or do they weigh too much?"

He did have a compass and a few nautical charts, which looked to me like topical maps of Hindustan. So, around five o'clock in the evening, we headed out to sea. Or tried to. The wind had chosen not to accompany us on our voyage, and we were going nowhere...slowly. Don't even ask about an engine. The SS Jenny Craig was also not weighed down by running lights.

Then a dense fog set in, and we were unable to see where we weren't going, so our Captain ordered us to drop anchor, the end of our first day.

I like speed with my adventures, and this wasn't cutting it for me. I had envisioned us slicing through the water at hull speed with the mainsail, jib, and spinnaker filled with wind and the boat healing over to the rail. What we got was three guys sitting in the cold, damp fog, drinking a few beers, but those spirits didn't do much for ours.

Anchors Away

Morning came early and it took over an hour to make instant coffee on a portable gas stove, which I was amazed Jus hadn't thrown over the side to save weight.

We left the safety of Buzzard's Bay and entered the forbidding waters of the Atlantic.

Then, an even greater reality struck. Religiously, after morning coffee, my next move is to the bathroom for a good dump. That day was no exception, and in the absence of a toilet—but not the need for one—I had to make do with what we had. That turned out to be me dropping my pants, hanging on to the shrouds, those wires on which the sails are connected to the top of the mast, and leaning over the side and polluting the ocean.

We were in the open ocean now, out of sight of land, desperately hoping that Jus had not saved money by buying the cheapest charts available and that he knew how to read the ones he had. It was a strange sensation. Our lives were totally dependent on those charts and the compass.

Around early afternoon, the mist turned to rain, and it got colder. It's one thing to be cold yet know it's temporary and that you'll soon be warm. It's totally another thing to be cold and wet and on the ocean, headed for a couple days of more cold and wet without a break.

Jus decided we'd have to put in to port for the night, so we headed to Point Judith, Rhode Island where we dropped the hook.

As night descended, we could see the lights coming on along the shoreline and imagined people in warm, dry clothes, having drinks and hot meals and perhaps a little after-dinner dancing. Instead, we ate baloney sandwiches on wet bread and froze our asses off, and I wondered if peacetime mutiny carried jail time.

It poured rain during the night, and when I woke up on Sunday morning, there was literally over an inch of water keeping me company in my sleeping bag. I leaped out of it, grabbed it, and emptied it over the side.

"You don't like water beds?" O'Brien asked. That got a laugh. It had to. We were so fucked it was almost funny, but not really. We just wanted to focus on getting to Westport and getting off this goddam boat. We hoisted the anchor and took off again at a snail's pace.

We plodded on, and in late afternoon, we got a little sun to celebrate day's end, but it didn't make the boat go any faster, and that was becoming a career challenge for me. As darkness fell, we left the ocean and entered Long Island Sound for the long run from Orient Point to the fabled Westport.

"Jus, not to be a pain in the ass and bring up a sore point, but didn't you say we'd be in Westport Sunday afternoon? And isn't this Sunday afternoon?"

"Yup," he replied, ever laconic. "Looks like it'll be tomorrow afternoon."

"Tomorrow is Monday for chrissake. I have to be at work." Back then, there were no mobile phones, so we couldn't make up an excuse and phone it in. We had reached such a low that it was clear we might even have beer left over.

Thus began a seemingly endless night. Night is very deceptive on open water. In a sailboat, you tack from side to side, and you see the lights of the upcoming shore and it looks so close, but it never gets any closer.

Night became morning at a very leisurely pace, and we accepted it without excitement as we bobbed along, headed for the elusive Westport.

Around nine o'clock, the sun came out, bright, strong, and hot. "Hey, Dick" the captain announced, "You're getting good color. At least you'll get an early season suntan out of this."

"Great. I'll just tell Lynn I was fortunate that the Emergency Room I spent the weekend in had a sun lamp."

And, finally, like all good and bad things, our epic voyage ended, and we docked in Westport in mid-afternoon. Jus chose to stay with the boat to revel in his good fortune while his crew called a cab and headed for the city. On the way, we stopped and I called Lynn to say I'd be a little late. When I explained the whole story to him, he laughed.

ELEVEN
It Ain't Christmas But I'm Carolin'

By then, Dorothy had gotten married and moved out of my life, so I sat there waiting for Miss America to straight-arm a few losers on her way to get to me. Always waiting...always hopeful...rarely fulfilled.

One night at Sparks Pub, life changed dramatically. Baron Bates, my Princeton friend, hadn't yet met Dorie, the attractive waitress and his future wife, but he showed up with his heartthrob of the moment, Ailene, an executive at Seventeen Magazine, who was accompanied by her assistant, Carol Streich. Carol was a good-looking twenty-one-year-old, who was new to the fashion world but didn't have to be taught how to wear a short skirt. A Milwaukee native, she had come to New York to study fashion at FIT, the Fashion Institute of Technology, and her first job out of school was at Seventeen.

Carol was intelligent and had a good sense of humor, two key elements in anyone I intended to spend more than a few late-night hours with. I was smitten with her, and despite my usual reticence, made an actual date for the next night. She lived in the upper 70s on the East Side.

I showed up on my motorcycle to pick her up. That was kind of a test. If the person didn't like the bike, it would be a short evening and even shorter relationship. Carol hopped on the Matchbox like she was saying, "I'm so glad it's not a Harley." We went to a party at Earl's apartment and then to the Village for some serious pub-crawling. She was great! We had a super time and agreed to meet again the next night. By the weekend, we were buddies and lovers.

JUST ANOTHER DICK

One Friday afternoon, on our way to the Hamptons, we were limping along the Long Island Expressway on the Matchless in heavy traffic. I noticed a lot of people staring at Carol. Naturally, I was proud of that, but also curious. When I looked back, I saw she was reading a book. Soooo cool!

Occasionally, on weekends, Carol and I would go upstate to Fishkill, New York where they held motorcycle races on Sundays called scrambles. Scrambles were races run on a dirt track with all kinds of turns and jumps. I was familiar with the track because, before I met Carol, that's where my friend Bob Sinclair and I would sometimes go on Saturday when no one was there, sneak onto the track, and ride it for practice. It was a giant thrill. Put yourself on the seat of the bike. You race down the straightaway, slide around a fifty-degree corner, gas it, go up a short hill, and when you reach the apex, you're airborne and absolutely free...until you land and get ready for the next corner. It's hard to compare that to playing right field at a baseball game, at least for me.

Carol wasn't a boozer, but she also wasn't a critic of my predilection, at least then. We were great buddies, sharing similar opinions on many things. After about six weeks of togetherness, one night, strictly on the spur of the moment and with absolutely no forethought, I asked her to marry me, and she accepted. I was very happy, but also terrified. I damn sure didn't want to get out of it, but the thought of any serious commitment was scary. Me, the emotional coward, would have to face my reality, but it was time. I was twenty-nine and I loved her.

The planning began. We would be married in late September. But where? Carol was Protestant but hardly fanatic about it. We settled on a Catholic wedding strictly to please my mother, since I was an only child and she was a widow. I got out the Yellow Pages and searched under Churches for the one nearest my apartment. Then we thought, "What the hell, let's go big." So, we settled on St. Patrick's Cathedral, not the big altar, but the small one behind it. Carol had to agree, not with me, you understand, but with the priest who married us, to raise any children we had in the Catholic faith. We went along with the gag, having no intentions to honor it.

My buddies gave me a bachelor party, but we were all such professionals in the game that I think I've been to more exciting Irish wakes. The rehearsal dinner was in a restaurant in the village and was highlighted by Carol's fifteen-year-old brother getting totally shitfaced and throwing up all over the place.

The reception was at the Penthouse Club on Central Park South, where my friends all had ample opportunity to demonstrate their social skills when given free alcohol. Carol's father, who was footing the bill, was visibly impressed and somewhat impoverished by their consumptive capabilities. Carol and I had no money for a honeymoon, so, after spending our wedding night at the Plaza, we went to work the next day.

My bachelor apartment turned out to be just that, a place suitable for single living, but not so hot for a couple after the romantic fireside dinners wore off. We needed more space, so we looked around and finally decided on Greenwich Village. We liked the vibe there and found a very cool apartment at 4 Perry Street, a small sliver between Seventh and Greenwich Avenues. It was a third-floor walkup. We loved it, although it was somewhat unconventional. It was a two-bedroom apartment, but you had to walk through the master to get to the second bedroom that was more bunk room than bedroom, size-wise.

The kitchen held one person somewhat tightly, and the living room floor was a bit off-kilter, as though it had barely survived a moderate earthquake. But the prime feature that sold us on the place was a spacious patio terrace that looked out onto the other patio terraces in the neighborhood. Maybe not too private, but a big plus for an NYC apartment.

Carol had somewhat eschewed the fashion world in favor of advertising. She was hired as a copywriter at one of the big "shops," Grey Advertising. Shortly after that, she thought of becoming an actress. She did some research and found HB Studios, a prestigious acting school on Bank Street in the Village, an easy walk from our apartment, founded by Herbert Berghof and Uta Hagen, thus the HB. While she genuinely wanted to do it, Carol was a bit intimidated at the thought and asked me to join her. I agreed, and it was fun, a whole new world for me; although, as I never got the bug to be an on-air radio personality, I also harbored no dreams of an acting career.

In acting school, there are two basic forms of exercises: scene study and improv (perhaps it should be called *improve*). I was not crazy about the discipline of learning the lines and the incessant rehearsing that was required for scene study, but I loved improv. The instructor would give you a situation, then you and one or more of your classmates would get up and go for it. I was good at the extemporaneous smart-ass one-liners, but I was never approached by any agents. Not true of everyone in the class.

One of the students was a young, fifteen-year-old girl who was strongly motivated, but intensely shy, to the point where she simply attended class religiously but didn't volunteer to do a scene or a monologue. After a few weeks, the teacher told her nicely that it was an acting, not a viewing, class and she either had to do a scene or drop out. He said she could do a monologue and could choose to use someone in the class as a foil if she felt more comfortable that way. Guess who she chose. Me. I thought she might need the help of a casting director in any future productions, but she probably felt safe with me, as my wife was also in the class and my acting ability was no threat to her dreams.

She elected to do what was basically a monologue from *Member Of The Wedding*. My role was John Henry, a six-year-old with no lines. If this were a stage production, can you imagine the time that would be required for hair and makeup, transitioning a mid-thirties guy into a six-year-old kid? She'd come to our apartment to rehearse around seven o'clock in the evening. Carol would serve dinner, and we'd go at it—or she would, as I had virtually no role. I was as important to the scene as a lamp. I felt more like a fool than a foil. Sometime around one in the morning, I'd say, "Let's bag it. I have to go to work tomorrow, or more accurately, today."

She'd say, "Just a couple more times. Please!"

It Ain't Christmas But I'm Carolin'

She once said to me, "You are so lucky. You're not afraid of people. You'll say anything to them. I wish I could do that. Agents and people like that scare me to death."

Somehow, she very obviously overcame those fears and has had an amazing career in film, television, and on stage. She was in *Annie Hall*, got an Oscar nomination for *Hester Street,* and was a principle on the long-running TV show, *Taxi,* while also appearing on Broadway in *Wicked*. Her name is Carol Kane.

Our acting instructor's name was William "Bill" Hickey. Bill was a highly respected, but under-utilized, character actor. A few years later, I had a Local Sales Manager who had been an actor and studied with (and was still friendly with) Bill. He had an idea: acting lessons for salespeople, taught by Bill. It hit at the core of many salespeople's problems. They don't listen. Good acting requires you to listen and be in the moment with the other actor(s) to be effective. Sales is supposed to be problem solving. People don't buy stuff they don't need. By applying acting techniques and getting your prospects to talk about their problems, you learn their needs and it opens the door to convincing them that your product will solve them. Dale Carnegie once said, "If you see John Doe through John Doe's eyes, you'll sell John Doe what John Doe buys." Very true! Unfortunately, the idea lives only in this tome. It never happened and I forget why, but I still regret we never did it.

Given my daily work schedule and its challenges, I was tired and wanted to get away for a while. I said to my wife, Carol, "I know. Let's go skiing in Europe for a couple of weeks."

She looked at me like I was suffering from severe dementia and suggested I take a glance at our checkbook to see if I could find any money there to finance my folly.

"Listen. I've worked my ass off and I need a break. I'm going. You'll love it and we need it."

It worked. We went to Zermatt, Switzerland for two weeks and it was a sensational trip. Zermatt is a magical town...no cars, great skiing by the

Eiger mountain, or just slip your passport into your parka and take a run down to Italy.

When we got back, it turned out Carol had been right all along. We clearly couldn't afford it and now the pressure was on to pay for it. What can we do to get some quick cash and get American Express off our asses?

I remembered that I was in a cab one day when the driver stopped to talk to a friend of his who was pushing a cart selling pretzels. When we drove off, he said he, too, had once been a pretzel vendor. I said, "Well, I guess you're glad you don't have to do that anymore."

"Are you kidding?" he responded. "That guy makes a lot of money selling those pretzels. Especially on weekends."

I took that in and, as the financial pressure was mounting, one day Carol and I happened to be walking down Fifth Avenue when we came to another pretzel vendor. We each bought one and I asked him, "You make any money doing this?"

"Hell," he said, "On a nice day in the park, I can pick up $125-150." And that was in 1969 money. Not bad. So, I asked how it worked and he explained. If I wanted to do it, I should go over to West Forty-Ninth Street to get the pushcart. That was free, but I had to buy the pretzels when I took the cart.

So, the next Saturday, we went over to Forty-Ninth Street, got the cart, bought the pretzels, and headed for the park. I was wearing a beret as a disguise. As we walked up Sixth Avenue, I looked up at the ABC building and hoped none of my friendly competitors were up there looking at me schlepping the pretzel wagon up the street.

It was a beautiful spring day, sunny and unseasonably warm, maybe more of an ice cream than a hot pretzel day. Anyway, we set up our pushcart at what we felt would be a good location in Central Park. One of our first customers was an NYPD officer who didn't want to buy pretzels; he wanted to give me a summons for unlicensed selling. He asked for my ID, and when I gave him my driver's license, he was shocked and asked,

"Is this your first day?" That made me surmise that my colleagues in the business carried no ID on them.

All in all, we got three summonses before we dragged our asses back to Forty-Ninth Street with a lot of unsold pretzels that, naturally, were not returnable. Since we were so late, the boss figured we'd been arrested. "Happens all the time," he said.

The following week, I took a half day off and spent it in court with my fellow entrepreneurs paying my debt to society. Thus, another career ended. Between the fines and the cost of the unsold pretzels, we lost our ass and still owed everybody money.

Despite that adversity, I was happy with my job and my life and anticipated no immediate changes, until one night, Carol announced she was pregnant. We were euphoric because, while we had not planned to have a child, we were now in love with the concept. One problem. The apartment was not exactly kid friendly. It wouldn't be a lot of fun for Carol, trying to balance a baby on one shoulder while wrestling the carriage up three flights of stairs. We needed a new place, but at that time, it seemed like every vacancy in all of New York City had multiple offers. It was an endless and frustrating hunt. There was a joke going around that when the single resident of a rent-controlled apartment died, the undertaker removing the body tried to rent the place but was told the physician who declared the person dead had already gotten it.

Then we got lucky. A friend of Carol's from work was getting married and she and her roommate were vacating their fifteenth-floor apartment at 200 East 71st Street off Second Avenue. It was a two-bedroom with a doorman and the works (if an elevator is considered the works). I had never considered the Upper East Side, too vanilla. But I now embraced it like a long-lost love. We got the apartment for $325 a month, proof of our upward mobility, but an absolute steal, grand larceny at today's prices. It was also an easy commute, as my office was on Forty-Second and Second. However, I soon found that walking the mile and a half was faster than waiting for the bus.

Anyway, as the birth date of our child became imminent, that naturally became our primary concern. We were super excited about having a baby, a boy. What about a name? Carol and I batted numerous choices around but didn't hit on any that dazzled us. A few months into her pregnancy, in an act of total ignorance and self-absorption on my part, we went skiing in Aspen. Carol was a gamester. One afternoon, after we left the slopes, we were standing outside a restaurant/bar having a drink and we heard a guy say to his young son, "Dillon, get over here." That was it! Dylan, with a "y" in homage to Dylan Thomas rather than some shit-kicking cowboy with two Ls in it. It was short and distinctive and difficult to make fun of. Now that he was named, he just needed to be born.

Carol was going to have a natural childbirth and I would be there to support her. Finally, ten days late, the labor pains started in the middle of the night. We grabbed her stuff and jumped into a cab for the trip to Mount Sinai Hospital. I remember thinking on the way, "Wow! Who will he be? What will he be like? I was in a state of high excitement while Carol had more immediate and, literally, more pressing problems on her mind.

She was in a great deal of pain, and on examination, the doctor found that Dylan was crossways in the uterus. They quickly put Carol on a gurney that raced out of the room, leaving me. I was no longer a key player in the production. I was relegated to a Waiting Room role, which turned out to be an apt name for it.

Finally, a few hours later, I couldn't take the worrying and waiting, so I went to the head nurse and asked if there was any news. She got my name and came back with a big smile on her face, saying the baby was born a couple of hours ago and he and his mother were doing just fine. Carol was in good spirits but rather depleted from the process.

Dylan, on the other hand, looked like he had gotten into a fight with the kid in the bassinet next to him, and following in my footsteps, had come in second. His face was a bit banged up from where they had to use the forceps or calipers or whatever they used to straighten him out, so he could initially see the world head-first like the other kids.

It Ain't Christmas But I'm Carolin'

Carol had left her job to be a full-time mom. We had bought a white cane rocking chair, and I remember giving Dylan his bottle in the middle of the night in that chair, and I loved it. As he got older and assumed the skills of a pedestrian, I would relieve Carol on Saturdays and take Dylan to Central Park where we'd visit the zoo, have lunch, and just hang out. Those were very special days. He was funny and tons of fun to be with, and after all my years of self-indulgence, I loved being a father and somehow slipped into the role, but I doubt I'd get any Oscars for my performance.

I now had real responsibility, a wife, a child, and a growing career. I sometimes wondered what had happened to the aimless drifter of my early days, but I didn't miss him.

TWELVE
Opposites Attract

Opposites rarely attract, but in my case, they had a head-on collision. How about racing and politics? Do they qualify as opposites? Racing I knew as a spectator; on the other hand, the politics, I basked in total ignorance, but not for long.

I was an avid racing fan, cars and motorcycles. I would rather sit in the stands for a local midget auto race than in the dugout for a World Series game. And racing was about to play a highly expanded role in my life.

After WWII, sports car racing, primarily European cars, became a popular, if somewhat minority, sporting attraction. Bridgehampton, at the Eastern end of Long Island, in the very heart of the fashionable Hamptons, had a proud history of that racing from its inception in this country.

The races were initially run on the town's streets and gained national recognition, but as the cars got faster, racing became too dangerous for local roads, and after a series of accidents, Bridgehampton canceled future races. However, the sport was good for local business. It put Bridgehampton on the map, so the town built a three-mile racecourse that scored high marks with both drivers and fans. It was both a challenging and picturesque track situated in the hills overlooking Peconic Bay.

Unfortunately, the local banks weren't such big fans and the operator/promoter who rented the track for the races eventually opted out. So, the track sat vacant.

Opposites Attract

Meanwhile, Earl Gandel, with whom I had become extremely friendly, bought a summer home in Noyac, just a few miles from Bridgehampton. Carol and I usually spent Saturday evenings at his place when we visited my mother.

One weekend, Bob Bochroch, a KABC-TV salesman and another racing fanatic whose father was a relatively prominent racing journalist, joined us at Earl's, and the conversation turned to racing and the unfortunate situation at "The Bridge", which was the in-crowd's name for the racetrack. At about two o'clock in the morning, after our brains were fully lubricated, we decided that, with our marketing expertise, we should be able to remedy that situation if we took it over ourselves. Unfortunately, the next morning, we somehow remembered the conversation and decided we wanted to see if we could make that happen.

Promotionally, we looked good. Earl was in advertising; Bob was in TV; I was in radio. However, if you stood the three of us upside down and shook us, only a little change would fall out, but we somehow felt capable of running a major facility in what was perhaps the world's most expensive sport at that time. That's an example of the power of alcohol.

A friend of mine, a Board member of the track, got us a meeting with them at which we gave them our thoughts, and in a move probably out of desperation, they wound up leasing us the entire facility, a three-mile race circuit on a six-hundred-acre parcel of land, for $7,500 a year.

We were now the operators of a renowned track on which we had seen our heroes race. In addition to being exhilarating, it was also frightening. We knew virtually nothing about the business of racing, and our only business dealings in the sport were with the folks who sold the tickets at the gate.

We each had full-time jobs, so this was to be a part-time undertaking, a word we sincerely hoped would not be used in the future to evaluate our performance.

I had a friend, Bill Conlon, who was and is a contemporary painter and another race freak. We spent many Saturday evenings fueling our interest with Jose Cuervo at the wheel. We obviously needed someone with vision and creativity to help us and Bill offered to be that person. An attorney was another essential, and our mutual buddy Peter Berla introduced us to John Lankenau who took over legal issues for us. John also became a good friend.

Bill took over creating a "look" for the track, while Earl, Bob, and I set about booking some local races and getting track sponsors to support that effort.

At the time, the unofficial headquarters of the racing community was a restaurant in New York City called Le Chanteclair, owned by Rene and Maurice Dreyfus. Rene had been a famed race driver in Europe for the legendary auto manufacturer, Bugatti, and Maurice was his riding mechanic. We took all our prospects and suspects to Le Chanteclair for lunch and hung out there ourselves in the hope of meeting someone, anyone, who could help us. The food at Le Chanteclair was very French and very rich, and I began to worry that our first racetrack casualty would be one of us coming down with the gout.

We achieved initial success in the sponsorship area, selling Castrol and Pirelli on sponsoring the actual bridges that ran over the track. Plus, we sold other minor sponsorships to put some money in the till.

We also convinced Fred Opert, a New Jersey racecar dealer, to open a race drivers' school at Bridgehampton. He used Formula Fords as classrooms. They looked like mini-Indy cars, rear-engined, fast, and super handling. We all got to flaunt our incompetence on the track in his cars, and that alone was worth our entire investment.

I never tired of driving one of Fred's cars or riding the Matchbox around the track at speeds that made me feel alive. Going into a corner on the bike and laying it over as far as I dared or sliding around one in the car...FREEDOM! Fuck baseball.

Most of our money would come from track rentals. We loved the SCCA (Sports Car Club of America) Nationals because there was a track rental fee, no winners' purses required, and we could keep whatever money we charged spectators for entry.

Opposites Attract

While club racing and rentals were our bread and butter, we longed for big-time racing, the stuff that would reestablish the track nationally and make us rich, simple objectives until you tried to attain them.

Around that time, a new racing sanction appeared, IMSA, the International Motor Sports Association. They agreed to stage one of their first races at Bridgehampton and we finally had our "money" race, or so we thought.

John Radosta, then the racing columnist for the New York Times, gave us his whole column the Sunday before the race. All my friends at other radio stations stepped up and traded out tickets they didn't want or need in exchange for commercials promoting the event. That week, I think our race had more radio advertising in New York than all General Motors products combined. It couldn't get any better. We had also secured a hot new Porsche 914, on loan from the local dealer, to use as our official pace car.

Race day dawned clear and sunny, and I was ecstatic. Carol and I were staying with friends in Amagansett, about twenty minutes from Bridgehampton. I had the Porsche, and on Sunday morning, we jumped in and headed for the track. I was taking back roads through potato fields, flying along about one hundred miles per hour when I said to myself, "Slow down, Dick. Don't get killed this morning. You're going to be rich tonight."

When we got to the track, my belief was underscored by a generous sampling of spectators already lining the first turn, the most exciting and desirable place to watch the race. Unfortunately, they were the majority, and the rest of the track was virtually empty and stayed that way. Like good promoters, we couldn't let on that we had the Suicide Hotline on speed dial. Newsday, Long Island's major daily newspaper, ran the headline, THEY DIDN'T MAKE GAS MONEY.

And, thus, our initial foray ended with a bank loan we couldn't pay and some public humiliation. We needed to figure out how to make some money and pay the bank. While Bridgehampton was in the fashionable Hamptons, the social elite were not there to tramp through sand

and dirt to watch a bunch of noisy cars duking it out. We should have put in a polo field.

Fortune smiled, or at least gave a bit of a grin, when we were approached by a guy who wanted to run motorcycle races at the track. He had a sanctioning body and he wanted to display his riders' talents on an appropriate venue that truly tested their skills, and Bridgehampton's three-mile track certainly addressed that issue in a highly positive way. Why not? We could stage a bike race at a fraction of what it cost for cars, and they are immensely fun to watch. When you see a string of "bikes" going into a corner in single file at racing speeds, each leaning far over as the bikes approach the apex, it's like watching a ballet.

We decided to do it up big. Make it an entire weekend event with all sorts of attractions including free camping on the track grounds. This didn't sit too well with the locals who felt we were inviting an unsavory element into their pristine environment. Local newspapers, like the Southampton Press, wrote disparagingly about the new promoters who were bringing an unseemly, and probably unsafe, element into their town. My poor mother was working at a Southampton gift shop and that wasn't her idea of how to get popular. The hits kept coming for her.

We got students from the local Southampton College to man the gates for us around the clock, and that was far less expensive than hiring a qualified security team. It also reminded me of my experience in Atlantic City, where the owner hired inexperienced friends of his son as bartenders with the idea that they could handle the money without becoming silent partners.

On the Friday night of our first motorcycle race weekend, we got to the track from New York City around midnight and went immediately to the gate. The guys in charge, students, appeared to be having a nervous breakdown. "THE PAGANS ARE HERE! THE PAGANS ARE HERE!" they cried, a note of sheer horror in their voices. After all, they were nice college kids and the closest they ever got to real terror was watching it on television. We weren't shocked. We were, in essence, providing the ideal asylum for some of society's misfits to exhibit their anti-social behavior.

Opposites Attract

It turned out that the Pagans were mostly a bunch of overweight characters from around New York City, sporting all the proper "colors" on their attire, like sleeveless denim jackets with "PAGANS" embroidered on the back in blazing colors with threatening designs. They swooped down on us in their aging Chevrolets with their ladies who paid homage to the literary world with tattoos covering a good part of their anatomies, consisting of clever sayings like BUBBA'S STUFF.

But it turned out the bikers were great guests. We never had a bit of trouble with any of them. I think they may have appreciated a place they were welcomed and not hassled.

Around that time, another form of motorcycle racing, already popular in Europe, was being introduced to this country. Motocross, a further developed and far more difficult form of off-road racing than its predecessor, scrambles. Earl, Bill (who had replaced Bob Bochrach) and I went to see a motocross race in Unadilla, New York, and we were sold. The terrain was as difficult as you could possibly make it, with hills, jumps, switchbacks, *et al.* We hired a prominent racer at the time, to set a course for us in the vacant, hilly area above our parking lot. We were now in business with a new, tough, and exciting form of racing. I got my kicks taking the Matchless around the track and got to understand how goddam tough motocross racing was.

As an aside, Bridgehampton is also where I found a new outlet for my motorcycle mania. Soccer on motorcycles. On race weekend mornings, we'd play what had to be the world's sloppiest form of soccer imaginable, on motorcycles in our parking lot before the fans came. A friend lent me a small 100cc bike. It was lots of fun, many low-speed crashes, no injuries but some hot tempers that resulted in many more crashes. It was kind of like motorized roller derby. I guess word got out and we became the intermission entertainment for the midget races at Freeport Stadium.

Virtually all our spring, summer, and fall weekends were spent at the track. Carol, Dylan, and I would head out on Friday afternoon and come back Sunday evening. My mother loved it because she got to sit for Dylan while Carol and I were at the track. It was her special time.

Given my mother's staunch Catholicism, and Carol and my eschewing all organized religions, I suspected that on one of those times when she was alone with Dylan, he would wind up getting baptized. The Catholics say you can't get to heaven without it. Frankly, I have greater faith in God's wisdom and feel the entrance exam may have more to do with how you have lived your life than with some water being sprinkled on your head when you were an infant and words you didn't understand being intoned. But I never brought up the subject. I figured if it happened, it couldn't hurt.

Jumping way ahead to the present day, Bridgehampton is no more, at least not as a racetrack. It is now a private golf course, and you, too, can apply for membership if you are willing to ante up the $750,000 for the initiation fee. Imagine the difference! From cars and motorcycles roaring around an asphalt track at 150 miles per hour to gentrified people being driven along the grass at about five miles per hour in a golf cart.

In retrospect, I'd have to say my Bridgehampton days, racing around the tracks on race cars, and my motorcycle, were incredible fun, a little scary, and a valuable, but not profitable, business experience. I wouldn't trade it for anything.

Politics, the other half of this *Opposites Attract* chapter title, also inadvertently originated in Bridgehampton. Politics became a highly disparate, but interesting and engrossing experience that I initially knew far less about than I did racing but ultimately embraced, and it has had a much longer life. John Lankenau, our track attorney, became a friend. John had a keen interest in Democratic politics, as his law partner was a guy you may have heard of named Ed Koch.

Ed, a Greenwich Village resident, was then a City Councilman, having defeated Carmine DeSapio, one of the old "machine bosses" for the office. Now he was getting ready to run for a seat in the U.S. Congress from what was then called the Silk-Stocking District, an area that ran from the Upper East Side of Manhattan down to Greenwich Village and was given the name in homage to the demographics of its residents. John enlisted my support for Ed's campaign, and I was an easy sell. Carol and I had planned to volunteer for Robert Kennedy's campaign that tragically ended with his assassination.

Ed was a progressive and a strong, outspoken opponent of the war then raging in Vietnam. He was running against Whitney North Seymour, Jr., a traditional Republican. Should Ed win, he would be the first Democrat elected from that district since Christopher Columbus. It was my first foray into politics, and I was stoked. I always assumed politics was way above my pay grade, so I hardly ever thought about it.

I was on Ed's advertising committee and was, in fact, instrumental in those decisions. One of the beauties of New York City politics is the accessibility of the candidate to constituents. Due to the density of New York City, a candidate for the United States House of Representatives can walk his or her district in a day, so a lot of the campaigning takes place on the streets rather than in the media, so it was critical to spend the money in the right places.

Carol and I also ran a storefront for Ed on Third Avenue and Thirty-Third Street or *"toid avinya an toity toid street"* as it was better known to some of the locals. That's where we spent virtually every evening and weekend in the months leading up to the election.

All politicians attract attorneys, and Ed was no exception. The fellow most responsible for managing all of Ed's storefronts was an immigration attorney named Stanley Mailman, who also became a great friend. Stanley would call me at the office and advise me when new volunteers would be stopping by the storefront to help. He would usually end the conversation with the good news that, "He (or she) is an attorney!" I could barely control my enthusiasm because most of these folks felt their main contribution was to stop by and talk issues and policies, while I wanted them to outsmart the doorman at Kips Bay Plaza and other apartment complexes so we could get our campaign materials into the buildings.

Finally, I told him, "Stanley! Fuck the lawyers. Send me some con artists who know how to break and enter without getting caught."

On many mornings, Ed would pick me up at our apartment because we were then living on East Seventy-First Street, a highly desirable location for his campaign activities. He and I would then go to a subway stop and pass out the info.

I also got to appreciate the honesty and lack of political correctness of New Yorkers during this time. In most locales, candidates and/or holders of high public office are treated with great dignity and respect, like celebrities. In New York, they're regarded on about the same level as vacuum cleaner salesmen.

I remember one morning some lady said something particularly insulting to Ed and he countered, in his high-pitched, squeaky voice, "Madam, I am not a beggar. I am a candidate for the United States Congress." Like she gave a shit.

Occasionally, Ed would have his "kitchen cabinet" come to his rent-controlled apartment on Astor Place in the Village for meetings, where he'd serve us cheap wine and cheese, and Carol and I would meet interesting people. They weren't characters or nearly as entertaining as the cast at the Dome, but they were intelligent and involved.

Ed was resoundingly elected and represented the district well for four terms prior to his subsequent successful election as Mayor of New York City, where he served for three consecutive terms, but I was long gone by then. Ed was a New Yorker. He never changed and I was truly happy when, two years prior to his death, the Queensboro Bridge, a major structure that connects Queens to Manhattan, was renamed the Ed Koch Queensboro Bridge, a fitting and well-deserved tribute to a great man.

For me, politics was a trip into reality and a gigantic leap from my perch on a barstool at the Dome. Now with a wife and family, a responsible radio job, a racetrack, and my work in politics, you might say I'd come a long way from 4Fs and 2Ds. The gang at the Dome probably wouldn't have let me in the joint anymore.

THIRTEEN
The Times They Are Changin'

When I had time for it, I loved my job at PIX, but that was soon to change. Lynn was an entrepreneur and visionary who had become disgusted with the WPIX-TV management's highly conservative outlook and its lack of both experience and interest in radio, as well as support for the station. Except for the price, we wondered why they bought it. Lynn saw tremendous opportunity in the FM medium and wanted to play a larger role in its growth. After the deal he put together (giving WPIX six additional FM stations in top ten markets for under a million dollars total) was rejected, that was the last straw for him. He resigned and put together a cluster of FM stations in major markets, got the deal financed, and resigned from PIX.

That left Charlie, the Program Director, and me vying for his position but pretending we weren't.

The station, through Lynn's leadership, was gaining a degree of respect, and with a powerful rep firm, McGavren Guild, selling us nationally, we finally had a shot at the big bucks. The only thing lacking was ratings.

Bob Williams, McGavren's National Sales Manager, set up a lunch meeting in Detroit where I was to pitch WPIX-FM to all the major auto agencies. It was such an important meeting that Lev Pope, founder and president, decided to come. I really didn't want to screw this up.

I put together an innovative presentation that compared the size of our audience favorably to that of major AM stations in other smaller markets. Due to the vast difference in market size, our station was drawing audiences comparable in size to some major stations in other markets, but due to the competitive size and nature of the New York market and our relatively weak ratings position therein, our spot cost was a fraction of what major stations in some major markets were charging. In my address to the assembled ad agency execs, I said, "How would you like to buy the WLS (a major Chicago station) audience for thirty dollars a spot? Well, you'll get that big an audience when you buy WPIX-FM at a fraction of the cost of other stations in major markets."

I hoped my presentation made an impact. Two weeks later, I was at a sales appointment when Lev's secretary tracked me down and said Lev wanted to see me...IMMEDIATELY. I wondered what I had fucked up this time.

I finished my appointment (can't give up a shot at a sale), raced back to the building, and showed up at Lev's office breathing hard and with a heartbeat equivalent to a pro bowler's score. He saw me immediately instead of the usual interminable wait. I took that as a bad sign when I slunk into his office, sat down, and looked at him, ready for the worst. But he had a huge smile on his face. I thought whatever it is that brought me here can't be all that bad, unless he's so fond of inflicting torture, he could have made it big in the Third Reich.

Lev warmly said, "Dick, we want to appoint you General Manager of WPIX-FM. You've done an admirable job in sales, and this is your reward." I was floored. I thought for sure that either Charlie would get it or they'd bring in someone from the outside, but I sure as hell wasn't going to argue with him. I wasn't just happy, I was euphoric, and in shock.

I became the youngest GM at a station in the nation's largest market. Truth be told, I wasn't ready for a GM job. I'm sure I got it solely on my sales ability, always their top priority. I called Carol to break the good news, and we celebrated.

One of my first moves caught the attention of the WPIX-TV executives who had always considered the radio station its poor cousin. We were making alterations to the offices to accommodate staff additions, and I was left to redecorate mine. The wood worker who did our apartment also did interesting, contemporary architectural-type designs, and I got him to design my office furniture. It soon became a *cause cele-bre* around the building because virtually everyone, top execs included, had the traditional, boring, cheap-looking Steelcase desks and support-ing furniture. Who the hell was this newbie with the exotic tastes? Lev took a tour of my office and questioned me on it. Fortunately, I had done my homework, priced out the Steelcase stuff, and got my friend to give me a better price. So, I told Lev I did it to save money.

The downside of my promotion was that I now had to deal directly with the WPIX-TV top management. The reality is they had no idea who I really was, or I'd have been lucky to have kept my old job, much less get the promotion. They were super conservative, and I was a scream-ing liberal.

Meanwhile, the FM audience was exploding. The simple fact was that, technically, music sounded better on FM, so auto manufactur-ers finally responded by equipping new cars with FMs. Programming was becoming more sophisticated, and our ratings began to languish because our format was outdated for this new group of listeners.

I proposed we switch to a pop music format. FM was generating a younger audience and there was a hole in the medium's programming spectrum in New York that a pop format with its huge potential audience could fill nicely. Wrong! To them, it was like telling the FCC it could take our license away whenever it was convenient. WPIX-TV's top manage-ment was comfortable with the PIX PENTHOUSE format, even though it appeared our listeners were leaping out its windows to escape from the dated music.

The war in Vietnam was raging and it changed just about everything in America from music to fashion, and more importantly to marijuana-fu-eled demonstrations. You could get high walking through Central Park. It seemed that, if you weren't in Vietnam getting shot at, you were in Central Park demonstrating against it.

It took me nine months, but I finally convinced the brass at the tele-vision station to let me move the station to a pop format. I knew that the business of pop was vastly different from the stuff we played. The record labels found no value in our format due to our older demographics and relatively insignificant audience figures, but they were gangbusters about pop. I soon learned that difference when a guy named Herbie called me. No announcement of the format change had been made yet, but I had hired a consultant to guide our new programming format.

Herbie was an independent music promoter. Payola, paying to get your music on the air, was illegal so labels hired independent promoters to do the job so that the label was not directly involved and could claim innocence if Herbie or his ilk got their ass in a jam by paying radio station Program Directors to play their songs.

Herbie opens the conversation in his best Bronx accent, "Hey Sweetheart, I hear you're goin' pop."

I said, "How could you hear that. There's been no announcement."

To which he replied, "I got good ears. Listen, we're gonna do business. We hafta meet. Not in your office. You come to mine."

I was curious about this new world, and so I did. Of course, Herbie knew all about the upcoming format change, probably from the consultant I had hired, who was supposed to keep it quiet.

Herbie opened the meeting with what I assumed was his familiar refrain, "We're gonna do big business together. What do you want? Broads? Bread? A house?" WOW! Talk about subtle. I figured this was going to be a seminal answer that defined my position in the industry, as well as in the mirror when I shaved in the morning. I replied, "Herbie, I want to be number one, and if your records help me, it won't cost you a dime. If they don't help, you don't have enough dimes. But let's stay friends."

And we did, kind of. However, it seems Herbie and my Program Director were even better friends. I expect there was a currency transaction somewhere along the way because, lo and behold, next thing you know, we have one of Herbie's records on the air. Unfortunately, it was the cover of a hit that was screaming up the pop charts. I asked the PD why we weren't playing the original hit, and I got some bogus answer about the one we were playing having greater musical value. It was a short conversation.

I ordered him to "Take that cover song off and put the real hit back on." Next call was from Herbie.

"So, what do you want now...concrete shoes?" I was starting to learn about the music business. By the way, I loved the new house...just kidding.

If you were going to be successful in pop radio, you had to walk the walk. I wanted personalities, not just announcers. I only had one, Cornelius, aka Neil Myers. Neil was a CHARACTER and I loved him. He would have been a prime-time player in the Dome. He was a New Yorker, then working on the air in Puerto Rico and wanting to return home. I hired him to do morning drive. He gave the station real personality and gave the people at WPIX-TV and the Daily News severe gas pains. A case in point...

At the time, the Long Island Railroad was being roundly criticized in the media for its apparent inability to get a train to go from point A to point B with any semblance of schedule. People were highly inconvenienced and totally disgusted. Nelson Rockefeller was Governor, and he took on the assignment of fixing it, declaring that "In sixty days, the Long Island Railroad will be the most efficient rail carrier in the country." Cornelius' on-air rejoinder was, "But let's not forget, he was also a spotter at Pearl Harbor."

My phone rang immediately, and I was invited to visit Lev Pope who told me about all the heat he was getting from the Daily News whose executives were getting blasted by their politically oriented advertisers. The Daily News was by far New York's largest circulation daily newspaper, and they didn't want any upstart radio station screwing that up.

"Well, it shows people are listening," I said.

"Fire him," Lev responded with a steely determination.

I thought fast. "Are you serious? You want me to fire him? I can't. We're in the same building with you and the newspaper. If I do, AFTRA, (the announcers' union) will picket the building. No union member will cross the picket line and both the television station and the newspaper will be paralyzed. Advertisers will bail too. You'll get horrible publicity and lose a shitload of money." I won, but I think it was a pyrrhic victory.

The WPIX-TV execs were also not ecstatic about my dress code, especially when I brought clients, prospects, and suspects to lunch in the Executive Dining Room, where they and the Daily News execs were entertaining the real nobility, their advertisers, and I looked to them like I was on the runway of a hippie fashion show with my shoulder length hair and my Nehru suits. I would get memos from Lev with quotes from Wall Street Journal stories about how executives didn't trust men with long hair and wild ties and funny-looking suits.

Lev, Fred Thrower (the president), et al were also particularly fearful of any association with the drug culture that was pervading the youth movement at the time. They probably felt that all of us at the FM station were dealers. We had a philosophical impasse on the music, and that was the beginning of the disintegration of my relationship with the brass at WPIX.

Fred was also concerned about the music we were playing having drug connotations and decided he had the time to attend the weekly music meetings where the new songs chosen to go on the air were selected. These should have been strictly the purview of my new Program Director (not the recipient of Herbie's benevolence) and the Music Director, the two who knew the most about the music. But we now had a mid-sixties Southerner helping to interpret the tastes of young New Yorkers. To defend the PD, a savvy and knowledgeable music person, I began to attend those meetings also.

It seemed that Fred had an amazing ability to discern color. He vetoed almost all Black artists, giving what I felt were specious reasons often connected with drugs. But he had no problem whatsoever with the Beatles' *Lucy In The Sky With Diamonds*, obviously never connecting the title to LSD, if he even knew what that was. How can you be a hit station when you're not playing the hits?

At that time, we were also trying to develop a slug line that described the station in a few words. Finally, when I'd had enough, I went to Lev and said, "Lev, I've come up with a line that I feel describes the station perfectly."

"What is it?" he asked.

"White rock," I replied.

His eyes narrowed like he was pissed, and he let that hang in the air with no response as he stared at me, but I went on to explain, "Lev, your boss is a fucking idiot when it comes to radio and he's going to ruin the station."

Shock would be a mild description of his reaction to my verbal indiscretion re his boss, and while he did not flog me on the spot, I expected an entry was made into my personnel file in capital letters, if there was still any space left.

I further alienated WPIX top management during the feared and hated negotiations with AFTRA, the announcers' union. At the time, we were making the switch from background music to pop, and you obviously needed a different type of announcer. I wanted personalities; we had voices. Management was afraid to fire people because of the threat of a potential union strike, an argument I had used successfully in defense of Neil. But now it was coming back to bite me in the ass. I was totally frustrated by their attitude, and if it didn't change, I felt it could make us the laughingstock of New York radio. It was like Willie Sutton selling savings bonds...not too credible.

I tried to explain to the union guys in our AFTRA meetings that our announcers, except for Neil, weren't cutting it. While they may have been proficient in reading live commercials for an automated format, they could not adlib without sounding boring; they didn't have any sense of humor and were not representative of the music we were playing or the audience we were looking to attract.

AFTRA's lead attorney asked me, "Well, Dick, what would you do if one of the guys you now have said something really funny?"

"I don't know," I answered. "It's never happened."

If Lev had a gun, I would've been dead.

But I wasn't done with the fun and games. I thought I'd liven things up at the meetings with another misguided act. At the time, the ILGWU, the International Ladies Garment Workers Union, had an advertising campaign in the subways showing a despicable early twentieth century sweat shop where women were horribly exploited. The headline was *IF YOU DON'T SHOW UP ON SUNDAY DON'T SHOW UP ON MONDAY*. I got hold of one of the posters and hung it in our meeting room before everyone showed up. For that move, I thought our lawyer might beat Lev to the gun and shoot me.

Despite my derogatory interpretation of their attitude toward the radio station, I must say that both Fred and Lev were highly respected in television. I think radio may not have been their medium, and I probably wasn't the station's best representative to them.

Despite the frustrations, we also had wins. One, a temporary victory, was with Gus Gossert. Gus had been a popular DJ on WCBS-FM, an old-ies station. He left the station abruptly and, a bit later, approached me on doing a specialized Doo Wop show on weekend evenings. Doo Wop was a new genre gaining popularity that, given a good imagination, might fit with our programming. Gus told me he could sell it out to advertisers, and since six o'clock to midnight on Saturday and Sunday were relative-ly unproductive time periods for both audience and advertisers, I figured we had little to lose and could possibly generate new revenue for the station, so we made a deal. We'd pay Gus scale plus a commission on the sales he generated.

Gus was an extremely talented air personality. Almost overnight, the show became a smash: number one in New York in the ratings for its time slot and sold out! In short order, Gus was making more money than I was. He became a leading Doo Wop personality.

On weekend evenings, Gus literally took over the station. His group of guests felt perfectly free to drop by and indulge their passions while he was on-air. Thus, when the staff arrived for work Monday, the first order of business was to chuck the empty wine bottles and get rid of the remnants of the joints that the weekend assemblage had enjoyed.

Ultimately, some of Gus' travels became a problem. It seemed he usually spent the five days between shows in Thailand and/or Rio apparently doing the kind of business that has led this country to having the world's largest prison population. The results of these wanderings started to become apparent on-air. He'd spend far too much time talking about the cures for addiction instead of music. The culmination was in a contest he ran on his show but neglected to tell us about, and for which he also apparently forgot to award the promised prizes to the winners. Unfortunately, the Attorney General or someone with whom he had a strong connection, was an entrant and there was subsequently a discussion of our broadcasting license being in jeopardy. By that time, Gus had pretty much worn out his welcome. Despite the success of the program, it wasn't worth losing our license.

Gus had to go. I sent him registered letters informing him the show was canceled and I called him frequently but got no response. The Program Director, Neil McIntyre, and I strongly felt he would pretend to know nothing about it and come in to do the show as usual. And we were right. So, Neil and I were there when Gus showed up with "Mike" on Saturday afternoon to prepare that night's show. Mike was clearly a torpedo (kind of a mob tough guy) brought along to scare the shit out of anyone who got in Gus' way, and he was effective in that role. Gus pretended to be shocked to see Neil and me there.

We explained the situation to Gus, and appropriate to my personality, I made a smart-ass remark. Gus said, "Don't go there, Dick. Mike doesn't have a sense of humor."

So, out of curiosity, I asked, "What's your last name, Mike?"

His reply, "I got four (pronounced "fawh"). Which one you want?" After a while, it became obvious that they had been briefed as to how far they could go with the intimidation, but Neil and I were, at times, genuinely frightened of this guy. We were a bit out of our element with two gentlemen whose incomes were most likely tax-free as proper reporting could result in incarceration.

Neil and I finally prevailed, and Gus picked up his collection of records and he and Mike left. Of course, we couldn't make public why we were firing him, so I looked like the biggest schmuck in town. A guy running a struggling radio station fires the DJ who is number one in the market in his time slot.

The explanation became clear about a month later when Gus was arrested in the safe deposit vault of a New York City bank in a sting operation mounted by the DEA. They found pistols, phony passports, a kilo of heroin, and a brick of illegal gold in his locker. Gus was convicted of tax evasion, the charge the government used to nail drug dealers, and he was sent to prison.

A couple years later, Neil was in a bar in the city one night and Gus, recently released from prison, walked in. They talked about old times and Neil asked what ever happened to Mike. Gus said they found him resting in the trunk of a car in New Jersey, but it was well ventilated... with bullet holes. A year later, Gus was found in the back seat of a car in Memphis with a hole in his head and a little white bag in his hand, the Boys' way of saying, "Don't sweat this one, Officer. We're just doing a little house cleaning."

The tragedy here is that Gus Gossert, while I was not a fan of him personally, was one of the very best on-air personalities I had ever heard. When he talked, you felt he was speaking directly to you and only you. A brilliant career totally wasted.

Another win, a real one, was with Volvo, a WPIX-FM advertiser. Volvo decided to have a promotional contest for the radio stations on which they were advertising. The idea being to get additional free exposure on-air and win the goodwill of perhaps the toughest audience in America, their car dealers. If you were a struggling station and fortunate enough to have their business, it made good sense to enter and try to make some waves that would garner the client's goodwill in the process.

At that time, Volvo ran a national ad campaign, "In Sweden, where the winters are really rough, the average Volvo lasts eleven years." Wow! That's terrific, because at that time, with built-in obsolescence, the average American car probably lasted less than a third of that time. But maybe it wasn't so hot if you were a Volvo dealer and the Chevvy store next to you was selling three or four cars to your one and Volvo owners might show up saying, "I've only had the damn thing for ten years and already I'm having trouble with it." So, we decided our entry in the competition would be focused on the dealers and their probable disdain for the campaign slogan (that was very powerful from a consumer standpoint). We bought an eleven-year-old Volvo, took it to a demolition site in Manhattan, invited all the NY area dealers and the media, gave them all hard hats with the Volvo logo on them and sledgehammers and told them to enjoy themselves.

They attacked the car ferociously and beat the living shit out of it. They turned it over on its side, then righted it, and the Advertising Manager got in and drove off, clearly showing the punishment a Volvo could take. WABC-TV covered the event, and it was broadcast on the six o'clock news. We won the contest and, as an added prize, they personally gave me an eleven-year-old Volvo.

On another positive note, I may have inadvertently done something of a public service nature during my tenure at the station. In my capacity as General Manager, part of my responsibility was to meet with civic leaders and key people in municipal services. The idea was that since stations were licensed by the FCC, they should use their airwaves to help solve community problems. Stations felt that the solution to these problems, whatever their nature, was to run PSAs (Public Service Announcements) around four o'clock in the morning.

One day, I had lunch with NYC Fire Department executives. I didn't know how WPIX-FM was supposed to put out fires, but it was a part of the hypocrisy of the gig.

During lunch, they spoke about a midtown office fire that had killed two people who died taking the elevator in an attempt to escape the fire. It had been a big news story. I told them there was a very large and respected ad agency based in the very building in which the fire had occurred. Since it was so close to them, they might help, and they certainly had the power. I wound up ghost writing a letter to the President of the agency on the Fire Department's stationery explaining how those people would not have died if they had known the dangers of getting on an elevator in a fire. It was obvious the public needed to be educated about safety in fires.

I thought no more about it, but I was then highly surprised when I saw a full-page ad in the New York Times, either paid for by the agency or donated by the Times, in which proper procedures for action in a fire were given with illustrations. Some are still in use nationally today. I can't really take credit for it. The agency did it, but if I was an initiator or a contributor in any way, I'm happy for it.

Life continued on the rocky road at WPIX-FM. There was less and less love lost between management and me, and there probably wasn't that much to start with, at least not on my part. I further widened the breach with increasing frequency.

At this point, you can probably figure out where my relationship with upper management was headed. We'd both had enough of each other, and I heard from my sources that Lev was talking to some other people about my job, so I took the initiative. I made an appointment to see him. I dazzled him with my first line.

"Lev," I said," I have a terrific idea."

"What's that," he said doubtfully.

"Fire me!" I countered.

He got this weird, quizzical look on his face and said, "What are you talking about?"

I said, "I'm talking about the fact that you don't like me, and the feeling is mutual. You're also looking for my replacement, and I must say, not surprisingly, doing a half-assed job of it. But the Daily News has a policy that if you are terminated (nobody in polite society says *fired* or *canned),* for every six months of employment you are entitled to a week's compensation. I've been here for nine years, from salesman to GSM to GM. I'm a paycheck junkie. I can't afford to quit, so please fire me."

Then he lapsed into corporate speak. "Dick, you may well be the best man for the job. All executives are constantly evaluating possible situation changes. Don't read anything into that. Let's table this conversation."

We did, but the table must have had uneven legs because three days later, the conversation fell off it. He called me into his office and "terminated" me. At which time, we had a disagreement over the definition of my compensation. I was paid a salary and an override on all sales. His proposal was salary only. I demurred rather vociferously.

He said, "Dick, don't get upset. This is just an emotional time for you."

"Bullshit," I said, "This is a very financial time for me." I called John Lankenau, our track attorney, and he called Lev the next day and John came away with the proper deal.

Dylan was then three years old and was enrolled at the Dalton School, a highly respected private school on the Upper East Side of Manhattan. At that time, New York City public schools were spawning grounds for the higher levels of education and job training that students would receive in places like Sing Sing prison. Thus, it was imperative to get your kid into a private school, and naturally, there was far more demand than supply. The competition was fierce. Think about it. How do you get your two or three-year-old prepared for an interview at a private school? One friend told me I had an advantage.

"What's that?" I asked.

"You're not a Jewish lawyer," was his answer. Personally, I think Dylan did it himself. He was cute, smart, cool, and a great kid. I would generally take him to school and sometimes also pick him up. I absolutely enjoyed that time with him. But once his school day started, I was on my own.

I half-assed looked for jobs in radio sales, but after the WPIX experience, my heart wasn't really into it, and it probably showed. But I really loved the racing world, and I thought about doing something in that arena, representing motorcycle riders for sponsorships. It was my first solo entrepreneurial effort since my black-market activities in Germany. I loved the idea...and I couldn't go to jail for it

Motorcycle racing in this country at that time had all the panache and press coverage of an Easter Egg Roll at a retirement community. To the public, motorcyclists were simply unarrested criminals and, as such, of little or no value to advertisers. But there was freedom, a world of great importance to me, in entrepreneurship. I was free of the corporate bullshit, but that may have been the only benefit, as it flat didn't work.

I also explored and tried to develop another idea: creating a network of radio stations in ski areas and selling upscale advertisers on buying time on the network. It was a creative but impractical idea. For one thing, when the listenership of all those stations was combined, it was still a very small, albeit upscale, audience. Also, when I was honest with myself and used myself as a model, I had to admit that most skiers on holiday in a ski area never find out there is a radio station there, so while it may look good on paper, it would be a form of larceny, however petty.

As I got closer to the end of the WPIX payout period, I took a good look at my dwindling bank account and the remote prospects for changing it in the immediate future and I began to evaluate my options. I had to stop kidding myself. I finally figured that my reality was to stay in radio. However, I wasn't sold on doing it in New York.

I started thinking about California. I needed to be in a big city to make a living commensurate with what I was used to. All signs pointed to Los Angeles, the second largest city in the country. There were miles and miles of beaches, and it was only a few hours away from spectacular western skiing. Carol agreed and we both thought Dylan might really love living there, rather than New York City.

FOURTEEN
California Here We Come!

I had never been to California, but I began to investigate possible opportunities in LA. I knew I'd have to take a step back from the GM position, and I was ready to do that, but it's tough to look for a job when you are almost three thousand miles away from a potential interview. My national sales rep for PIX, McGavren Guild, provided the solution. Ralph Guild also owned a few radio stations in California with his partner in that venture, George Fritzinger. There was an opening at the LA station and Ralph told me he'd get me an interview with George, fly me to LA, and put me up at a hotel while I was there. You sure as hell don't say no to that.

I asked Ralph what the job opening was. "We're looking for a Retail Sales Manager," he replied.

Hmmm! Maybe you do say no. Retail put me back at the vacuum cleaner sales level, talking directly to small shop owners that probably didn't have the money to buy radio.

"Ralph, are you serious? Retail Sales Manager? Are you sure they have enough janitors? By the way, what is the station's format?"

"KFAC is a classical station."

I had never even listened to a piece of classical music so, being a guy with no job and less money, I threw away my maturity and immediately donned my always-handy asshole cap and told Ralph, "You can't be serious. I was GM at a pop station in the nation's number one market and I'm supposed to fly three thousand miles to interview for a minor sales job at a classical station in an unsophisticated market like LA?"

Ralph responded appropriately, "Gee Dick, please forgive me. I thought I was doing you a favor. You want to get to LA, and this could be your shot. You don't have to retire from the station, and you'll probably be making more than you were at PIX."

Tough to argue with that kind of logic, especially when I glanced at my check book. I don't know who I was kidding other than myself. I had practically no money left, no job, and no prospects, and I was busting the balls of a friend who was trying to help me. I apologized to Ralph for being me and he set up the meeting with George.

It was early January and I departed New York on a dark, damp, windy, cold Sunday. When I arrived at LAX, guess what? It was sunny and warm. I caught a cab and my first question to the driver had absolutely nothing to do with Hollywood, its stars, or landmarks. "Where is Ascot Park?" I asked. Ascot was the site of a famed half-mile dirt track noted for its premier motorcycle races.

When I got to the hotel, I looked at a map of LA and practically went into cardiac arrest. I was astounded at the complexity and scope of the city. I thought, "Shit, I'm too old to ever learn how to get around here." In New York, if you know the alphabet and can count to ten, you can find your way anywhere. In LA, it looked like you'd have to get a PhD in geography to find a restaurant.

Nevertheless, I did find my way to KFAC and I met George Fritzinger on a Monday morning. He was born and raised in the coal mining region of Pennsylvania, an area not famed for turning out wimps. No silver spoon sticking out of George's ass. He secured an appointment to the Naval Academy, where he became an All-American football player, and after his military service, he went to Harvard where he earned an MBA. Although we were about the same age, it was obvious George had spent his time more productively than I had.

I really liked him, and as he explained the job, I warmed to the concept of classical. It was certainly not about selling audience numbers. You simply didn't have them and never would with that format. It was more of a creative, conceptual sell, ala my early days in FM. George and I clicked. We were both outspoken and honest.

I got the job and what amounted to a raise in pay. A new BMW (George had a trade with the dealer) also came with the gig. I was going to start in ten days. All I had to do was find a place for our family to live, get back to New York, pack up everything we owned, head out to Southampton, explain to my mother why our visits would be less frequent (the most difficult task), get Dylan out of school (also not an easy or happy task), make arrangements with my track partners for my departure, and get to the airport on time.

The most immediate task was finding a place to live. There was no rush; I had two days! LA is so fucking BIG! You can probably walk from one end of Manhattan to the other in less time than you can drive from one end of LA to the other. They built the city out instead of up, like New York.

Please note, we were house, not apartment, hunting because most people in LA live in houses. I went from Malibu to Hollywood with many stops in between. Given rents in New York, I thought I could live like a baron in LA, but that dream soon vanished as I was introduced to the LA economics. I found a place I thought would work. It was a house near the Hollywood Bowl, brand new, two bedrooms, nice neighborhood. Mission accomplished! I headed back to New York to deal with the other preparations. Our New York landlord was ecstatic. He couldn't wait to get rid of us so he could get more rent from the next tenant.

At Dalton, they gave Dylan a going-away party and that was bittersweet. Sad, but he, like us, seemed excited rather than bummed. Tough to leave my mother. I felt sorry for her. She had lots of friends, but it would be sad to be a widow and see your only "child" (of thirty-seven) leaving to live so far away. Our friends gave us a nice going-away party, and the next day the moving van came.

We landed in Los Angeles, rented a car, and drove to our new home. Dylan loved it. "I can go in and out; in and out; in and out," he exalted, excited by no longer having to be a prisoner in the confines of an apartment.

Getting used to Los Angeles took a bit of practice. First of all, the weather. It's terrific. It seemed that every day was the same...glorious, sunny, and clear with temperatures around the 70s. Radio stations seemed fixated on giving constant weather reports. Why not just record it once and play it every day. Tom Donohue, a progressive rock DJ, came out with a classic line when asked why he never gave time checks or weather reports. Said Donohue, "If you want to know what time it is, look at your watch. If you want to know the weather, look out the window."

To kind of introduce Carol and me to LA night life, George invited us out for an evening. First, we went to the Polo Lounge at the Beverly Hills Hotel for drinks. This was a must-stop for all the phonies in LA, but not George's style in any way. He was just showing us the sights. They used to have a dwarf dressed like Johnny in the old Philip Morris commercials, who would run through the bar announcing phone calls for guests in his high squeaky voice. Some people actually had friends call them there, so they'd look important.

As luck would have it, it turned out that George and I shared the same reverence for alcohol. We had a couple of drinks there and then went to a trendy Sunset Strip restaurant for dinner. After that, we were all feeling good and he suggested we stop in at the Classic Cat. It was a strip joint! So, there I am with my wife and boss at another of LA's must-see attractions. When the check came and George, who has a wallet FULL of credit cards, looked uncomfortable. I offered to pay, but he said, "No. It's not that. It's just that we used to have a trade deal here, so I hate to pay real money." Imagine! The classical station in the country's second largest market had a trade deal with a strip joint. That was George, and I loved him. By the way, I never saw George be anything but faithful to his wife, Grace, whom he obviously loved deeply.

I thought some of the signs on fast food restaurants were sacrilegious, especially the ones that advertised BURGERS TACOS PASTRAMI on a single sign. To a real New Yorker, that's like seeing a sign on a

California Here We Come!

Jewish synagogue, MUSLIMS WELCOME. They just don't mix. Pastrami is a delicacy verging on its own religion and deserving its own sign.

A major plus was that California sated my need for sand and sun in a big way. On Saturday mornings, Carol would take the day off from mom-mying and Dylan and I would hop in the car and drive through the San Fernando Valley on our way to the beach. We'd motor through the beautiful and rough Malibu Canyon to get to Zuma Beach where we'd spend the day. I loved those days with Dylan, just the two of us.

I felt that one of the minor character deficiencies of many Californians was apparently well-intentioned but insincere communication. I got so sick of hearing "Have a nice day," I finally told a person, "You really should wipe your mouth. Your insincerity is dripping."

I settled into my new job as Retail Sales Manager at KFAC. My responsibility was to generate new non-advertising agency business for the station. I soon found out just how low on the totem pole that position was. It seemed that even the guy selling hot dogs out of his car had an advertising agency, and one of the KFAC salesmen had claimed it for himself, even though it never generated a dime, and he probably couldn't find it on a map.

I was relegated to the status of scavenger, scrounging around for obscure and under-performing businesses when so many viable ones were not covered.

Soon after I arrived, George told me about a friend of his who sold jingles and had done very well for their Sacramento station, which had a pop format. Jingles are musical commercials. Many major advertisers used them in those days. This guy claimed his name was Danny Kaye. Got a hint of what's coming? George was a realist with no pretensions, and despite the fact jingles were anathema to the high-brow classical music audience, George wanted to give him a shot at KFAC.

Danny Kaye was a piece of work. A middle-aged, cigarette-smoking guy whose sartorial presentation looked like it was created by the wardrobe mistress at Ringling Bros. My job was to get him appointments, take him to them, and help him close sales. But I got to know LA from its innards to its exterior on our travels. It would literally take me hours trying to get a single appointment. I felt like I was back at Kirby Vacuum Cleaners but without the William Rogers dinner set as a purchase incentive. It was frustrating and scary. I was now in a city where I had no contacts. And, while I really liked George, I began to hate my job, a situation that was getting far too familiar for me.

Then, when Danny and I showed up at an appointment representing this classy, upscale, cultural icon of a radio station, he would go into his pitch. This is a guy who, among his other penetrating sociologic observations, described Asians as "puss eyes."

His spiel must have been one of the early indicators of the need for lie detectors. He would make outrageous claims about his company and the totally bogus work they had done, citing major national commercials and the works of important songwriters and artists his company used, when he was his entire company. He farmed out work he got to some boiler room production company. It was depressing, and not very profitable. Most prospects could smell the scam. That's just not the way you advertise on a classical station.

One appointment was with Frank Ponder, a bright, ambitious young fellow who managed Bel Air Camera in Westwood Village. Frank realized that KFAC might have a good audience for his clientele, but he also seemed highly skeptical about Danny's bogus claim that Jimmy Webb (who wrote *Up Up And Away,* the smash hit that also became the music for TWA commercials) had written some of his jingles. It's one thing for a songwriter of Jimmy Webb's stature to collect a fat check from a major national advertiser who buys the right to use one of his songs in commercials. It's an entirely different scenario to think he would sit down and compose a song for a retailer with one store. I was surprised Danny didn't claim the Mormon Tabernacle Choir did the vocals for classical stations.

After Danny's pitch, Frank, perceptively, looked directly at me and asked, "Dick, what do you think? Is this the best way to advertise my store?" Damn, why did he have to ask that, especially in front of Danny? I had a set of ethics and wanted to be able to do the right thing for clients. I wanted them to win, and I felt they were essentially entrusting their money to me. I had had enough of Danny's bullshit and prevarication, and even if it meant packing my bags again, I couldn't go along with it. I said, "Frank, for your store I would recommend spoken word commercials that both image the store and allow the flexibility to announce sales and special deals and work with your vendors on co-op advertising." To my great relief, that's what he did.

On the trip back to the station that day, we were like two Buddhist monks practicing the vow of silence. He knew KFAC wasn't working for him either. It was too sophisticated for his Atlantic City carny-like act. He finally convinced George he was more valuable in Sacramento or Fresno, and he left. I felt like I'd been paroled.

On the home front, after I settled in at KFAC, Carol got Dylan enrolled in pre-school and we adjusted to life. But we wanted to get a new place. Turns out we weren't dazzled by my find, so without any money, we started looking to buy a house.

My mother, having sold her house in Water Mill years before, had decided not to build another. She solved our immediate problem by offering us the money she had cleared from the sale for us to use as a down payment on a house in Los Angeles.

Ultimately, we found a super place in Los Feliz, a somewhat upscale community above Hollywood. The house was a Monterrey colonial, over four thousand square feet in size, in the Laughlin Park section of Los Feliz, a supposedly private neighborhood, but one without a gate at that time. Our departed neighbors included Cecil B. DeMille, W.C. Fields, and Charlie Chaplin. In fact, we had a DeMille Drive address because Cecil was our across-the-street neighbor; although, he had vacated the premises upon his death in 1959.

Unfortunately, and most likely the reason we could afford it ($72,000 in 1973), was that the former owner had marginal taste and was obviously not a fanatic about maintenance. It had great bones but a severe case of acne. Carol and I didn't have the money to have it professionally restored, so we'd have to do it ourselves, which we did.

Meanwhile, the station was not doing that well. I was frustrated that all these agencies that weren't doing any business with the station were protected territory for the other sales reps. I bitched to George about it, and he was also aware and frustrated by it.

George confided his unhappiness with the sales department to me and indicated he thought I might do a better job of running it. That may have been my toughest audition ever. George wanted a comprehensive plan detailing how I would organize the department—and I had never been famous for details. We went back and forth many times, and I ultimately passed the audition and was appointed General Sales Manager.

In realty, despite my early snobbish attitude toward classical music, I loved selling it. It was a creative sell, rather than ratings sell, so I immediately canceled Arbitron, the radio ratings source universally accepted in the industry as a credible source for audience measurement. We had to sell ideas, not spots, and that was much more fun.

The sales team seemed to like the creative sell, and we developed a lot of client-specific promotions. I was working my ass off creating them, going to meetings with the sales team, entertaining clients at night, travelling to out-of-state McGavren offices, etc. But, it was working! Revenue increased significantly and George seemed happy.

FIFTEEN
Big Changes

Unfortunately, my ratings at home weren't so good. I was in my own world. My job was pretty much my life. I left early and came home late. That wasn't great for Carol who wasn't working and didn't know anyone in LA. One Saturday morning at breakfast, Carol asked for some time to discuss an important issue.

"What's the topic? I jokingly asked.

"Dick, this is serious. We have no life together. You leave before the birds are up in the morning and don't get home until they've long been asleep. Your job is your life and it's not working for me. I want a separation."

"What? You can't be serious. This is totally out of the blue. I know I've been working too much, but I'm trying really hard to be successful and provide a future for us."

"This isn't the future I want. I'm too young to be a widow,"

The conversation went on, but the decision didn't change. You can't imagine how it blindsided me, this once aimless, directionless, don't-get-serious guy who was now getting successful and had a family he was now going to lose, all because he worked too hard. Frankly, on later reflection, I realized she was entitled to a life of her own and wasn't getting one the way we were living. Plus, I don't think my drinking added to the experience for her. At times, I knew it annoyed her, but we never had any serious discussions about it.

We talked about trying to make it work and saw a shrink together, but we ultimately decided we would have to be apart before we could get together again. It was an extremely civilized split without a lot of acrimony. I think we still liked each other, but the love seemed to be gone.

Our main concern was Dylan. We decided he and Carol would stay in the house, and he would be with me one night during the week and on most weekends. Breaking the news to Dylan was horrendous. I loved him so much and wanted to be a big part of his life. He was too young to fully understand the importance of the situation, but he did know there was going to be a major change ahead. I tried to soften the blow by saying we were going to be together a lot and have fun, but he just cried.

The morning I packed my things and left the house in Los Feliz for the last time as a resident was one of the worst days of my life. After Carol took Dylan to school, I went into his room, looked around, re-lived some of the memories, thought about the future, and cried convulsively with my body wracking for what seemed like the whole morning. Years later, he questioned me on it, and I explained that in separations, someone has to leave. I was the logical choice. Carol was the full-time mom and my job was to support us all.

My first logistical challenge was finding a place to live, and George stepped up and fixed it for me. The station had a trade deal with the Beverly Rodeo Hotel, a small boutique hotel on the famed Rodeo Drive in the heart of Beverly Hills. George told me I could use the station's trade, including room and restaurant, and all I had to pay was room tax. And I did...for seven months, thanks to George.

Life changed for me that day. Instead of a husband and father, I became a bachelor living in the epicenter of the LA singles scene. There were lots of singles-type bars that were highly proximate to the Beverly Rodeo. This was the beginning of an odyssey in my life that, were it closely investigated, would forever preclude my becoming a U.S. President. It would leave me more open to indictments than endorsements.

I pretty much settled into a routine where I worked hard during the day and played hard at night. As the evenings progressed and the libations took effect, I'd meet and talk to a lot of young women. There's a country song, *The Girls All Get Prettier at Closing Time*, and if a young lady is still hanging in the bar past 1:00 a.m., the guys are probably all getting better looking too. It all made for an active social life. Suffice it to say, I became very single. I apparently was not aware there were movie theatres and other places, many without liquor licenses, where people whiled away their leisure hours.

Wednesday nights I would be with Dylan. We'd have dinner and then I'd drop him at home because it was a school night. On weekends, he would stay with me at the hotel. It was undoubtedly a strange environment for a six-year-old, but he seemed to like some of the perks, like room service. We made it fun.

One Sunday morning, I saw an ad in the LA Times for a brand-new riding and tennis club in Malibu. It looked interesting. I hadn't played tennis since I left New York, so Dylan and I drove out there to check it out. I wound up talking to the owner and making a trade deal with him for the station. That was a bit presumptuous of me since it wasn't my station and I had to get George's approval.

On Monday, I went in to see George. I said, "Hey George, good news. My third quarter bonus (there was no such thing) is handled." And I explained the deal.

He smiled and said, "I have one question. Did you get one for me too?"

"Of course," I responded, and we were golden.

I don't think George ever went there, but Dylan and I became weekend regulars. Private clubs were never my thing, not that I had the choice, but this wasn't a stuffy club at all. I made some good friends, including Lou Drobnik, the tennis pro who had a racquet cut down for Dylan. We'd play tennis and go horseback riding, and eventually, we even camped there on weekends. That was real fun for both of us and great bonding, something that is critical when you upend the life of a child the way separation and divorce do.

My office at KFAC was on the ground floor, facing a parking lot with passerby foot traffic. There were floor-to-ceiling windows in the office, putting me somewhat on display.

Dylan, at the time, was doing lots of art. Inasmuch as he was only six, his style was a bit primitive, and he signed each piece at the bottom with a clearly legible "Dylan." One day, I noticed a lady peering through my window with a curious expression bordering on amazement.

She looked at me and mouthed, "Are those real Dylans?"

"Yes," I mouthed back.

She asked if she could see them, and I invited her in. The truth was that, at that time, Bob Dylan was getting into art and some of his works were primitive in style. She asked if I knew how she might get one. I told her I would speak to the artist. Then I confessed who the real Dylan was. She was a good sport and still wanted one of his drawings, so we negotiated. After consultation with the artist, we settled on the price being a new toy, a Tonka truck. His first commission.

George and his partner in the stations, Ralph Guild, were innovators and visionaries. They believed that sophisticated training for salespeople would bring far better results than the old-fashioned "sell what you got" routine. They booked Alan Laykin for a full day seminar. He had recently written a popular book, _How to Get Control of Your Time and Your Life,_ that basically was intended to take one's efficiency, effectiveness, productivity, and personal satisfaction to a higher level.

Alan was a tricky dude. He had us write down our personal and business goals for the next six months. A couple hours later, he had us write our five- and ten-year goals. Then he asked us to compare them to see if we were on track to reach our long-term goals. He nailed me. My six-month goals were primarily dedicated to my personal satisfaction and lacked any depth whatsoever in comparison to any life goals I might have had but was unaware of. It made me think. The obvious conclusion I quickly came to was that my days at the Beverly Rodeo were numbered.

Around that time, I started a new relationship. Her name was, and still is, Erika. She sold time for another radio station. Erika was very attractive, smart, and ambitious, not a bad combination. She was only about twenty-five years old, but she didn't want anyone to know that because she was overachieving for her age. She didn't want the possibility of advancement stalled by some jerk thinking she was too young to do something she already was doing well.

Meanwhile, in my naivete, I thought things were going well at the station. I had made a couple of changes in the sales department, and research I commissioned showed our listeners were real people and actual consumers. They weren't freaks or oddballs because they preferred classical music. This was having a very positive effect on the bottom line. We set sales records for the station for a few months in a row.

Then I got the shock of my life.

George called me into his office late one afternoon. He looked really nervous, and I soon found out why. He was firing me. I could see in his face that he hated to do it. We had a strong business as well as a personal relationship, and I had significantly increased station revenue. But politically, there was someone in the national company's hierarchy, one of the founders, that wanted to move to LA, and they needed to find a respectable position for him at the station. As strong as he was, I could see George faltering in his explanation. The person in question was one of the leading men in the McGavren Guild organization, highly competent, respected, and a guy I knew and liked. That didn't make me feel any better, but at least I understood. George gave me a very soft landing with extended pay and let me keep the car for a generous amount of time. We both felt badly, unlike the WPIX-FM situation, and we parted friends.

Immediately after that meeting, I went back to my office. As I packed my things, the phone rang. It was Erika. She had great news. She had just been named the General Manager of the Metromedia FM station in Boston, an amazing accomplishment for someone so young without management experience. Of course, she wanted to celebrate. She had a business dinner planned but asked if we could meet for a drink first. What an incredible juxtaposition! She gets the opportunity of a lifetime the same day I get canned. We met and I tried valiantly to share her joy. I didn't want to spoil it by sharing my angst, so I never mentioned my situation. I told her the next day. She moved to Boston and the relationship ended. But years later, she told me she thought that my not sharing my situation at that time was a very noble thing to do.

So, there I was. Thirty-eight years old with no job, no wife, and now, no girlfriend. Plus, I hadn't really been in LA long enough to have built strong relationships in the industry, so I was kind of starting my job search fresh. I assumed there probably appeared to be a bit of an odor of failure attached to my resume, going from General Manager to Sales Manager and now willing to settle for a sales position.

No matter how hard you work at it, looking for a job is not a job. I would make a list of all potential prospects and try to follow up with them. Finally, I got a lead. KPOL, a background music station then owned by a radio powerhouse, Capital Cities Communications (later sold to ABC Radio), was looking for a person to develop new business. I was never a fan of background music as a results producer for advertisers, and it would be like going back to Kirby Vacuums for the umpteenth time. But I needed a job, the money wasn't bad, and I really liked Paul LaGasse, the Sales Manager, who would be my boss. Paul offered me the job, and I took it gladly and appreciatively.

Meanwhile, one Saturday as I was driving along the Pacific Coast Highway in Malibu, I saw a FOR RENT sign on a house on the beach. I had always wanted to live right on the ocean, so I stopped to check it out. The house itself, a rather dilapidated dump, wasn't for rent. It was the bootleg apartment below it, a very small space that was basically a studio, but with a sleeping alcove, another candidate for a feature in Architectural Disgust, but it was right on the sand. To say it was primitive would be complimentary. There was no dry wall or insulation in the sleeping alcove, and you could see the ocean through the cracks between the planks and the two-by-fours that served as the wall. But with my keen eye for design, I loved it and rented it on the spot. It was on a rather funky section of PCH known as Dog Beach for the obvious reason.

I moved in on March 1st. Daytime temperatures in Malibu were generally mild to warm, but the evenings went from chilly to cold at that time of year, and that was definitely the case on moving day. I rounded up a couple of friends to help me. For only the cost of a case of beer and a one-day truck rental, we got it done. That accomplished, I returned the truck and prepared to spend my first night in my new home.

But, when I returned to paradise, I thought I was in Antarctica instead of Malibu. After a comprehensive and unsuccessful search for any possible dial, button, wheel, or lever that might activate heat, I went upstairs to the landlord, Don Beach as he preferred to be called. He was a genuine character, a white-haired, red-nosed Irishman who did his best to uphold his nation's tradition. You could generally smell that tradition on his breath.

"Don," I said, "The place is freezing. I can't find where to turn the heat on."

He laughed and answered: "You wasted your time looking. There's no heat in there. The heat's in here. Come on in and have a shot of tequila and a joint." My kind of landlord.

After that, I found it best to pay my rent in the morning, so I'd remember doing it.

A real benefit of my new living quarters was that Don's live-in girlfriend, Jones, had a son, Sam, who was Dylan's age. When Dylan was with me, they hung out.

I loved the shack. I even tried to decorate it with quirky art that I purchased at a local gallery. But the *piece de resistance* was a poster from the Koch campaign. It was about three feet by four feet and said in bold black letters, "KOCH FOR CONGRESS." Ed had also put a personal note on it thanking me and he signed it.

My neighbors were all cool young people who had moved to Malibu for the right reasons, not the ones who should have worn pitons for their climb to the top of the social pecking order. That gang wouldn't be caught dead on Dog Beach, nor would they have been welcomed.

There was a lot of social interaction from spontaneous parties to volleyball. An added scenic enhancement was that, in addition to the ocean, many of the ladies were topless. My friends from Beverly Hills would come out to my place for a day at the beach, but despite these scenic attractions, when they saw my place, I could tell they felt sorry for me. And when they left, I felt sorry for them having to return to a boring one-dimensional city.

I developed a routine where in the morning, I would get up, slip on my bathing suit, and go for a run on the beach. I followed that with some long distance (at least for me) swimming and would conclude by riding waves. As I later drove to work, I couldn't believe how good I felt and how undeserved it was.

At that same time, I also managed to prove that I was a true real estate ignoramus. There was a small, beat-up house a few doors down the beach that went on the market for $67,000. Someone asked me about it, and I said, "Only a moron would pay $67,000 for that shit hole," The "moron" who bought it is now sitting on a multi-million-dollar property.

I complemented my beach living by skiing as much as possible in the winter with friends. Mammoth was my favorite. For a former East Coast skier, Mammoth was heaven, a massive area, super snow, and lots of it, and it was soft, not icy. We'd ski our asses off all day, hit the sauna after that, then have a few beers and dinner. Around eight o'clock in the evening, we'd start wishing it was eleven so we could go to bed with dignity.

The holidays were coming, and my plan was to spend Christmas morning with Dylan, Carol, and Gary Markowitz, Carol's boyfriend and a good guy. After that, I was headed to Mammoth, but a strange and unique situation occurred. For once, Mammoth had lousy snow. A friend of mine said there was spectacular snow at Alta, the legendary Utah ski area made famous in Warren Miller films. I had never skied in Utah, and, from Miller's films, I thought Alta was probably the jaws of death and you had to be Stein Eriksen to attempt it. But I figured, *what the hell*, I really wanted to go skiing and my friend told me they still had available reservations.

I managed to get one, not a room but a bunk in a dorm at the Rustler Lodge, a quaint but not very large hotel directly at the base of the ski area.

Big Changes

Alta was the most difficult terrain I had ever skied, a tough no-bullshit mountain that offered virtually no amenities. They just wanted skiers. If you weren't ready to lay it on the line, go someplace else. I didn't and I had the best skiing of my life.

I really wanted to take Dylan skiing, but Mammoth didn't allow kids under six in ski school, so when he achieved that plateau, off we went. As a town, Mammoth was weird. There was a totally insufficient parking lot at the ski area. If you weren't one of the early arrivals, you'd have to park on the street and schlep your equipment up to the mountain. But, on the way, you had to pass Lift #2 where you could buy tickets and take the lift to the summit. I thought that was a lot easier than walking all the way up, especially for Dylan. I had rented skis for him, and from the top of the lift, I figured he could ski down the mountain between my legs and I'd drop him at ski school.

On the lift line, as we got closer to the front, I told the attendant Dylan had never been on a lift and asked him to slow it down so we could get on. Maybe if I had used sign language or a blackjack that would have worked, but my plea made no impression whatsoever on this guy and, as the chair approached, I grabbed Dylan, lifted him, and tried to get us both on the damn thing. It only partially worked, and we were each precariously perched on the front portion of the seat and about to fall off, but they never slowed or stopped the lift. I was frantic. I thought for sure we were going to fall off. I was trying to hold Dylan on the chair, but I was half off myself. I even considered dropping him, thinking broken legs weren't as bad as dying. But I gave it one last try, got him fully on and managed to do the same for myself.

I feared the experience might be traumatic for Dylan, so I tried to distract him from thinking about it. "Look in the woods over there," I said. "Are those dancing bears?" He looked at me strangely, but he seemed fine. He skied down between my legs and I enrolled him in ski school. In the afternoon, after his class, I picked him up and we headed for the car. I chose the same route as in the morning. I put Dylan between my skis and off we went. As we got to the scene of the morning's debacle, Dylan screamed, "Lift 2! What the fuck are we doing here?" Out of the mouths of babes...

Selling KPOL, as it turned out, was another bad fit for me. It was like believing in God (radio) but being in the wrong church (station). Capital Cities was a very successful but conservative (bad word for me) company. The format was one step ahead of euthanasia, a dreary background music sound that was so passive it could have been recommended as a sleeping aid.

Then, something fabulous and life-changing happened, socially not professionally. Stephanie Levine, a client with whom I had become friendly on a professional basis told me she was moving to New York. In the interim, she was staying with another single female friend that she was sure I'd like, and she wanted to fix us up.

"What does she do?" I asked.

"She sells for KABC-TV,"

"Forget it," I countered.

The last thing I needed was to spend my evenings talking about work, especially television and most especially KABC-TV. The station was tremendously successful, and I assumed it worked well for its advertisers, while I felt like I was standing on a corner with a tin cup, emblazoned with KPOL on it, looking for donations.

Apparently, Steph got the same reaction from her friend who expressed a total lack of interest in meeting a radio salesman.

As a parting gesture of friendship, and to let her know our relationship hadn't just been about the money, I invited Steph to have a drink the night before she left for New York, and I told her she could invite her friend since she was staying at her place. I also advised her I had an 8:00 dinner, a total lie but a convenient exit strategy. We set it up for 6:30 at the Rangoon Racquet Club, a popular Beverly Hills watering hole and restaurant.

Stephanie was on time but her friend, Elsa Holtz, was fashionably late. When I saw Elsa, I began having second thoughts about my earlier recalcitrance. She was very good-looking, smart, and sophisticated.

Big Changes

I was entranced, a totally different experience for me. Around eight o'clock, Steph said, "Dick, what about your dinner?"

"Oh shit, I forgot. I'll bet I can get out of it. Let me make a call." And I went over to a relic of the times, a pay phone, and since I was in sight of the table. I pretended to insert money, dial a phony number, and pretended to talk.

I went back and informed them I had successfully extricated myself from the obligation. We stayed there until the joint closed.

I remember looking at Elsa and thinking, "Wow! She's going to be beautiful for the rest of her life." I was obviously smitten, and she also seemed interested. And the fact she was from New York didn't hurt, so we made a date for a couple of nights after that. When I arrived to pick her up at the charming cottage she was renting in Beverly Glen, a very cute, small, stand-alone place, with heat no less, I saw she was upset and had been crying. Her mother had passed away a few years before of diabetes and something had occurred that made Elsa fearful the same might be in store for her. When she composed herself, we went out and, believe it or not, had a romantic dinner. Could I be falling in love so quickly?

Whatever the case, in addition to my romantic feelings, I was also concerned for her. She was alone, scared, and thousands of miles from her family. I assumed they were also very worried, so me, the apparently irresponsible, self-indulgent, shallow guy that I was, phoned the father of a girl I'd known for about forty-eight hours to tell him not to worry, I'd take care of his daughter.

We began to see each other nightly and both felt it was meant to be. I remember telling Elsa, "I want to tell you how I feel about you, but I feel it's more than love and I don't know how to express it."

She said, "Well, love would be a nice way to start."

We looked for a place together within two weeks of meeting. It certainly wasn't going to be my place because I wouldn't dare ask anyone to share that with me.

I remember the first time Elsa saw my shoddy little beach dump. I was afraid it might kill the relationship. I figured she must wonder how an employed adult would choose to live like that. What probably saved me was the Ed Koch poster. What nice Jewish girl from Queens would not be impressed by a personal message of thanks from the man who was then a member of the U.S. House of Representatives, and soon to be the Mayor of New York City? Saved by a poster!

I loved all the aspects of living in Malibu. That's where I wanted to live, on the beach of course. So, we decided to give Malibu Road a try and we struck gold. We found a brand new two-bedroom apartment right on the beach. It was on two floors with a cathedral ceiling and a fireplace in what was like a great room, a combination living room, dining area, and kitchen with sliding glass doors to a deck that sat about six feet above the sand.

After Elsa and I got settled, our weekends were idyllic. As with the place on Dog Beach, we found a social spontaneity with our neighbors, albeit a slightly upscale version of the Dog Beach gang, but still cool and fun. Lots of impromptu cocktail parties broke out around 5:00 p.m. on Saturdays and Sundays.

I had noticed a couple of Hobie cats out on the ocean. They were small, high-performance, twin-hulled catamaran sailboats, and they got my attention. It looked like a version of motorcycling on water as they executed turns with one pontoon (hull) high in the air. One day, I arrived in Newport Beach early for a business call. I had some time to kill, so I dropped in at a Hobie showroom. I asked a few questions, kicked a few tires, and the next thing I knew, I was the owner of a fourteen-foot Hobie. Of course, despite my limited forays with Jus Fisher, where I was merely crew, I knew absolutely nothing about the art of sailing, but the salesman said I'd get a lesson when they delivered it.

Being from the East Coast, where there's a high population of sharks in the Atlantic, and because Hobies are so close to the water, when I had my lesson after the boat was delivered, I spent most of the time looking for sharks and missed many of the pertinent details. That created future problems when the instructor was gone and I was on my own.

It's one thing to know how to sail, and it's another to know how to get your sailboat through ocean waves so you can sail. That was the trick, and I was slow at mastering it. Even experienced sailors had a problem with this. I'd have the boat sitting on the beach and someone would come along, look admiringly at it, and ask if it was mine. I'd counter by asking them if they knew how to sail. If the answer was affirmative, I'd suggest we take the boat out and they could be skipper because I was still learning.

So, we'd push it out, hop on and have a meeting. Meanwhile, the boat would turn slightly sideways in the current, a wave would come along, grab the boat, flip it over in the surf, break the mast in half, and continue its route to the shore. While not a good sailor, I became quite proficient in getting to Steve Curran Yacht Sales in Marina Del Rey and back with a new mast in record time. Eventually and expensively, I learned the trick and had great fun on the Hobie. I was always hanging it out on the edge until it capsized. My favorite part was when it was time to beach it, surfing through the waves to the sand. Exhilarating!

Elsa's and my respective stations were near each other, KABC-TV in Silver Lake and KPOL in the bowels of Hollywood, and both a far drive from Malibu, so we'd carpool. She had the cooler car, a convertible Fiat, so we'd take hers. We stopped for dinner so many times on the way home that we could have written restaurant reviews. On Fridays, we'd usually stop at Tonga Lei, a Polynesian restaurant in Malibu that served kick-ass Navy Grogs. Once you had a few of them, you became very groggy.

Professionally, Elsa was riding high at KABC, and I was riding it out at KPOL. KABC was number one in the market and Elsa was their star. She was smart, knowledgeable, innovative, and honest. She wound up being the go-to person on the staff. When they were having a problem with an ad agency, they'd assign it to her and she'd fix it.

I, on the other hand, was bored and frustrated at KPOL. I really felt like I was shoveling the proverbial shit against the tide. It was hard to get new advertisers, and the ones I got expected directly attributable business, but didn't get it. I thought the ideal advertiser on that station would be NoDoz.

One morning, Paul who, as I've said I really liked and respected, had undoubtedly picked up my vibe, and innocently asked, "How's it going, Dick?"

"Fine," I replied too quickly.

Then something snapped and I said, "Actually Paul, it's not fine. Actually, it sucks. This is the most frustrating thing I have ever tried to do, worse than selling vacuum cleaners." I continued ranting for a minute or two in that vein until I got it all out.

"Wow! So, what do you want to do?", he asked.

I'd thought only of my frustration, not the solution, so I quickly replied, "I don't know, but I don't think this is it."

I had become quite experienced at giving my employers the opportunity to can me, but Paul, on the spur of the moment, said, "Tell you what. Take a month's paid leave. Check out your options. Then come back and let me know your decision. If you want to leave, OK. If you want to stay, that's fine too. But let's not have this conversation again." That's probably the classiest thing that had ever happened to me in business.

So, I hit the road in search of those flowers I was dying to smell. Not a particularly good year for flowers. One thing I knew was that I was through with selling radio. When you're trying to develop new business instead of answering calls from ad agencies with budgets to spend, it's a tough world. No matter what the prospect's problem, your station must always be the best solution. I thought, "What would happen if my radio station didn't have to be the answer to every advertiser's problem? What if I could recommend what I really felt was best for them?" Did I have the chops for that? Who knew? But I'd better find out. The only thing I knew for sure was that I wasn't going back to KPOL.

Regardless, Paul and I stayed very good friends.

SIXTEEN
So What's New?

Once again, I was in familiar territory, no job, and no dough. This time I was determined to do something I liked. I still had the motorcycle racing bug and I had kept in touch with some of my friends and colleagues from that world, one of whom was Peter Starr. Peter was an English motorcycle racing film producer who wanted to syndicate half-hour racing shows on television in the U.S. Being English, he wasn't that familiar with how television syndication works in this country, but he wanted to set up a syndication company here. I knew nothing about TV syndication but knew someone who did...Elsa.

So, Peter and I made a deal. I'd head up his company...with no pay until we were on the air and the cash began to flow. It never did. He lived in LA, and I religiously went to his apartment/office every day, set up appointments and made pitches. No hits, not even any foul balls. I couldn't even get Yamaha or Kawasaki to go for it, especially without a station lineup, and I couldn't get that until I had the advertisers. Would you like the chicken or the egg first, sir?

Finally, someone explained that this country was totally unfamiliar with, and uninterested in, motorcycle racing, and the time slots in which these shows would run, usually Saturday afternoons, wouldn't attract enough viewers to outdraw a neighborhood bocce ball tournament. Thus, my career as a motorcycle television impresario came to a quick and merciful end with no checkered flag. Back to the drawing board.

I then started to pursue the advertising world, thinking that rather than working for a station that had to be the answer to everyone's problems, if I had my own agency I wouldn't be bound by any media, and I could make the best decisions for my clients. Why not? I called it Richard Gary Enterprises, not from a vanity standpoint, but because new agencies at that time were named after the founder(s). Strange that some of the most creative businesses should have the least creative names. I had kept in touch with a couple of the successful direct response clients I had generated at KFAC and/or KPOL, so I started with them, because there's no bullshit in direct response. You run the spot and the phone either rings or it doesn't. I liked getting a scorecard and I had done well in that area, primarily because of my copywriting ability, inasmuch as I didn't have a choice of media.

The first was a drapery cleaner. I chose talk radio rather than smooth music on the premise the talk audience remained awake during the commercials. It worked, and I was off and running. Forgive the exaggeration. Staggering might be more appropriate.

What followed was a series of acquisitions from former clients. Then, I hit the yellow pages and started cold calling. That's where I developed my mantra, "I can take no for an answer, I just can't take no answer."

After the drapery cleaner, the next logical prospect was a carpet cleaner. If you can get business for a drapery cleaner, it should be even easier to get it for a carpet cleaner.

I finally got a "yes" from a guy who was doing so well, he was considering filing for bankruptcy. He couldn't afford the advertising, so I made a deal with him that should have earned me a Guinness Book award for business stupidity. He couldn't afford to buy advertising, so, cocky bastard that I was, I said I'd buy the time on my dime and sell him the leads. He had nothing to lose. It worked so well that I was making more on the leads than I would have on standard agency commission, twenty-five to forty percent instead of fifteen percent.

Elsa was already contributing to my efforts anonymously, We collaborated on everything, including copy. That was interesting because we are such different people. Elsa tends to be highly factual while I am ethical, but more a salesman. In defense of this position, I would say, "It's just a radio spot. We don't have to defend it in court." I wouldn't go over the line, but sometimes I would push it and Elsa would pull me back. Good balance.

Then, a miracle!

Elsa was getting bored at KABC. The station was doing gangbusters; there was huge demand from advertisers; and clearances for commercials became a big problem. There was nothing to sell, not the greatest way to build commissions. Being number one became more of a pain-in-the-ass than a source of pride for her.

One morning we went to a romantic breakfast, if there is such a thing, at a place on the beach, and talked about Elsa leaving KABC and officially joining me. We agreed to become partners in business as well as in life.

We weren't concerned with making a killing. We both just wanted to make a living doing something that challenged, motivated, and inspired us (if drapery cleaning is inspirational). We never even talked about the quality of the living.

Despite that humility, we were living on the beach in Malibu. In those days, I thought anybody without credit card debt was filthy rich. In reality, we wound up financing some of our early business lunches for a few years. The fact of it was, we had more chutzpah than experience. We knew media sales and that was pretty much it. We didn't even know what a type face was or have the vaguest idea of how to create and produce a print ad. I, of course, knew radio production, so that's where our clients went. Kind of like when your only tool is a hammer, every job has to be a nail.

Our apartment building on Malibu Road had three apartments and two bonus rooms that were empty. We convinced Larry, our landlord, to let us use one of the rooms and we went shopping for office furniture that day. Richard Gary Enterprises became The Gary Group, a very broad hint at what was to become of our personal lives.

I got lucky and signed a couple of former clients of mine, the Pittsburgh Paints West Coast Region, and Dale Carnegie. We came up with a cool line for PPG: *PITTSBURGH PAINTS TAKES THE PAIN OUT OF PAINTING.*

Then, I'd get on the phone and start cold calling. My research director was the Yellow Pages. My first score was the Continental Home Loan Company, a second mortgage provider. The founder was quite happy with our radio results but wanted to add television to the mix. For our first spot, we tried to get Ed Mc Mahon, Johnny Carson's sidekick, to voice it. At the time, Ed was doing spots for several financial institutions. He'd start Johnny's TV show off every evening by bellowing, "HERE'S JOHHHHNNNYY!" We wanted him to start ours off with, "HERE'S MONNNNEEEYYY! Everybody but Ed thought it was great. Next was another company founded by the same guy that created Continental. It was Vestcorp, a pension fund investment company. We kicked that one off nicely, especially at a CPA convention in LA where, to get attendees to the booth, we rented a three-foot high robot, dressed it in a fedora and tie. We had him carrying a briefcase, identifying himself as C-3PA (after C-3PO in *Star Wars)* and telling people to get over to the Vestcorp booth. It was a hit with everyone but the Feds who leter called Vestcorp a Ponzi scheme and any further meetings with that client would be held at the Orange County Jail.

Next, Elsa got a lead from a major agency about an account that was too small for them to handle, a guy who sold adjustable speaker stands to keep your speakers off the carpet so the sound of your stereo wouldn't get muffled. We called them Speakeruppers. We also did the fulfillment on that one and it paid our rent, until the guy stopped paying us for everything despite his success.

Another lead brought us McArthur Home Builders, a home improvement and renovation company. Our deal with the owner was that he'd pay the media and we'd get five dollars per lead, and fifty dollars for each sale. We got a shitload of leads, but he got virtually no sales. I asked the owner if he had trouble counting, or did he have a lousy sales staff. The latter he said, and Elsa and I wound up spending our evenings following up on leads with our Stanley 25 Ft. PowerLock tape measures and a pack of graph paper. To show his respect for us, we were the ones he called to pick him up when he was released from jail on his DUI charge.

So What's New?

The classic was Public Insurance Company. They specialized in problem drivers with unenviable driving records for a multitude of reasons, too many tickets, DUIs, etc. We figured these drivers knew what their problem was and didn't need an insurance company humiliating them in their commercials as the ones running did. So, we created a humorous spot ala a mob guy talking about protection. It went over big, but when the client called and got our answering service, he figured, successful or not, we were too small for his big ego.

You may be getting the idea that while adding new direct response clients was highly doable, making money on them was another story. We thought of becoming our own clients and developing a couple of our own products. One was selling packs of assorted nuts via mail order under the banner, NUTS 2 YOU. The other was creating an assortment of wines called Malibooze.

The final coup was Larry, our landlord, who had a hot tub business that was anything but hot. He traded our services for the rent on our apartment and offices. Same story there. We got leads and he couldn't sell them, so, classy guy that he was, he advised us of the problem via an eviction notice.

Given that, we thought it might be a good idea to move...and we fell up! Elsa found a spectacular house, still in Malibu, that more than solved the problem. It was a two story with two large bedrooms on the ground floor that we used for offices. On the upper floor a great room with living room, kitchen, and two bedrooms, one for us and one for Dylan. Outside the second floor was a deck that ran the entire length of the house and had a super ocean view.

Being in our own business was teaching me a bit of verbal self-control. I even learned to practice a little tact and self-restraint. I no longer felt I had to say exactly what I was thinking to my available audience, especially if they were clients. It was OK to leave a couple of bridges standing. Maybe the best part of being in our own business, especially for me, was that I no longer had to put up with the corporate politics I despised so much and that had gotten me into so much trouble for sharing my unedited views with my superiors.

SEVENTEEN
Do I Hear Music?

A chance meeting changed our business and our lives. I had kept my account in the bank located in the building next to KFAC. One day, when I was there probably making a withdrawal, George Fritzinger walked in. We had stayed friendly despite the mutually uncomfortable circumstances of my departure, but we hadn't really seen one another. However, George and I had always liked and respected each other, so, to ease any potential awkwardness, I asked him, "How's that fuck who stole my job doing?" When he saw I wasn't serious, he laughed and asked what I was doing. I explained, "Man, I was getting sleeping sickness at KPOL and I had to quit before it became terminal. Then I got lucky, met a super woman, who incidentally sold for KABC-TV. We started living together; she got bored at the station; and we started an ad agency. We're mostly doing media stuff." George suddenly got highly interested, not just cocktail party interested, and he told me why.

"When I was a senior at the Naval Academy in Annapolis, as you know, I was on the football team and got lucky and was named an All-American. One Saturday, we played our big geographic rival, the University of Maryland. Playing opposite me for Maryland was another All-American, Ben Scotti, a very tough guy from Newark, New Jersey whose father was a labor organizer on the docks there. Needless to say, but I'm saying it anyway, the docks of Newark are a world away from the playing fields of Eton."

Do I Hear Music?

George continued, "We didn't know each other but, as opponents, we hated each other, and spent the afternoon trying to beat the shit out of each other."

"Fast forward to 1975. I'm at PIPs. You know the joint. It's that very trendy bar in Beverly Hills. I'm enjoying a few when somebody, I forget who, introduces me to Ben and the light goes on. We both remember the game. But that was a long time ago, so we had a few drinks and kidded each other about our past rivalry. It was weird but we found we really liked each other. Then we compared our post-college careers."

Ben, post-college, had played pro ball for the Eagles, Redskins, and 49ers. He wasn't big, but he was tough and feared and respected, even in the company of rugged professional football players. After his pro career ended, Ben went to work for an independent record label. His job, a thankless one, was to collect money from the record stores that were notoriously slow in paying independent labels for product they had purchased and sold. Independent labels had little clout and were last on the payables list, but an amazing thing happened when Ben visited them. Virtually, every time he went out to collect money, he came back with it. The label was impressed and soon decided to see if Ben's charms would also work on radio station Program Directors in getting their songs played. Another win for Ben. He's a tough man to say no to. Let's just say he could be highly persuasive. Later, I kidded him about being a great philosopher, as he had a sign in his office that read, "When you go you grow. When you stop you flop." It's true.

After graduation, George did his tour of duty in the Navy and then got an MBA at Harvard and met Ralph Guild, whose national radio sales rep firm had worked for WPIX-FM and KFAC. They went into the radio business together as station owners.

"As soon as Ben found out that I was co-owner of a few radio stations, from the look on his face, I thought he might be getting an erection."

"Given what you're doing, I'm thinking there might be something here for you, with us." Ben was, and is, extremely close with his brother, Tony. Tony is a tall, very handsome man and a hard worker with a brilliant, creative mind who had, by his choice, a short career as an actor and singer, appearing in films such as *Valley Of The Dolls*. But Tony's brain was too big to be sated solely by performing, and he didn't have the kind of enormous ego that reveled in attention, so he turned to entrepreneurial pursuits that worked his brain. The two of them started a record promotion company. Tony was the architect and Ben was the guy who went out and made it work.

"Are you starting to get the picture, Dick? I'm in radio and they're in record promotion. So, Ben introduces me to Tony and the next thing you know, we have a joint venture, but it's not about me playing their records. It's about bigger projects. You, Tony, and I should talk. You know the record business. Maybe you could be involved too."

At that time, Jon Peters, a former hair stylist whose scissors may have been getting dull, was living with Barbra Streisand. He became enchanted with the lure of the silver screen and Barbra was his ticket to film production. I don't know if he ever actually did anything, but he got a producer's screen credit and probably a basket full of money. Thank you, Barbra. Warner Bros. was about to release a new version of the classic, *A Star Is Born,* starring Streisand, and co-produced by her and Peters. Naturally, there would be singles and a soundtrack. Tony got the film and record companies to work together, a totally new concept. The idea was that if the single, released well in advance of the film, was a hit, it would be a great lead-in and help the film. The film's success would then be a terrific intro for the soundtrack. Masterful and unheard of at the time, but highly indicative of Tony's business acumen.

Tony's company would handle the record promotion of the singles on-air and, to give him more leverage at radio, be responsible for placing the radio advertising for the film and then also handle advertising for the soundtrack. Tony wasn't versed in the nuances of advertising, so that's where George came in as a silent partner.

George obviously knew and respected my knowledge of radio and, although he didn't know her at the time, Elsa's credentials in both radio and television were a huge plus. George set up a meeting for us with

Tony. There was instant rapport. We liked him and we sold him. The deal they offered us was very fair. The first film we worked on was *The Main Event* starring Streisand and Ryan O'Neal. It was a smash.

One film followed another and pretty soon Tony was by far our biggest client. We had a ton of work to do and had to hire a couple of people to help us do it. In fact, we were so busy that there was a week when Elsa never set foot out of the house. We'd start buying radio in the Eastern markets at about six thirty in the morning (PST) and work our way across the time zones until we finished with the West. Then we'd figure out what we had done all day and plan out the next day. When that was finished, it was frequently hard to find a restaurant still serving dinner, but it was exciting, and we were starting to make some money. And the music business was a tad more exciting than carpet cleaning.

Tony also got into the "crossover" business, where he would take a country artist and cross them over, i.e., get their music played on pop stations. That, too, was a natural for us, and was soon another valuable revenue area, as well as a lot of fun. Dolly Parton was our first project, for *TWO DOORS DOWN.* She was the first, but far from our last country project.

I spent a ton of time in Tony's office... or my classroom as I called it and got a Ph.D. in music marketing just sitting there. I remember one Friday night I got home from his office after eight o'clock and told Elsa that Tony was going to Europe for a month. "Really," she said. "What are you going to do with your Friday nights while he's gone?"

Tony and Ben went from being clients to being good friends. Like many Italians, they were a very close-knit family, and Elsa and I knew our non-business relationship was true friendship when Tony invited us to his home to spend Christmas Eve with his family. Ultimately, Elsa and I would spend time with him and his wife, French singing star Sylvie Vartan, in France and Italy and we remain good friends today. I have enormous respect for Tony, both personally and professionally.

Given that success, I began making some cold calls to labels in LA and New York. We were developing an awareness in the industry. Then Disco popped its ugly head up and it all went to shit.

Disco became a lifestyle sport with young people. They dressed the part, filled all kinds of new clubs to capacity, and danced to exhaustion… but they stopped buying records. They didn't just want to listen to the music, they wanted to dress for it, and dance to it, and live it. Suddenly, the projects we were working on went away and we were powerless to stop it. It was frustrating, very frightening, and a true and imminent financial dilemma for us, just when we were starting to emerge.

One thing became certain. Getting out of the parking lot at what was then our fancy Century City address would no longer be a problem. In fact, having any address at all was not a certainty, but we got lucky. On Saturdays, Dylan was in a youth soccer league, and we had gotten quite friendly with Tom Baker, the father of one of Dylan's teammates, Tommy Jr., with whom he became best buddies.

One day, I shared our lodging problem with Tom, and he solved it on the spot. He was the CFO of Aurora Films, an independent production company with offices in Beverly Hills. In fact, a couple of extra offices in Beverly Hills. Tom made us the sweetest (and kindest) deal imaginable, and this on-its-ass young agency now had a Beverly Hills address…and we wound up getting film business from our landlord.

EIGHTEEN
Nashville Aka Smashville

Tony also had an artist management company with a partner, Stan Moress. Sometimes Stan and I would both be waiting in Tony's office to get a minute to talk to him about some business, and we got to know each other very well in this environment. It reminded me of a quote by the famed English poet, John Milton, on his blindness: "They also serve who only sit and wait." I know. He actually said "stand," not "sit," but what the hell.

At the time, Stan was managing Eddie Rabbit, a white-hot country artist who was burning up the charts. He was booked into the MGM Grand for his first-ever Las Vegas appearance and Stan wanted to hit it out of the park. Casino bookings were very important for country artists and not just for the money. They were true road warriors, travelling endlessly from gig to gig, as opposed to pop artists who only had a major tour every couple of years when they released a new album. Vegas gave country artists a chance to get off the bus, take a shower, get a good night's sleep in a real bed without wheels, have some fun in a town that kept hours like they did...and make good money. We got the job promoting Eddie's first appearance. It was at the MGM Grand, one of the premier Vegas hotels.

I'd never been to Vegas, so I went there to scope it out. Wow! I had never even imagined the extent of its glitz. Gaudy would be a massive understatement. Architecturally, Las Vegas might best be described as "glopulent." Lots and lots of gaudy gone mad.

Having no idea of what was being done to promote casino acts may have worked in our favor. We did some research, used some street smarts, and came up with some highly creative and innovative ideas. The campaign was a success. The MGM was very happy and, obviously, so were Stan and Eddie, who was invited back. That was the beginning of a lot of work there for us.

Stan thought we could do a ton of country business and he invited me to Nashville to meet agents and record labels. That was like inviting a Mormon to a cocktail party. Being brought up in the New York market where there were no country stations, my awareness of that music and its artists was virtually non-existent.

I wound up going to Nashville frequently for meetings with Stan's artists, so I figured, if I was going to be there, I may as well make use of my spare time, so I started calling the managers of other acts being booked into casinos. We had the Eddie Rabbit success story as credentials as well as Stan's recommendation that was immensely helpful as he was highly respected. It worked and the more I went there, the more I liked it, especially the people.

Stan called one day and said, "Dick. Good news! I got you on a prestigious panel on country music concert promotion."

"Are you crazy, Stan? The closest I've ever been to a country concert is Eddie Rabbit's booth at the MGM."

He laughed and said, "Don't sweat it. You can carry it off." So, I agreed.

The panel went well, and I did not embarrass myself...or Stan. He couldn't be there, but he found me after and asked how it had gone. I told him it was OK, nobody laughed, and nobody left. I told him I spoke with a couple of guys, and one gave me his card.

"Who was that" he asked.

"I don't remember his name but here's his card," and I showed it to him.

He looked at it and then gave me this incredulous look. "That's THE OAK RIDGE BOYS, you moron!"

Nashville Aka Smashville

I responded, "Who are they?" At that time, The Oaks were also dominating the country charts. After that, I thought maybe I should follow that stuff a bit more closely since Nashville was becoming such an important stop on my route.

I did follow up with The Oaks' manager. He was tough. It turns out the Oaks had been booked into the MGM, Eddie's stomping ground, for their first-ever Las Vegas appearance and he wasn't taking it lightly. I gave him a proposal.

By that time, we had developed all kinds of promotional tricks and knowledge based on our experience there with multiple acts. And they were working.

All these and more were included in our proposal. Then one afternoon, his assistant, a very nice young woman, called and said that our proposal was approved with a couple of minor revisions. Then she began to be more specific. Instead of this, the manager wanted to do that, and there were a couple of things in the proposal he didn't want to do at all, plus he wanted to add a couple of things. If these revisions were minor, then so was the bombing of Hiroshima. To me, it looked like a formula for disaster, so I slipped on my New York attitude and asked her, "So, why doesn't he just do it himself?" She sounded terrified and said, "I'll call you back in ten minutes."

Ten minutes later, the manager calls. "So, do you want the deal or don't you?"

I responded somewhat arrogantly but confidently, "Look. We want to be a part of your success, not your failure." He bought the deal, probably because he realized we had the experience, and if he did it his way and it didn't work, it was his ass, not ours.

The Oaks' engagement at the MGM was another success and the manager then hired us to help promote their summer State Fair dates. These were critical for all country artists, as they paid very well. The fairs were municipal events and, as such, nonprofits. So, after expenses were tallied, any remaining money was split between the local organization and the artist, with the majority going to the act. It paid to do well.

JUST ANOTHER DICK

We convinced a television station in each market to sponsor and stage a talent contest for quartets of young boys and girls. We provided contestants with music tracks of The Oaks songs without vocals. In each market, the winning group got to take the stage and open for The Oaks at their fair. The television promotion gave The Oaks' show super on-air exposure and helped sell tickets. We called it *The Little Acorn Talent Show,* adding the line *Because Little Acorns Grow Into Mighty Oaks.* It was a winner for all.

Another very good thing had come out of our relationship with The Oaks. Donna Jean, a young woman on their staff who did a lot of their marketing coordination, called and told us about a friend of hers, Connie Baer, who had worked for a West Virginia promoter, had recently moved to LA and was looking for a gig. Donna Jean suggested we meet with her, and we did, more to appease a client than to hire someone we didn't need for a job we didn't have. We set up a lunch with Connie, who was in her late twenties, attractive, bursting with energy and ideas, and obviously knowledgeable about the business. Elsa and I really liked her. We hired her on the spot. We'd find something for her to do.

The more I went to Nashville, the more I liked it. Someone in LA snottily asked me "What's the difference between doing business in LA as opposed to Nashville?" He made it sound like it was the difference between heaven in LA and hell in Nashville.

"Well," I said, "In LA, you need a subpoena to see someone; in Nashville, they invite you to lunch."

Stan essentially became our "doorman" in Nashville, opening a countless number of them for us. In recognition of all his efforts on our behalf, we presented Stan with an actual door with all the hardware on it and a proclamation stating, "You've Opened So Many For Us, We Wanted You To Have One Of Your Own."

At that time, Larry Gatlin and the Gatlin Brothers were on the charts with lots of country hits. Larry was the songwriter and lead singer, Steve, and Rudy the backups. The group was known for its amazing harmony and hit songs. Larry had a reputation as being rather temperamental, and

Steve seemed to be the one charged with keeping it all together. They had just been booked into the Riviera and I made my pitch to Steve. He was interested and told me I'd have to get Larry's approval, a fairly daunting proposition. I caught up with him during a break at a rehearsal for a TV show in LA. I introduced myself and told him about our prospective plans. He said, "I have one question. Do you work cheap?"

I quickly thought that question defines any possible future relationship with them and responded, "No!"

"Good," says Larry, "You're hired." I never did find out how he got the rep. I found him great to work with. He was smart and I loved his sense of humor.

I was essentially on the road with them in Vegas, and they included me in everything. No act ever treated me better. Larry had a good line on being in Vegas: "Man, this goin' to bed at six forty-five and gettin' up at quarter to seven will kill you. When I don't have anything to do, I go down to the casino and play a little 22."

One night, I was standing in the wings backstage watching the show when one of the crew approaches me and says, "Tonight's the night. You ready?"

I say, "What for?"

He replied, "It's your initiation. Everyone new has to do it."

"Do what?"

"Go on stage and sing with the guys," he says with a smile.

"NO FUCKING WAY," I adamantly replied.

"Well, it's your ass and your job if you don't. They're expecting you. They like it."

The next thing I know, I'm walking out on stage. I go up to Steve who's smiling, but surprised, and I pretend to join in, but I lip synch the lyrics. I can't carry a tune in a backpack and I'm trying not to embarrass myself, and them, in front of a packed audience who are wondering who the hell I am. Plus, I'm so nervous I was wishing there was a urinal onstage. Meanwhile, as the song is ending, Larry turns around to see what's going on, sees me onstage and laughs his ass off. He explains

I'm the marketing guy and he doesn't know what I'm doing there but I'm welcome. I exited the stage quickly in utter embarrassment and went looking for the wiseass who fabricated the sham.

I tried to time my Nashville trips so I'd be there when Stan was. Frances Preston, who was running the Nashville office of BMI, was probably his best friend in Nashville, or anywhere, and we'd spend many evenings by her pool. This was prior to her ascendancy to CEO and relocation to New York. Frances had a beautiful home in a fashionable section of Nashville, or Smashville, as I later came to call it.

One night, Mary Ann McCready, the marketing guru for what was then CBS Records, and a good friend of both Frances and Stan, was there and we got to talking. She was very friendly and a bit curious as to what I did. I explained that our company promotes artists' events. She became highly interested and thought it might work for labels too, possibly for Mark Gray, a new artist on the label whose first album, *Diamonds in the Dust*, would soon be released. Mary Ann set up a meeting with Roy Wunsch, head of the label. When I met Roy, his first remark to me was, "What can you do that we can't do?"

My answer was, "I can fly across the country for a thirty-second meeting. Can you?" He laughed, and I then explained what we do and said, "If you can do what we we're doing, why aren't you?" Roy took it in the right spirit, and we made a deal.

Connie Baer and I put together a sensational promotion for Mark around the album's title, *Diamonds in the Dust*. We got top radio stations to promote it on air; we traded out airfare for the station winners to fly to Cancun, stay in a hotel, and search for a diamond in the dusty ruins of nearby Tulum. The winner got to keep the diamond and Mark Grey entertained on Saturday night.

The promotion was enormously successful for the label, popular with radio, and thus started a new stage of our growth, working for labels on new releases. Pretty soon we were doing it for virtually all the major country labels.

Nashville Aka Smashville

Roy was a terrific guy. He was smart, creative, and straight. He and Mary Ann were later to marry and become our lifelong friends.

I was spending a considerable amount of time in Nashville developing country music business. As such, I was getting to know a lot of the key people there and getting visibility for our agency. At the time, the Nashville music community was very close-knit, and because of my exposure, I was invited to join the Board of Directors of the Academy of Country Music, a Los Angeles-based group founded by Dick Clark, who created and produced the *Academy Of Country Music Awards Show*, an annual network TV show.

NINETEEN
Wedding Bells and Baby Toys

Prior to our evacuation from the Bill Mack house, the house became very significant to Elsa and me for a reason that had nothing to do with business. That's where we had our wedding reception.

After a little over two years together, we decided to make a lasting commitment to each other. We set the date for April 30, 1978. We wanted to really do it right, but on a very limited budget. This was Elsa's first stab at marriage (and hopefully her last) and Abe, her father, was a very serious practitioner of the Jewish faith, having been Principal of a Hebrew school on Long Island. Elsa's mother had passed at a young age. My mother had already had her fling at St. Patrick's, so we decided to have the ceremony at the Wilshire Boulevard Temple in Los Angeles, a magnificent, historic, awe-inspiring, structure.

That was my first experience as a minority. The Rabbis weren't rushing to perform the ceremony for this lovely Jewish woman marrying this infidel. We got one of them to do it...but he wouldn't let me break the glass, a tradition in Jewish wedding ceremonies, because I was from a different tribe. The ceremony was to be in the grand Sanctuary, a magnificent, stately, and very large space, that would always hold fond memories and far more friends than we could invite.

To minimize the expense, we chose our home as the site for the reception. We wanted it to be special, so we got an Indian restaurant we really liked to cater it. The morning of the wedding, Elsa and I drove to the Temple in her spiffy Fiat for the big event.

Wedding Bells And Baby Toys

When it was time for the wedding, there was something missing...my best man, Paul LaGasse. It seems that the night before, Daylight Savings kicked in and he had neglected to set his clocks ahead, so I enlisted Les Goldberg, one of the ushers, as a highly capable stand-in. Stand-in is a good description for the job because that's about all a best man does... stands around. Les was over-qualified.

The magic hour came and went, and Elsa, in the vestibule with the bridesmaids, kept scanning the Temple's vast expanse for guests. It looked empty, so she wanted to delay the start until she figured every-one who was coming was there.

Meanwhile, I'm standing on the altar, or whatever the proper name is for the main stage of the Temple, wondering if she'd met someone else. Finally, the lady running the operation informed her to get on with it. The hitch went off without a hitch...and they saved the glassware for a more deserving groom.

To give the day some added pizzazz because our house was about a one-hour schlep from the Temple, Elsa and I rented a Rolls Royce, with driver, to convey us home to the reception after the ceremony. As we were leaving the Temple, we waved to the guests on the steps of the Temple and noticed the arrival of the intended Best Man, who looked so embarrassed I felt sorry for him, but he had relinquished his title.

The reception was great. The caterer did a super job. The female waitstaff wore native Indian garb. Our wedding cake was a massive bowl of whipped cream with giant strawberries dipped in chocolate and inocu-lated with Kirsch, a fruit brandy made from cherries. No bride and groom standing atop a cake or, in our case, drowning in the whipped cream. It was a superb Malibu day and the guests crowded onto the deck and enjoyed the ocean view. Despite all our prior anxiety, we had a terrific time and totally enjoyed our reception.

The next morning, rather than a romantic honeymoon in Hawaii, we got up, cleaned up the detritus from the prior evening, and rushed off to a 10:00 a.m. meeting at the Pittsburgh Paint Company. Even *they* thought we were overdoing the responsibility bit.

Life and business progressed. We weren't nuts about the commute from Malibu, but we genuinely liked our Beverly Hills offices, courtesy of Tom Baker, and we were now far more in the mainstream and our label business was growing nicely.

Around August 1979, it turned out that Elsa was building something else...a baby! We greeted that news with great joy and anticipation. Our lives had truly become one. We worked and lived together and now we would be parents together; although, I have to say Elsa always treats Dylan like her son and he, in turn, shows love and respect for her. But wouldn't you know, Elsa's pregnancy killed the ski season. Just kidding!

The upcoming blessed event did put some additional demands on us apart from parenting. Like housing. We had moved from the Bill Mack house when we got the office in Century City because we couldn't afford that luxury without it also being an office. We were then living in a tiny two-room condo and there was no way the four of us could survive in those limited quarters. Elsa and I had wanted to buy a house, but it seemed out of the question. We had no money...NO MONEY!

Elsa's sister, Barb, offered to lend us $10,000, which was spectacular, but not nearly enough because, with my beach addiction, I still had to live in Malibu. Nevertheless, we started looking...every weekend. After a while, I think we could have qualified for real estate brokers' licenses. We knew just about every listing in our price range in Malibu...and given our price range, there weren't too many. Finally, an agent told it like it was, "You're lousy buyers and, to close on anything, it's gonna have to be a desperate seller who's a heartbeat away from foreclosure." Fine, but we still had to love the house. We were not on a rescue mission for over-extended homeowners.

We finally found a house that fit our taste and budget and the seller's sense of emergency. It was a small but attractive and functional place about three miles up Corral Canyon, a very winding, twisting road. To get there, I would imagine myself at the wheel of a modified sports car racing through the mountains of Italy in the Targa Florio.

The price, in 1980, was $210,000. The agent suggested we do a lease option where we gave the seller the $10,000 as a good faith gesture that would go against a final purchase deal, and then rent it for a year with the monthly fee also reducing the final price by the amount we paid. That's where we were headed until we figured that in a year, the guy who owned it could have all kinds of other problems and lose the house anyway and we would be kissing the ten grand goodbye.

We wanted to buy it then, not wait, and here's what we worked out. We gave the seller the $10,000 as a down payment. In those days, you could assume a first mortgage without qualifying, so we assumed his mortgage. Continental Home Loan was still our client at the time, and they gave us a second mortgage (with points and at a usurious but competitive interest rate). The seller, who had no choice, took back a third, and the realtor, who would have lost the listing anyway, took his commission as a fourth. We felt we should have qualified for some kind of creative financing award.

When asked where we lived and I replied, "Malibu," people frequently asked, "Are you on the ocean?"

I'd reply in the negative and get back from them, "How far are you from it?"

My response, "About five to ten million." I think that's why they asked.

After her early morning sickness, etc., Elsa had a relatively easy pregnancy (I know, easy for me to say). At about two o'clock in the morning on May 18th, Elsa said, "This is it!" We were all packed, got in the car, and drove through an intense fog to get to St. John's Hospital in Santa Monica. We had discussed names and, in honor of Jewish tradition, had decided the baby's name would start with an A after Elsa's father, Abraham. It would be Anthony for a boy and Amanda for a girl.

We had taken the Lamaze courses so I would be present for the actual birth, something that had not been possible for Dylan due to the emergency whereby he chose to recline sideways in the uterus. Late in the morning, after a lot of pain and pushing, which she withstood amazingly, Elsa gave birth and out came the baby. Since I had a better vantage point than she, I saw the sex before Elsa and I shouted, "It's Amanda!" and that girl owned my heart right on the spot. I was instantly in love, and I hadn't experienced such sheer happiness since July 1, 1969, when Dylan appeared on the scene. I think there is no greater joy a person can experience than the birth of a child, especially for the mother who has had to do all the hard work and bear all the discomfort—but I'll take my share of the joy anyway.

The middle name was tougher. We wanted it to mean something to us and not just be a repetition of a family name, so we finally settled on Brooke, paying homage to our mutual birthplace, Brooklyn, a dirty, seedy, dangerous place at the time. We put the "e" on Brook to soften it. People thought the name was very classy, not being aware of its true origin. Now, given what's happened in that infamous borough, they'd probably accuse us of pretension.

When Elsa and Amanda were released from the hospital, an experience we had on our way home defined the frantic style of our lives. We had painted Amanda's room a light blue with cutouts of white clouds sprinkled all around, but we still hadn't bought lamps and some other stuff. So, with the newborn infant safely stored in the car, we went shopping at a baby store on the way home. I'd run in, look around and run out and tell Elsa what I liked and what aisle it was on, and she'd run in and do the same while I watched Amanda. Elsa was such a great mother. I think she started to teach Amanda how to read on the drive home.

Dylan came over that night to meet his new sister and brought her a Teddy Bear that was promptly named Theodore and is still a favorite family companion who Amanda enjoys seeing on her visits home.

One other major detail we had to work out was who was going to care for Amanda while we were at work. We converted the basement into living quarters for whoever would be lucky enough to get the job as

Wedding Bells And Baby Toys

Amanda's daytime caretaker and, hopefully, friend. Our first hire was our first mistake. We thought we wanted someone young with energy and experience, and we found a young English woman who had done the job before. But, as the days progressed, we became aware of the change in her attitude, and her appearance. She couldn't wait for the day to end and the evenings to begin, primarily at the bars in Santa Monica patronized by English ex-pats. When we'd come home and ask how the day went, she'd reply, "She was a dear. Slept all day." Not exactly what we'd hoped for. We didn't expect her to be giving math classes, but we were hoping for more interaction in this developmental state.

One day, we left for work but forgot something and came back to the house to retrieve it, having been gone less than ten minutes, and there was the keeper of our kid, lying on the chaise on the deck slathered from head to toe in suntan oil. We then realized we were day care for her and not the opposite, so we decided to upgrade. That's when we got really lucky.

Through an agency, we found a late middle-aged African American woman, Alberta, who had grown children and, obviously, the experience of rearing them. Alberta was a quiet, nurturing person who treated Amanda with a mother's love. It's impossible to judge what a positive and subliminal effect Alberta may have had on Amanda's persona, but I'd bet it was significant. Alberta lived with us Monday to Friday and went home on weekends. I'd drive her the three miles down to the bus on Friday and pick her up when she returned on Monday morning. I think that was the part of the job she liked least, driving with me on that winding canyon road.

Alberta was with us for a couple of years until she opted for a less demanding schedule. Ruth, a wonderful Hispanic lady, replaced her and was also good for Amanda, but those things don't seem to last forever, and when Ruth left, we realized that Amanda was getting older and was not in need of such full-time attention.

JUST ANOTHER DICK

I was travelling constantly. In fact, I considered changing my name to Shlep 'N Fetchit. On every trip, I'd bring back a doll or a plush animal for Amanda. One day, as I was leaving, I said to her, "Hey Amanda, I'm going to Dallas. What kind of animal should I bring you?"

Her reply, "No animal. Don't go, Daddy." Wow! I almost didn't.

We had decided that for her future care, we would go the Au Pair route, hiring young European girls who had one-year visas and wanted to experience life in the United States. We thought Amanda would be better off with younger people who spoke English, at least better than she did, and could relate to her. I think we called that one correctly. We would provide the girls with a car, and they would clean the house, shop, pick Amanda up after school, play with her, and make dinner. After that, they were free to explore the LA nightlife.

Our first au pair was Jenny, a nineteen-year-old Berlin native. She was terrific and we are still friendly with her. She has visited us, and we have seen her on her home turf. She would also figure into our lives in another way, but I'd be getting ahead of myself to go into that now.

Another standout was Slavka, also nineteen, from Prague. Slavka was different from the other girls. In the evening, instead of heading for Merlin McFly's Bar in Santa Monica, an ex-pat hangout, she would sit on the couch with her Czech-English dictionary, watching television and learning more about the language. On weekends, she'd go to a film expo at UCLA or to some other cultural event.

One Christmas, we rented a condo in Park City to go skiing. We flew up but told Slavka we had an extra room if she and a friend of hers from Prague, also an au pair who was working nearby, wanted to experience an American Christmas, they could drive up to Park City in the car we provided her and stay with us. They did, and, on the way back, they wanted to see Las Vegas so they decided to drive through it. When stopped at a light, her friend recognized someone from Prague who was with an American. It was the beginning of a life change for Slavka.

The American fellow managed the art collection of a wealthy Houston oil family's charitable foundation. He and Slavka got friendly, and she would sometimes visit him in Houston. Once, during Amanda's Spring vacation, Elsa, Amanda, and I were going to Santa Fe and Slavka was going to meet the fellow in Houston and then go to New York with him.

While in Santa Fe, we visited a Tibetan art gallery, and as we headed out the door, the manager stopped us and said, "Please stay. The Dalai Lama is coming, and you can be here to help welcome him." We instantly agreed, and when he arrived, we barely saw him get out of his limo, wave to the small group of us gathered and disappear into the gallery. But we did see him, and when we told Slavka about it, she said, "Oh, I had dinner with him in Houston. He's very nice." It was at the home of the family with the foundation.

So, I jokingly asked, "Where did you stay in New York? At Gracie Mansion?"

"No," she laughed. "We stayed at Milos Forman's place." Milos Forman, of course, was the famed Czech film director whose credits included *One Flew Over The Cuckoo's Nest*, *Hair*, and *Amadeus*. I felt like maybe I was the one that should be doing the dishes that night.

Meanwhile, I was proving myself totally worthless around our new house. I have absolutely no practical or even basic technical skills or knowledge and less ability in fixing things. I had always rented, and when something broke or misfired, I simply called the super or the owner of the property. Not anymore. Elsa and I were the owners now and, as a man, I was expected to pull my weight.

During our first summer in the house, there was an excruciating heat wave, and our air conditioning chose to go on strike. We were melting. I finally got a heating and air conditioning guy on the phone. He said he was very busy, but I begged him to come. I told him we had a new baby, and I was fearful for her health.

He finally grudgingly and very reluctantly agreed to come and see what the problem was. He arrived, went outside, and returned about ninety seconds later, looking like he was ready to roast me on our driveway.

"I found the problem," be barked.

"Great, what is it?" I was afraid the repair would be very expensive.

"It's your circuit breaker," he said disparagingly. Circuit breaker. Shit, that really sounds expensive.

"What's a circuit breaker? Can you fix it? "I innocently asked. He looked at me with real disgust.

"I fixed it. It was a very complicated process where I had to flip a switch." I was appropriately ashamed of my ignorance, and he played it to the hilt. This guy belonged in New York. I wondered how he'd be at writing commercials.

About two weeks later, the stove chose to go on unemployment, and I managed to put my ignorance on exhibit once more. Having no shame, I again called my man and, before he had the chance to belittle me or ask questions I couldn't answer, I said, "Listen, I checked and this time it's definitely not the circuit breaker."

"It wouldn't be," he said disgustedly, "You have a gas stove."

TWENTY
One Less for The Road

At this point, you may be nursing a hangover from reading about all the drinking I was doing. Alcoholism is a disease and the main deterrent to getting clean is denial that you have the problem. Drinking was undoubtedly a factor in my getting kicked out of college, and I had more than one experience with the law. It also probably figured in Carol and my break-up. Booze really controlled my life, and I wasn't getting any better at it. As mentioned before, one drink and I was a passenger with no idea of my destination.

Amanda was young and I didn't know how my drinking might have affected Dylan, but if it had—and I expect it did—I didn't want to repeat that with her, and it wasn't fair to Elsa. I owed it to the three of them to stop. Plus, at some point, it stops being fun and you realize that you aren't in control.

One night, before I knew Elsa, shortly after the bars closed, it turned out I was accompanied home by a Highway Patrolman, a fact unbeknownst to me until I saw the red lights and heard the siren. Fortunately, when he pulled me over, I was home and I parked in front of the shack on PCH, and then the field sobriety test started.

I didn't think my recitation of the alphabet backwards was going to get me into MENSA. For the next part of the test, he told me to put my head back, close my eyes, and touch my nose with my forefingers. I was sober enough to realize that the end result of that trick would be me getting a concussion from falling over backwards and hitting my head on the sidewalk, so I kept my eyes open, and he didn't catch it. Finally, I asked how I was doing, and he said, "You're marginal and you're home, so I'll let you go." I thanked him profusely, and in the morning, when I woke with my traditional hangover, I promised myself I would NEVER drink again. EVER! And I didn't...until about five o'clock that evening.

I also remember that sometimes on weekend mornings, after Elsa and I had been out the night before, I'd wake up and go through the mental drill. I'd ask myself, "What did I do last night? Did I embarrass or disgrace myself or, worse yet, Elsa? Did I drive the winding three miles up the canyon like it was the Nürburgring and put her life in danger? And, finally, how pissed will she be?"

I was more of a jovial than a nasty or falling down drunk, and Elsa never seemed to be mad at me for that. But, as you start to get over the denial and realize and accept that you have a problem, you sub-consciously want some help, even in the form of anger. Some reason to quit TODAY! I started to get a bit frustrated at her lack of anger, thinking, "Don't Jews understand anything about alcohol? The Irish all have PhDs."

I finally accepted that I was a functioning alcoholic. The word "functioning" could raise legitimate questions. It's kind of like a professional typist who isn't very good at his or her job and makes lots of mistakes but does it every day. I didn't get drunk every night, but I drank every night, and I wouldn't start until I knew I wouldn't have to stop.

In January 1984, I decided it was time to stop bullshitting myself and really quit. It should have been easy, as I'd had so much experience trying it. While alcoholism can't be cured, it is one of the only diseases that can be successfully treated by the patient.

I got some help from a friend who had kicked booze and cocaine. When he knew I was serious, he brought me to a few AA meetings. I originally thought AA was just a bunch of alkies getting together to tell war stories. Was I ever wrong! It's a dose of reality. The first time I properly identified myself, "Hi. I'm Dick and I'm an alcoholic," I felt committed.

I've never liked clubs or organized religions, and I thought too many people probably used AA as a crutch, which, by the way, is what you're supposed to do. I decided to do it by myself. I bought all the books and when I travelled to Vegas or Atlantic City on business, my modus ope-randi was dramatically changed. Instead of checking in at the bar, I'd hit the concession stand to pick up a large packet of peanut M&Ms and head for my room where I'd devour them to get the sugar rush and then order room service to avoid the places where alcohol flowed freely. And then I'd read my AA books.

So far, it has worked...for forty years. I ultimately realized what a chokehold the shit had on me and how it totally controlled my life. Personally, I found real freedom in sobriety and consider it one of the greatest gifts of my life. And I've still got the fun stories, at least the ones I remember.

TWENTY-ONE
The Road Back...With Detours

The disco disaster had finally outlived its welcome and the music business slowly returned. It appeared that our re-build of the agency was working and some of the financial pressure was off, but Elsa and I had too much to do. We needed to add staff. To do that, we needed more space, and Aurora Film Partners, our landlord, didn't have it. In fact, they were lusting after the space we had, which was actually theirs. We started looking around and our exploration led us to Venice.

At that time, Venice was a forgotten part of LA. Main Street was pretty much thrift shops and biker bars with a measurable part of the foot traffic being ladies of the evening shopping for johns. To add to the aura, parts of it were gang infested. But how long can you have a slum that's only two blocks from the ocean? Best of all, the rents were cheap! Our kind of place.

We found a space in what was laughingly called the Main Street Design Center. It had about as much design incorporated into it as an Army barracks. The space we rented was basically an empty shell, devoid of walls, partitions, or any human signs of habitation.

Any "design changes", aka renovation, would have to be done by the tenants at their (our) expense. But it had high ceilings and loads of promise. We hired an architect and wound up with a very cool, contemporary, and highly unorthodox office space. We totally dug it and got ooohs and aaahs from our clients and vendors. We loved the offbeat vibe of Venice and were there to witness its evolution from a seedy, supposedly dangerous, slum-type environment to a hip, trendy destination.

Ultimately, with the onslaught of high-tech companies, it became known as Silicon Beach.

Our agency was small and did not have an industry profile, so when we were looking to add a highly creative Art Director, we took a small, classified ad in *Adweek*, the premier trade publication for the advertising industry. The headline: "We're The Closest Thing to Chiat Day," a premier creative agency and a neighbor. Surprised we didn't hear from them.

One day, we were at a planning meeting when, off in the distance, I could hear my phone ring. To me, the phone is like a religion, and a call could be from a savior. This one wasn't. It was from Herbie Nanas, a good guy I really liked who Stan hooked up with after he and Tony had a friendly split. Herbie is an inveterate native of the Bronx, who was then managing Albert Brooks.

The night before, they had been at The Tonight Show, hosted at the time by Johnny Carson, where one of their acts was appearing. Also on the show that night was an unknown comedienne. It was highly unusual for any total unknown, without even a manager or an agent, to get a gig like that, but she was highly recommended to Johnny by Mitzi Shore, then the owner of a popular club in Hollywood, the Comedy Store. Johnny trusted her judgement, so he gave the nobody a shot. She was a smash! Herbie and Stan signed her on the spot.

That prompted Herbie's call to me. In his native Bronx tongue, he asks me, "Hey sweetheart, you wanna be in the PR business?"

"Huh?" I replied.

"Listen, we signed this broad last night and she's sensational. She's gonna be a huge star, but she's got no publicist and she's got no bread, but if you wanna get inta this biz, here's your shot."

"What's her name?"

"Roseanne Barr."

Meant nothing to me, but what the hell, why not? Something new and different. Connie Baer, in addition to her other duties, now became our in-house publicist. The only problem was that none of us knew a damn thing about the PR business, nor did we have any connections with the press. But we were fast learners.

Roseanne's shtick was that she was the Domestic Goddess, and she was hilarious. She pretends to be worthless in the kitchen and men tend to be useless everywhere, regarding women as domestic help. In the act, she kids about the fact that men can't seem to find anything themselves and always have to ask the woman, and she says, "Men think the uterus is a tracking device."

Herbie and Stan began to get Roseanne some bookings and then scored big. She would be the opener for Julio Iglesias' entire summer tour. Julio was a monster act at the time and, with his stunning Latin looks, a real favorite of the women. We took an ad in the trades with the headline:

Roseanne Barr Has What Every Woman Wants
50 Hot Summer Dates with Julio

For the Caesars Palace engagement in Las Vegas, Julio didn't need any press and gave us the green light to do whatever we wanted for Roseanne. What we wanted was to plant her Domestic Goddess shtick in the media, so we talked Caesar's into letting us have our press conference in the kitchen instead of one of the regular press rooms. Then we sent invitations out to the press on spatulas with the note, "You're going to flip for Roseanne Barr." Everyone who attended the press conference received a copy of the *Official Roseanne Barr Cookbook*, a three-hundred-page book with a lovely yellow plaid jacket and not a single word written in it.

In developing our music business across both artists and labels, the artist managers were a critical link. Ken Kragen was one of the more powerful. He represented Lionel Richie and Kenny Rogers, both major powers at the time, and a host of other important names. Ken was also the author of the book, *Life is a Contact Sport*. That title says it all. We felt it would be smart, and hopefully profitable, to develop a relationship with Ken. His office was on the Sunset Strip in West Hollywood, directly across the street from Le Dome, a restaurant very popular with music industry execs. Ken, we heard, had an appreciation for creative ideas, so we made a deal with one of the Le Dome waiters to go over to his office, formally attired in waiters' official mufti with a white towel over one arm and a small silver tray in his hand with a glass of wine on it and a card that read: THE GARY GROUP...WE DELIVER. It worked and Ken became a valued client.

I remember being in Ken's office one day when he was on the phone, obviously talking about one of his artists who had burst on the scene with two powerful albums and then a third that was kind of a stiff. I heard him explain the possible reason for that situation. "Well, you know it's hard to write hit songs in the back seat of a limousine." That's what happens to too many artists that start strong and are distracted by the fame.

To prove the power of Ken Kragen's book, *Life is a Contact Sport,* a chance encounter led to something spectacular for Elsa, me, and The Gary Group. We were in Palm Springs to see an aspiring young singer and client perform. At breakfast the next morning, who do we run into but my Nashville friend, Frances Preston. Frances had just been appointed CEO of BMI Worldwide and had moved to New York.

Frances knew we were involved in music marketing but not specifically how. So, during our conversation about her new gig, she said, "What I really need is a new advertising agency. I wish you guys did that." I drove an eighteen-wheeler through that opening. We talked briefly and she asked me to come to New York and meet with some of her executives. If I could sell them, we were in. I almost left her sitting there to race to the airport for the next flight out. BMI was a prime account for anyone in the music business. If we got it, it firmly embedded us as legitimate industry player at a high level, and meant that our work would be seen by all facets of music...labels, publishers, agents, managers, promoters, etc. It was exciting from many aspects, not just money. Mostly, it was the challenge and the opportunity to image an important company in the industry from which we were generating most of our business.

I went to New York and met with BMI executives. It worked! They liked what they heard, and we were hired. We were ecstatic. Frances was now a friend and a client and, we were highly appreciative of the opportunity. It had to work for a couple of reasons. First and foremost, she had put her trust in us. Second, if it didn't work, we would be displaying our ineptitude to the entire industry.

When Frances took over, BMI was a distant second to its major competitor, ASCAP, and her goal was to close that gap. She immediately hired Robbin Ahrold, a very bright, talented, collaborative, and knowledgeable executive from RCA, as VP/Communications, a task that encompassed advertising and publicity. He would be our day-to-day boss at BMI.

BMI's main tasks include signing songwriters and publishers and negotiating agreements with radio and anyone who uses music for commercial purposes; collecting money from the users, and dividing it between songwriters and publishers according to the amount each earned based on airplay. It is a billion-dollar-plus business. Fortunately, Elsa talked me out of my first idea. I thought that for our first ad directed at the songwriters, we might say, "You do the *re mi fa so la ti* and BMI will handle the *dough.*"

Over the years, we were able to provide BMI with some strong and effective imaging in campaigns for songwriters and publishers as well as the retail licensing group. Two examples of our out-of-the-box thinking stand out most in my mind.

To attract and add awareness for young, new, and foreign writers to its roster, BMI wanted to give them exposure via ads on college radio where playlists are looser and new artists are more welcome. We suggested that, instead of ads they create a syndicated weekly radio program featuring the music of these artists and writers, containing some relevant facts about BMI, and send it to all college stations free of charge. Thus, *Planet Stereo* was created, which turned out to be far more effective and less expensive than commercials because the music became part of the stations' editorial environment and, thus, more credible than paid advertising.

Another idea of ours created amazing, instantaneous results. BMI was engaged in a campaign to recruit new songwriters through its six domestic offices. At the time, the internet was in its infancy. Nevertheless, I asked Robbin, "What if you could have an office in every town and city in the country that was open twenty-four seven?" He looked at me like I had just ingested a jar of stupidity. "You can! Here's how." And I introduced the idea of a non-branded website whose content genuinely informed, educated, and helped young songwriters...and, of course, directed them to a link to BMI to sign up. We called it SONGWRITER 101. Robbin jumped aboard immediately, and in its first year, they got more new songwriters from that than ALL the six offices combined. For someone as ignorant of and disinterested in technology, it was a miracle I came up with that one.

BMI was far more than a client; they were a partner.

Frances had been a founder and was a lifetime member of the Board of Directors of the Country Music Association (CMA). One day, my phone rang, and it was a CMA executive, informing me that they wanted permission to place my name on the ballot to become a CMA Board member. That was the top of the mountain in country music. I was flattered, but also greatly surprised. Of course, I didn't win...but I got another call soon after, telling me I had been appointed to the Board. "How the hell did that happen?" I asked her.

"Let's just say you have friends in very high places." Frances again. I wondered if she could declare me a dependent on her tax return.

The CMA had their Board meetings in exotic locales. My first was in Vancouver. At the time, whenever I went out of town, I always brought back a stuffed animal for Amanda. She had quite a collection. In Vancouver, in honor of its Canadian heritage, I selected a Mountie, i.e., a Royal Canadian Mounted Police Officer that looked a lot like a bear. It was a big mother, and I was carrying it back on the plane. Fortunately, it was not a crowded flight. I put the bear on the seat beside me. It was very popular with the passengers as they boarded, but not so much with the flight attendant who said she'd have to check it. The whole plane booed her.

Next was London. At that time, although I had spent a lot of time with Frances, Elsa hardly knew her because I was Mister Schlep 'N Fetchit, the wandering frequent flyer, and she was charged with staying behind and running the show...and the home. I would describe our individual roles as, "Elsa's the brain; I'm the mouth," although she was also highly effective in my area. During our down time at the London meeting, Frances, Stan, Richard Sterban, who is the Oak Ridge Boys baritone, and I went shopping. I wanted to get something for Elsa and Amanda. I got Amanda a game from Harrod's, *My First Computer*. Elsa wound up with a pair of crotchless panties, gloves with no fingers, and a sweater with three sleeves. I gave her the stuff and she said, "Who the hell is this Frances Preston you hang out with?" She, of course, was kidding, but got a kick out of it, and she even wore the sweater.

I learned a lesson in humanity at another CMA Board meeting. After dinner, a few of us were walking back to the hotel, one being Norm Epstein, then the General Manager of KZLA, LA's country station and a Gary Group client. On our walk, we encountered a panhandler, a local homeless down-and-outer, about sixty. You could see from looking at the cardboard boxes around him that the street corner was also his home. He obviously had not showered in a long time; his hair was scraggly; his clothes were dirty and torn; and he was asking for money for food. A couple of the guys were way too slick to fall for that old trick, but a couple of others and I gave him a couple of bucks. Norm gave him a twenty. Trust me, he wasn't trying to impress us; he had a heart and felt compassion for this poor man. It genuinely moved me. That was one lesson I learned and still practice.

During Frances' tenure, BMI did rise to virtually equal ASCAP in size, revenue, and stature. Frances was truly an MVP in the sport of contact, but to Elsa and me, she was much more than a client. She became one of our best friends, and it had nothing to do with money.

The Road Back...With Detours

In addition to her gig at BMI, Frances also found time to reign as President of the T.J. Martell Foundation, a charity founded by Tony Martell, then a CBS Records exec whose son T.J. contracted leukemia at seventeen and, before he passed at nineteen, asked his dad to raise a million dollars for research so others after him might have a better shot at life. It became the unofficial charity of the music industry and has raised almost $300,000,000 for research into treatments and cures for cancer, leukemia, and AIDS, much of it through events.

One afternoon at the office, my phone rang, and it was Frances. She informed me, "Dick, you and Elsa are going to be invited to join the National Board of the T.J. Martell Foundation. Is that something you'd be interested in?" Well, as she was arguably one of the most powerful people in the music industry, nobody in their right mind, not even me whose mind is not always right, would say "No" to Frances, and certainly not someone who had been the beneficiary of as much of her amazing kindness as we had.

I didn't really know what it meant but being slightly wary of the commitment, I kiddingly responded, "Thank you very much, Frances. We are truly honored and, of course, we accept. And you'll want to be very careful when you start your car from now on." I was just kidding but little did I realize that Elsa and I would soon be kissing a part of our lives goodbye for that worthy cause. Also, this Villanova castoff was perhaps starting to make them wish I was a graduate, because they can't ask someone they kicked out for any money.

Martell had offices in New York and Nashville at that time, and a decision was made to open a Los Angeles office. Elsa and I were then asked to Co-Chair the West Coast Board of Directors. We were now committed to raise some money, not just sit at meetings looking alert. How do we do it?

The logical move was to have a dinner gala. We thought that was too traditional and too boring, especially for the West Coast. We wanted to have an event that people might WANT to go to. We also felt that while the music industry is populated by creative people, they generally are a lousy audience for music with kind of a "been there, done that, and got the T-shirt" mentality, unless it's their artist, in which case they pay rapt attention, or at least appear to. So, that was out, but we wanted to do something unique that would be appealing and motivate the industry to participate, something creative.

We finally settled on an art show, but not in the traditional sense. It was perhaps a strange choice for us because, while we like and buy art, we know nothing about it. We just buy what we like regardless of its pedigree...or perhaps don't buy it because of its price. One time we were having a conversation with some folks and the subject turned to art. Someone asked, "Are you collectors?" To which another person who knew us well replied, "No. They're gatherers." The reality is, we don't want to know enough to become critics because then we'd have to find fault with everything, and that takes the fun out of it.

We wanted the show to be different. I'd say "off the wall' but that's a weird description for an art show, so we settled on offbeat and eclectic. We named it *Artworks For The Cure*.

We had no idea what we were getting into...the total domination of our lives for the next four years. I guess the easy way is not our way.

The revenue for this type of charity event comes from a few areas. The biggest source is people with industry gravitas who are selected to be "honored" at an event. They provide a list of potential donors, not so much relatives and friends, but rather people who owe the honorees something or want something from them. So much for philanthropy.

The next largest revenue generator in many cases are the live and silent auctions. If the right people are in the room and the auctioneer is good, the live auction can be a phenomenal source of revenue. One of the things we learned is the persuasive power of alcohol on live bidding.

Naturally, at an art show, the sale of the art itself adds measurably to the success of the event. You must have the right art for the crowd and price it accordingly. Elsa and I wanted to have a kickass show with brilliant and original art.

The Road Back...With Detours

I must give credit here to all the artists, who were fantastic, generous, cooperative, and supportive. We did not spend one cent on art; it was all donated. We had never worked with a greater group of people than we did on the shows. In fact, many also participated in a program we initiated where, about once a week, an artist would visit Children's Hospital Los Angeles, a major recipient of T.J. Martell research grants, and spend an afternoon working with the kids, all of whom were pediatric cancer patients. They couldn't go out and play, but they could paint, and through this program, the artists provided some relief for them.

We wound up doing three shows. The first two were successful and raised about a half million collectively. The third one was a sensation and brought in over a million bucks.

We found a super venue, the Barker Hangar at the Santa Monica Airport, a thirty-five-thousand-square-foot, EMPTY space. Hard to call it intimate. How do we fill this gargantuan cavern? Elsa and I spent the next eighteen months addressing that question.

In the end, we had 152 painters, photographers, and sculptors represented. Visual artists from the music world included Graham Nash, John Mellencamp, Dave Matthews, Janis Joplin, Leonard Cohen, Yoko Ono, and Julian Lennon. Street artists/photographers participating included Shepard Fairey, RISK, Mister Cartoon, Hank O'Neal, Chor Boogie, Justin Bua, and a host of other incredibly talented and innovative artists.

So, how to make the show an event? We called on the creative talents of our former agency Creative Director, Tom Nikol. The show Tom put together was "awesome," the word most heard at the event.

We got lucky when Amanda's first Au Pair, Jenny Vogt, a Berliner with whom we had remained friendly over the years, stayed with us on a visit to the States and gave us, as a gift, a coffee table book of graffiti art from the Berlin Wall. Turns out her father, Herman Waldenburg, took all the shots and made them all available to us in whatever quantities we wanted at no cost. But how do you display it all?

Using art walls, Tom recreated the Berlin Wall by creating a long art wall, twelve feet high, with a guard tower at the end and curled barbed wire over the top. On the west side, we hung photos of the graffiti art that had been on that side of the wall and did the same on the east side. From the quality of the images, you'd think the Berlin wall must have been an art gallery.

We also had a lot of paintings and photographs featuring New York City, and Tom created a New York subway station. Dylan, by then a Brooklyn resident, took shots of an actual station and subway cars and sent them to Tom who edited them and had them printed on vinyl. On one side of the "station" was a subway car, rendered in vinyl that was forty-two feet wide and twelve feet high. RISK, an internationally-known Southern California graffiti artist who had illegally painted subway cars early in his career, graciously came in and tagged it, and at the show, we had markers for our guests to do the same.

Mister Cartoon, a highly regarded street and tattoo artist provided us with a display of amazing classic low rider Chevrolets that he had totally customized. They were immaculate, spectacular, and strictly for viewing, not touching.

You're getting the idea. It wasn't a traditional art show, and it was enhanced by our cadre of Honorees, an all-star cast that collectively raised almost $700,000 themselves. There was a dinner for six hundred, including music impresario Clive Davis. Colbie Caillat entertained pro bono. All in all, the show exceeded Elsa and my fantasy goal of $1,000,000. It was by far the most successful T.J. Martell West Coast event ever. *Artworks For The Cure* raised more than $1,500,000 during the years with the Foundation.

TWENTY-TWO
It Pays To Ski

Back in the office, a precipitous phone call came from Larissa LaGasse, Paul's wife, with a fabulous lead, the Mountain High Ski Area in Wrightwood, California, about seventy-five miles from LA. Holy shit! A ski area as a client? What could be better, at least for me who had a ski for a brain? I'd already had a racetrack and now, even though I wouldn't be running it, a ski area too?!

Terry Tognazzini, an entrepreneurial type, was the new owner. Elsa and I drove down to Wrightwood to meet with him, and it turned out to be a good trip; we got the business.

Terry was tough. But he was smart, and he listened and usually went along with our proposals since, although a highly successful man himself, marketing was not his strength, and he knew it. Neither was public relations. Mountain High was strictly a day trip ski area for Southern Californians. There were virtually no beds in the town of Wrightwood, which made it tough to compete because its neighbor and major competitor, Snow Summit, had thousands of beds and was a larger area with better facilities. To his credit though, Terry put his money where It counted most, into lifts and snowmaking. There were seasons where Southern California ski areas didn't get enough natural snow to warrant buying a shovel, so the importance of snowmaking couldn't be overestimated.

Terry soon bought the adjacent ski area, Holiday Hill, well named because it certainly wasn't a mountain. At the time he bought it, Mountain High languished in terms of market share, drawing something just a touch higher than a hash mark (too small to measure) in the ratings.

For us, it was the ideal client...we thought. I loved skiing and knew something about the business end of it from my days hosting my ski show back at WBFM, and there were unlimited opportunities for great promotions if you were media savvy. In those days, radio was highly competitive, and some stations would still barter or at least do a cash/ trade deal. Lift tickets, believe it or not, cost sixteen dollars a day. To put it in perspective, as I write this, one ski area in the U.S. charged $300 for a single day lift ticket in 2024.

Elsa and I believed that for Mountain High to get competitive, which it was not at that point, it would have to be innovative. Our audience was basically young guys, seventeen to twenty-four years old, with more balls than skills. Skiing there was like being in a roller derby. Given the demo, rock radio was our preferred medium, and we had good connections there from our work in music and film, so we put together some kickass promotions. At the time, Prince's *Purple Rain* was a #1 song on the radio, so we did a Purple Snow promotion and dyed the snow on one run purple.

Def Leppard had a smash hit with *Rock 'Til You Drop,* so we created *Ski 'Til You Drop*, a twenty-four-hour marathon promotion that started at midnight on Friday and ended at midnight on Saturday. We had DJs competing in three-legged races. It was the only place in the world where you could ski at three in the morning, and at that hour, we had over two thousand skiers on the mountain.

Of course, that didn't mean Terry was happy. He seemed to be one of those guys who couldn't share success but was highly adept at inducing fear. Occasionally, he'd call us at home at night and say things like, "You guys are killing me." We assumed he meant that he was getting a double hernia carrying his money to the bank. The next season, we were able to bring him two groundbreaking promotions that lasted far longer than we did. We got Ralphs, the largest supermarket chain in Southern California, to do a promotion whereby, if you bought seventy-five dollars in groceries, you got a free one-day pass to Mountain High. They promoted it heavily on television and it was a smash.

Also, that year, our sales rep at KMET, the rocker, had moved over to KBIG, a "beautiful" music station that would have been a better advertising fit for a nursing home than a ski area. We told him, "The only way you'll ever get a dime from us for this client is to bring us a promotion so strong that we don't give a shit if you even run the spots." And he did. He shows up with the Southern California Chevrolet Dealers Association. The deal was simple. For everyone who takes a test drive and mentions the promotion, that person gets a free day pass to the ski area; for every sale, the buyer gets a season pass. And, wow, did they promote it with advertising we never could have afforded!

Business was booming for Mountain High. They rose from nowhere to number two in skier days in the market, a miracle given the fact there were no accommodations in the town.

None of this success seemed to affect Terry's bargaining position. Each year, prior to the season, we'd meet with him to painfully hack out our deal. When he was on a mission, he could not be distracted from it by personal insults or anything else. He knew what he wanted and went for it, and you couldn't argue with his success. Of course, given our track record of success for him, we naively thought we had considerable leverage; although, he would never acknowledge it. It was very frustrating for us because we gave it all we had; it worked amazingly well, and it was never really acknowledged.

At one of our pre-season soirees, I'd had enough, and I told him there was no personal or professional satisfaction working for him. The only reason to do it was for money. It didn't faze him. You could not insult the man. You also couldn't argue with his success. Finally, we both gave ground and made a deal.

However, there was an unexpected bonus in working for Terry, a big one. Radio stations would run first quarter promotions to beef up their revenue, as that was traditionally the slowest time of the year. The promotions were geared for business owners, the decision makers, and not their agencies.

JUST ANOTHER DICK

Advertisers that spent a certain amount in the first quarter qualified for an exotic station-run trip to some fantastic destinations. Mountain High always qualified because we spent ALL our money in the first quarter. But Terry's wife preferred not to fly coach on very long excursions, so he gave the trips to us. I must give him credit for that. It may have been his way to say thank you without having to admit there was anything to thank us for. Via this perk, Elsa and I made our first foray to Hawaii; went to Tahiti and Cancun; and even got to bring Amanda to Borneo where we kayaked in the South China Sea, rode rafts down a delta, saw monkeys swinging from trees, and visited an orangutan preserve.

Ultimately, Terry sold the area to a New England ski conglomerate that did everything in-house, and we became history. But for years, we still saw the Ralphs and Chevrolet promotions on the air. It would be an understatement to say that pissed us off, but we did take pride in a job well done. This was inadvertently told to me years later when I was introduced to the General Manager of Snow Summit, our biggest competitor by the then owner of the Park City Mountain Resort, who identified Elsa and myself as having promoted Mountain High. Our former foe said, rather disparagingly, "Mountain High was the most over-marketed ski area in the country."

"Thank you," I replied.

TWENTY-THREE
Park City, Utah

Given our successful experience with Mountain High, we jumped when we saw a story in ADWEEK, one of the advertising industry's weekly trade journals, about a new ski area planned for Provo, Utah. I had an incredible time on my maiden trip to Alta, and I knew from the Warren Miller films that Utah was the mecca of skiing in the U.S., so I arranged a meeting to pitch them on our services. We flew up and gave them our spiel. We had a strong story of success in their industry, and they seemed impressed. We were confident we'd add them to our roster when they got the place built. I had cleverly scheduled the meeting for a Friday and, if we were going to be in Utah, we decided to spend the weekend skiing at Park City, an unexplored mountain for us but one that I had heard good things about. It turned out that the ski area we pitched was never built, but that weekend started another major change in our lives. We loved Park City...the mountain, the town, the vibe, all of it, and it replaced Mammoth on our ski itinerary.

We began to spend Christmas vacations there and at the new area up the street, Deer Valley, where we had first skied compliments of Bill Cooper, prior to his pulling up stakes and relocating to an Orange County jail.

We always made a big deal of Christmas, not from a religious standpoint but as a fun family event. Elsa and I would totally overdo it. Since we had little time and less inclination to shop throughout the year, we let it all hang out at Christmas, and we didn't want it to be any different just because we'd be away. We had to rent two cars to get all the stuff there.

One year, the place we rented was a bona fide dump with ripped window shades and bare bulbs hanging from the ceiling by a cord. This was 1987, pre-computer and pre-Airbnb or VRBO, where you now get to see actual photos of what you're getting. But the owner of this place could have had a brilliant future as a copywriter. It looked more like a hideout than a ski rental. I kept waiting for John Gotti to show up and shoot us. Anyway, one day Elsa didn't feel like skiing and certainly wasn't going to hang around that joint, so she wandered into a real estate office and began researching inexpensive condos. I was ecstatic when she told me how she'd spent her day, and we looked at several places the next day with a young, smart, and honest agent, Rob Karz. That was the beginning.

We went back for a long weekend that summer on a serious hunting expedition. Rob had shown us a unit we really loved, a three-bedroom, 1,655-square-foot condo with a great room with high ceilings and fireplace, a deck out back with a built-in spa, and a terrific location that was an easy walk to town. $133,000. We couldn't afford it, but Rob said to be patient. There was a real estate depression at the time due to overbuilding in Park City and lots of new construction in Deer Valley.

The unit we liked was owned by a Phoenix bank, and they were running out of patience with the state of the market and not impressed by the phenomenon of snow. Rob did a little negotiating, or a lot, on our behalf, and a few days later, he said the new price was $87,000. SOLD! I remember Elsa and I buying a lot of stuff for it, loading it into our SUV, and Dylan and I driving up to our new ski condo in Park City. It was also a very special day because he and I got to spend it together, just the two of us, a rare experience.

We used the condo whenever we could and tried to rent it out the rest of the time. We'd run small, classified ads in SKI and SKIING with our phone number in them. The one thing we quickly learned was, if we were busy when the call came in, the "I'll call you back" line didn't work. The caller would rent the first place where someone talked to him or her.

After we figured that out, we took the calls and wound up with a positive cash flow. We were making money on a self-indulgence.

We began to come up to Park City for Thanksgiving week. We'd take Amanda out of school for a couple of extra days on the premise that it gave the other kids a chance to catch up to her. Then from pre-Christmas to post New Year's and at spring break, we'd go up to flaunt our incompetence on the slopes.

Elsa and I were a good balance on the mountain. She was conservative and I was insane. Dylan got my gene, although he wasn't with us as much as I would have liked. When he was, he was something to watch. Without a lot of lessons, his style and Stein Erikson's may have been different, but we'd be on a black run, and he'd take off and ski it until he fell. Then he'd get up and take off again for an encore performance. We put Amanda in ski school, and it wasn't long before one of the instructors told us she could ski anything we could...and it wasn't long before she could do that better than we could.

There were only two units in our complex, complex being a big word for only two units, and during our first year of occupancy, the bank had rented the other one to a very social and very single group of guys, not ideal neighbors unless you were hard of hearing. The bank came to us after the ski season and said, "We're from Phoenix. Get us out of here."

We said, "Give us inspiration," and we got the second unit for $80,000 and made money renting that one too.

During our winter hegiras, we frequently needed ski equipment, especially Amanda who grew out of clothes and equipment on an almost annual basis. As a result, we became very friendly with "Goose," one of the sales guys at Jan's Mountain Outfitters.

After a few years and several dinners, we started talking about going into a business together. Goose had dreamed of having an adventure company that provided unique and fun experiences for Park City visitors, things like dogsledding, snowmobiling, and snowshoeing in the winter; white water rafting, kayaking, mountain biking, and stuff like that in the summer. Elsa and I got pretty stoked about the prospect, probably more me, as I subconsciously felt it added to my desire to be an adventurous spirit.

Thus, All Seasons Adventures was born. Goose would run it, and Elsa and I would provide the financing. We bought tons of equipment, including a fifteen-passenger van, reputed to be top heavy and the most unsafe vehicle on the road, but one we needed to transport customers and equipment. All Seasons also provided Amanda and a friend with a summer's employment.

Goose always provided a quality experience for our customers. Elsa and I personally enjoyed rafting on the Weber River, kayaking at the Jordanelle Reservoir, and all the other activities. But the day after Labor Day and as soon as the ski lifts closed, All Seasons Adventures could sleep it off for a couple of months until the next tourist season began.

After a couple of years, we were still losing money and the thrill of having an adventure company was wearing off. Elsa and I were also worried about liability. For example, when an inexperienced college kid was driving that unsafe fifteen-passenger van, towing a trailer full of, kayaks or rafts, there seemed to be a good chance that if it might wind up upside down, and we would learn the hard way that the signed waivers we had were simply an exercise in penmanship. We thought it was time to end it, but Goose wanted to keep it going, so we arrived at a friendly parting and are still friends.

After years of being winter-only visitors, we had begun coming up in the summer and found yet another super facet of Park City. It is absolutely beautiful in the summer. The air is fragrant; the humidity is low; the sun doesn't go down until around nine o'clock; there is hiking and biking on the trails we fell down all winter; outdoor music; and lots more. We quickly decided that we wanted to spend more time there and work from there part-time, but the condo wouldn't really provide us with the workspace we needed. Our business was good, and we thought the town was a good investment, especially since Park City had been designated as the site for most of the 2002 Winter Olympic Games. So, we began the hunt for a house. The house in our minds kept getting bigger. We each wanted a workspace or office and we wanted to provide space for Dylan and Amanda and any possible future families they might have.

It was amazing how many houses we found that didn't take advantage of a gorgeous mountain view. Then a providential occurrence presented itself. We found a house that had recently been for sale but was taken off the market. It was a five-thousand-square-foot home on three levels with a twenty-foot ceiling and a river rock fireplace that extended up to the ceiling in the great room. There were also magnificent mountain views through floor to ceiling windows in virtually every room, plus an expansive deck in front. The upper floor had a bedroom and bath, a loft-type office, and lots of storage space. The basement was simply a large rec room.

What's not to like? The main floor! It must have been designed by an architect who, at some time, had been seriously wronged by the initial owner and decided to get even. The living room, entry, laundry, and mudroom were OK, but the kitchen and dining room were a joke...that fell flat, but we saw the possibilities.

We got an architect, contractor, and interior designer who were all superb and helped us make it the house of our dreams. We simply gutted the kitchen and dining room and created one large great room that was handsomely appointed in a style appropriate to a mountain home. In fact, if you saw both our Malibu and Park City houses, you would not believe the same people had lived in both. The realtor also pointed out that the basement had not been fully built out to the footprint of the entire house. We had paid about $200 per square-foot for the house and found we could build out the basement to the footprint for around seventy dollars per square foot. So, we added another bedroom and bath, a sauna, a media room, and an office/gym; a little over 1,300 additional square feet, so we now had a 6,300-square-foot second home for the two of us.

However, during escrow, we kind of decided we didn't want our offices in our home. To alleviate this situation, we eventually rented an office in town, but never went there because we'd start working at home and it made no sense to stop just to drive to an office to start again. Thus, we had a very expensive parking space on Main Street. As far as the "kids" went, Dylan is a confirmed city guy and only comes to Park City under subpoena. Amanda lives in Argentina and that's a tough commute for a weekend. Plus, they are both still single. But Elsa and I love the house and are very happy with all our decisions.

A few months later, in February, the 2002 Salt Lake City Winter Olympics opened, and they were spectacular! Most of the ski events took place in Park City. A spirit pervaded the entire town, one that I never experienced before or since. Main Street was closed to traffic and there were all kinds of interesting, unique displays in stores rented by large companies, especially for the event. The hot clothing article was a Roots beret. It cost twenty dollars and there was a long line outside their store every day to buy them. There were even scalpers selling them for around $150 to those way too busy or important to wait in line.

The whole town was turned around for this once-in-a-lifetime event. We filled the house with friends in two shifts and got tickets to nine events. The feeling of camaraderie everywhere was unforgettable. Amanda got a job as a "slipper," smoothing the runs between racers. They gave her the halfpipe, both a sign of her ability and a supreme challenge. It was also an opportunity for Elsa and me to brush up on our cooking and entertainment skills. If we had ever thought about running a B&B, we got over it during the Olympics, but we had a spectacular time.

Around that time, we also became interested in Sundance. Why not? It's in Park City, so we had the big expense, lodging, already covered. The film festival runs every year for ten days in the last half of January, and it provided us another opportunity to fill the house with friends and clients and to indulge our growing interest in independent cinema.

It turned out that it was harder to get tickets for Sundance than it was for the Olympics. At that time, it was a three-step process. First, sometime in September you register to buy tickets during a prescribed time. You can't just buy them; you must register to do it. The next step, in mid-October, you are given a half hour on a specific day to purchase the package(s) you want...if you got a decent time and they're still available. If your designated time is not near the front of the week, you're not going to have a great package selection. To get a better time, Elsa and I began to register multiple non-existent names. One year, I was George Greenberg and she was Florence Wambaugh. The third and final step comes in early January after the schedule is announced. You are then then given another half hour to make your film selections...if they are still available. And, if they're not, you must decide on the spot what your alternatives are...and it ain't cheap. One year, we paid $500 for a parking space.

We typically saw twenty to twenty-five films during the festival. Prices seemed to increase every year as demand increased. In 2020, we estimate it cost us each about one hundred dollars a ticket. You really don't want to miss one of your films at that rate.

But with the cost comes the bragging rights. Months later, when one of the films is released, you can always say, "Oh that one? We saw it at Sundance. You might enjoy it."

During the ensuing years, Elsa and I also got more involved in Park City and its activities. The realtor who sold us our house was then President of the Park City Ski Team, a prestigious local organization that feeds qualified candidates to the U.S. Ski Team. He invited us to join the Board of Directors. It certainly wasn't for our skiing ability. Had that been the criteria, we would have probably been cleaning the latrines for them. No, our joining the Board was more about our potential to help them raise money via our entertainment connections. And we did...with a lot of help from our friends, especially one in particular, Robert Earl Keen.

Robert, a Texas singer/songwriter in the Americana vein, has a terrific cult-type following. His songs range from quirky to fun to touching. He is absolutely one of my favorite songwriters and also a consummate entertainer. Robert agreed to do a benefit for the ski team. That was immensely generous as, in the end, it cost him money.

We made a deal with the biggest club in town at that time, Harry O's. It could hold nine hundred people if the Fire Marshall was on vacation.

We got the door receipts and Harry O's got the bar. Robert did it for a few years and it was one of the Park City Ski Team's biggest fundraisers, not to mention the most fun.

Robert's opening act was the Mother Lode Band, headed up by Dana Williams, then the Mayor of Park City. We got to know and like Dana. He was raised in an exclusive Los Angeles suburb. His father had a successful company that insured music tours and films, so, following not too closely in his footsteps, Dana naturally studied agriculture in college. He became a farmer and then, somehow, morphed into real estate. When we met him, after the financial world collapse had killed the market for second homes, he was a barista at the coffee shop adjacent to the local art center. He did an amazing job of guiding a fast-growing small town—but one with high visibility—through a period of substantial growth. Regarding his career as mayor and the attendant compensation, he once remarked, "I feel like I took the Buddhist oath of poverty."

While shopping for art for the new house, we met Karen Terzian, the sister of Kristi Terzian Cumming, a former member of the U.S. Women's Ski Team and wife of the then owner of the Park City ski area, John Cumming. Karen was on the Board of the Park City Performing Arts Foundation, a group that booked and promoted music shows with name artists throughout the year. When she learned of our entertainment background, she introduced us to Teri Orr, the Executive Director of the foundation, and, after several conversations we were on the Board.

Back then, in the summer, the Deer Valley Ski Area put up a band shell and various entities like the Utah Symphony, local concert promoters, and the Performing Arts Foundation (now the Park City Institute) all ran concerts there. It is a magnificent venue. It is still light when the concerts start with the mountains serving as a backdrop. Then, it morphs into dusk and nature's sunset. Finally, it gets dark, and the stage provides beautiful lighting. A spectacular place to see a show. It has a five-thousand-person capacity, both in seats and on the lawn. That experience made us feel closer to the town. We felt we made a genuine contribution and met some very nice people in the process.

Park City, Utah

There's a lot more than skiing to Park City. In addition to all the winter and summer outdoor activities, it could also be called Dark City...in a positive way, because when the sun goes down, there's still tons to do. There are ten movie screens in town, plus a film series that shows an indie film each week, a legitimate theatre for stage productions, and tons of music all over town, as well as excellent and diversified restaurants.

One night, we saw *West Side Story* at the beautiful art deco Egyptian Theaters. It was funny for a New Yorker seeing an Ogden, Utah acting company present a version of this edgy, rough, very New York play. Tony, the hero of the play and a gang leader, looked like the Pillsbury Doughboy. His gang, the Jets, supposedly a group of tough New York street kids, looked like they had their meetings at the local library. But I love the music and they did a great job; it worked for me.

Given our bleeding hearts, we also became peripherally involved with two charities at opposite ends of the spectrum: Adopt A Native Elder, which gives support to elderly Navajo Indians, and Futures for Children, which worked in educating Native American kids who live on reservations and pueblos in New Mexico and Arizona. We have had an "adopted" grandmother for over thirty years. I wonder sometimes if we got her right out of high school, but we're glad she's still with us. In the Futures program, we mentored a young girl who grew up, married, and had a son whom we mentored once he reached school age.

When he graduated from high school, he earned a college scholarship. We are proud to have been even an indirect part of his life, and he has success written all over him in both English and Navajo.

TWENTY-FOUR
Business As Unusual

Since our business was doing well and we had long ago rolled all four of our initial mortgages on the house in Corral Canyon into one, we decided to lose the canyon and find a better place, closer to civilization. We sold our $210,000 investment for $489,000 and had the money for a down payment on a better place.

After surviving the Malibu sticker shock, we found and fell in love with a house in Malibu Country Estates, adjacent to the Pepperdine University campus on the landside of PCH. The house was over four thousand square feet with three bedrooms, an office, plus an additional attached room and bath we could use for Amanda's au pair...and a pool, plus an ocean view. We opened escrow at $1,020,000.

One day, while still in escrow, Elsa told me there was a new art gallery in Malibu and she loved their stuff, especially some mobiles by Andre Miripolsky, an LA artist who was being heavily promoted in Japan. She said I should check it out. The next day, Amanda, who was then nine, and I visited the gallery and Elsa's observation was spot on. There was one piece in particular that blew me away.

Elsa and I both have quirky, offbeat tastes in art and, fortunately, we agree on almost everything. She was next door getting her nails done, and I went over and asked her to come to the gallery when she was done. She did, and we both focused on the same piece, a seven-foot mobile that we decided should grace the entryway to our new home.

Barry, the gallery owner, was so low key I was going to call an EMT to revive him. "Are you sure it will fit? It hangs too low in most rooms." I thought maybe he hated the artist. Then he said, "Tell you what. Have the realtor let us in tomorrow. I'll bring it up and we'll see if it works." That made sense and we did. It turns out that he was right. It did hang down too far from the ceiling, but we didn't care. We wanted it. It was going to be the focal point of our new home. People could just walk around it. Barry said he would get the artist to touch it up and then come to the house to hang it in two weeks, after escrow had closed.

Two weeks later, the house was ours, or at least twenty percent of it, and Andre came to hang the mobile. Barry also came. Elsa and I were almost as excited by that as we were about the purchase of the house. I was taking pictures of Andre hanging it, so we'd have that memory, and, at one point, he said, "I'm so happy I got to meet the people who bought this. I always knew they would be really cool with a great sense of humor." We thought he might be overreaching but we sucked up the compliment.

Barry left before the installation was completed; as soon as he had the check in his hand and, as Andre walked out the door, he turned and asked, "Would you like to know the background of the piece?"

"Of course," we responded.

"Well, it was originally commissioned by a Malibu pornographer..." and he went on to share the man's travails. Meanwhile, Elsa and I were experiencing a powerful foreboding. We're trying to sneak looks at the piece, and we genuinely just wanted Andre to get the hell out so we could view the enormity of our mistake.

When he finally finished the story that we were no longer listening to and left, we spun around to discover that we now had seven feet of dripping penises hanging from our ceiling to welcome guests.

"Get it out of here," Elsa said with utter desperation.

"Let's not let it ruin the day," I lamely responded, thinking mostly about spending the afternoon by our swimming pool.

"The day? What about our lives?" She had a good point, so I called Barry. He began, "You and Andre sure hit it off."

"I think it's going to be a short relationship." And I went on to tell him the story.

Elsa and I, the advertising creative gurus with the sharp eyes for design that we were supposed to have, felt like two blind assholes, but then Barry admitted that he'd had it in the gallery for a few days before he recognized the subject matter, and that was the reason for his initial reticence. It actually was a bit abstract. He agreed we could return it, and he'd give us a credit on any other Andre piece.

So now we had our million-dollar dream house. No novel, short story, or news brief is complete without mention of the Kardashians. It turned out the house across the street from us was, at that time, a rental, and a few years after we moved in, who became our new neighbors? With my big hint, you got it. At that time, Bruce (now Kaitlyn) Jenner was married to Kris Kardashian. They moved in with her daughters Kim, Kourtney, and Khloe. The girls were very young at the time and Elsa told me that one day they came over, rang the bell, and introduced themselves. She said they were very nice and polite. From all you read, they may have outgrown that.

On another day, I saw Bruce in the driveway working on his mountain bike and, in a gesture of neighborly friendship (or was it star fucking?), I went over to introduce myself. He said, "I guess you're the guy from across the street." I laughingly replied, "I thought you were."

Another fast and offbeat meeting was with Anthony Hopkins. People started telling me I looked like him. The clerk at Blockbuster asked me if she should put the rental on his bill. One day, Elsa and I were at a Santa Monica mall and who do we spot? Anthony Hopkins! I couldn't let it go by without doing something, so I went over to him, explained I wasn't a stalker, and told him a lot of people said he and I looked alike. He looked at me closely and said, "Yes, maybe in the eyes." So, I asked him if a lot of people told him he looked like Dick Gary. His response, "That's how I get all the work."

Yet another Malibu experience, this one very flattering, came our way. The Malibu Times, our local paper, gave out an annual award, the

Dolphin Award, to a local or locals who had distinguished her, him or themselves in some humanitarian way in the previous year. One year, Elsa and I were honored with the Dolphin Award for our T.J. Martell work. The previous year, Dick Van Dyke, who was a friend, had been the honoree. Dick and I, in addition to being Dolphin Award recipients, apparently also shared another fact from the past: we'd both given up the sauce, so I asked Dick, "Do you think we got the Dolphin Awards because we drank like fish?"

While our advertising business was booming, our PR company, never having reached great heights, should have been renamed Muck & Mire. Emilio Estefan, Gloria's husband and manager, figured out he wasn't with Rogers & Cowan and moved on. Roseanne went over to television.

The real truth was that we didn't have any experience or media contacts in that field and didn't really know what we were doing, so our effectiveness could definitely be called into question no matter how hard we tried. Another truth is that some of our other PR clients were so far down on the awareness/importance list that they couldn't get any press coverage unless they killed someone. The highlight of that venture was when we were sued for discriminating against men for job openings. We decided to close that department. I was covertly pleased, thinking maybe we really were ahead of the times.

We had had great experiences with women employees, and never took advantage by paying them less than the men. I thought they wanted to get the job done, while the guys wanted to have lunch with the clients. So, we left the PR world. The end of an era, OR AN ERROR.

With the addition of BMI to our client roster, we had added an in-house creative department, and we were also doing more media buying. We had become a full-service ad agency. As proof of our expansion, we now occupied three rather small spaces in the Main Street Design Center in Venice and were looking for a fourth. We decided the smart move was to consolidate everyone in the same space. I found a small ad in the LA Times for "Creative Space" in Culver City, which then was kind of a dumpy, forgotten section of LA.

"Creative Space" was quickly becoming a nice term for oddball spaces that the owners didn't know what the hell to do with but soon found success renting to "creative" companies that didn't need a formalized office structure or a lot of parking.

In any event, I called the number in the ad and spoke to the owner of the building complex, Frederick Smith, who turned out to be an interesting and visionary guy. Frederick had acquired a bunch of non-conforming buildings, and his personal mandate was to put art in architecture in the properties he owned. We had to qualify creatively before he'd talk about renting us space. We did just that when he learned the nature of our business. He was attracted to entertainment, as that industry best appreciated his vision...or maybe he thought we were all nuts and he found that appealing too. I personally equated creative space to low rent and found that concept highly desirable.

Of course, the space he offered was untenantable (is that a word?) and would have to be gutted and re-built to our specifications, but at his cost. It turned out that Frederick was working with a very cool, contemporary architect, Eric Owen Moss, on all his buildings and they WANTED creative renovations. We said we envisioned something unique like the Hard Rock clubs with the car sticking out of the side, and thus began the saga. The exterior that Eric designed was sensational. It was a one-story building, so he added a fire escape to nowhere. My office was so big I could have raised cattle in it.

The receptionist's desk had a commanding view of the reception area and vice versa. It was essentially a metal desktop with nothing underneath it. We generally had attractive young receptionists and were concerned the desk might also offer a commanding view of their knees and on up, ala Sharon Stone's famed and notorious scene from *Basic Instinct*. But we wound up with a very cool office. It got a lot of coverage in contemporary architecture magazines, and for the first few months we were there, it seemed most of the visitors were Scandinavian architectural students with backpacks and Birkenstocks.

Business As Unusual

Frederick and Eric did change the face of Culver City. It went from a dump to its current reputation of hip and trendy. Channel 5 in LA was doing a story about them, and they interviewed me. They were mostly interested in Eric, but I wanted to get a plug in for Frederick, so I said, "In order for something like this to be outstanding, two things are required...a creative mind and a visionary client...Eric and Frederick." I said it reminded me of the Renaissance when artists had patrons. Without the patron supporting the artist, there would have been no art. Eric was fortunate to have Frederick as his patron and Frederick was lucky to be the beneficiary of Eric's creativity.

Meanwhile, the face of our business had changed. Thanks to the success we originally had with Mary Ann and Roy at Sony Music Nashville, we had long since evolved from just working with artists on their personal appearances to working for major labels in New York, LA, and Nashville on new releases.

In addition, we were hired by Procter & Gamble to work on Folgers Coffee's initial foray into automobile racing, a NASCAR sponsorship where they incorporated a country artist, TG Sheppard, into the promotion. TG was a popular country artist at the time with a lot of "turntable" hits, i.e., songs that charted well but were not strong sellers. They were smart to sign him instead of some major star whose agent they probably couldn't even get on the phone once the check cleared. I couldn't believe that this college flunk-out was hired by one of the most sophisticated marketing companies in the country. Maybe it was Elsa.

It should have been heaven. I loved racing, and we were now combining that with country music and making money in the process. Our job, essentially, was to give Folgers an identity with race fans. Folgers' job was to sell coffee. They rated their success not on race attendance but rather on the size of the order that their sales rep extracted from meetings with the chain buyers in race cities. Kiddingly, they claimed they didn't care if anyone showed up for the race...but it better be sold out.

Soon after came the opportunity to work with Marlboro. They were beginning to sponsor music tours and were looking for a promotion company to support the effort. We were a natural and they approached us. We perhaps should have been ecstatic but, for us, it raised an ethical dilemma. If cigarettes caused cancer, did we want to promote smoking? Could we take the money without the guilt? Was it worth it? We were not in the habit of turning down major national companies, but Elsa and I decided we'd rather be poor than hypocritical and, thus, established a policy that remained in force for the duration of the company. We would not work for any tobacco company.

A couple years later, we were pitching the PBR (Professional Bull Riders) on supporting their events. They were very interested in our ideas. We were going to build enormous awareness for their events through country music concerts in advance of the shows, a natural audience for bull riding. They invited me to the National Finals Rodeo in Las Vegas. There, I met with their marketing executive who gave me the good news (I thought). He said they wanted to move ahead with us, and they were going to use their existing sponsors. That was terrific news for us because lining up sponsors was the toughest part of the deal, and if we didn't get them, we didn't have a deal.

"U.S. Tobacco is going to love this," the exec said enthusiastically. I told him I doubted that very much because they couldn't be a part of it.

"What are you talking about?" he asked in a very perplexed voice.

I said, "We don't work with tobacco companies."

He was astounded and replied, "That's crazy. Why?"

I didn't want to get on my soapbox, so I said, "It's just a decision we made."

Not good enough. He pressed the point. "But why make a decision like that?" he asked incredulously.

Bingo! I'd had enough. "Because when you work for a tobacco company, your success is measured by how many people die before they have to. For them, cancer is a sign of success. All you have to do to understand that is read the labels on their packages."

Business As Unusual

To this day, I don't understand how men or women working for a tobacco company can come home after a day at the office and share their experiences with the family. "How many did you kill today, Dad?"

Meanwhile, along with media buying, we were still doing a lot of label promotions. One of our staffers, Bentley, a young guy, had been a vegetarian for six years. He and I were going to New York, his first trip there, on a Motown promotion, and Bentley, who was Jewish, told me that what he really wanted to do was go to a good Jewish deli and have a pastrami sandwich. I told him that even though I loved the stuff, I thought it was a shame to blow six years of vegetarianism on a greasy pastrami sandwich. He disagreed vehemently. I suggested, "Why don't you start with corned beef and work your way up." Nope, it had to be pastrami. I took him to the Carnegie Deli on Seventh Avenue, famed for its "mile high I dare you to finish this you pig" sandwiches. We were seated and Bentley asked me if it was a really good Jewish deli. I retorted, "For crissakes, Bentley. Look to your left. That's Jackie Mason sitting two tables away."

Parlaying our label experience to other music-related businesses, we landed KZLA, LA's premier (and only) country station as a client. At the time, there was no country station in New York, and as LA was the nation's second largest market, we assumed KZLA was the number one station nationally and began developing a campaign. We called it, KZLA, THE BIGGEST COUNTRY IN AMERICA. It sounded like fun until we found that a Chicago station, despite a much smaller population to draw from, had a bigger audience.

We morphed from KZLA to Y-107, a rock station with an undesirable dial position but a good sound and a strong desire to expose more listeners to it. The budget was small, but the creative freedom was big. We wanted to do something different, and they were up for it. We decided television gave us the strongest, most powerful palette on which to apply our creativity. To give us a new and younger perspective, we brought in a bright young talent by the name of Dylan Gary. You may have read about him here in his earlier days. Dylan had gone to film school, had been in bands, and clearly got the picture.

He came up with a super concept. It involved a guy (Dylan) driving along a desert road trying to find a good radio station to listen to. He kept looking at the radio and switching the dial. He lost track of where he was going and had a head-on collision with another car...that happened to be driven by a very good-looking young woman (Dylan's girlfriend, an actress). The next scene showed the girl's car with the windshield smashed. Dylan, who obviously had flown through it, was in a pile on the front seat, her at the wheel, the radio blasting, and Dylan, groggily hearing the station being played, brightens and asks "Hey, what's that station?" to which, of course, she replied, "Y-107." Our agency won a WEBBY for the spot, the first and only national award we ever received. Thanks, Dylan!

In Nashville at that time, there existed a certain mystique about LA. Subconsciously, a lot of Nashvillians thought there was a higher level of marketing sophistication in LA. I remember one potential client who wanted what, in my estimation, was a fairly simple job, and he asked for a quote. I gave him a fair price based on other similar projects and he replied, "Wow! That's a lot of money. Are you worth it?"

I told him, "You may be asking the wrong guy. We always try our best, but we can't promise results. It works more often than it doesn't, but there are no guarantees. But you can probably get it done cheaper in Nashville."

"Oh no," he countered, "I want the best and I'll pay for it." It's interesting that the less eager you appear for something, the more likely you are going to get it.

One thing that encounter reminded me of is that it's fun to be honest. There's so much bullshit going around that plain, blunt honesty really stands out, and the people who appreciate it usually go for it, and you can build a solid relationship with them. I almost got to thinking that honesty was a ploy, a sales technique. But it's one that I am very comfortable with.

Fortunately for us, the music business was considered different from other product categories in that it was OK for an agency to represent more than one company in a category. Given the amount of work we were doing for numerous labels in New York, LA, and Nashville, The Gary Group came to be considered music's most prominent and dominant agency. But the office wasn't big enough anymore. We had dramatically expanded our roster of music clients and had outgrown the Culver City office. It was time to move again. We liked Santa Monica. In addition to being closer to home, this one-time retirement community was now becoming vibrant headquarters for several entertainment companies. As usual, we eschewed the big traditional office buildings in favor of smaller "creative space" dwellings. We found a six-thousand-square-foot space on Broadway, perfect for us. Another buildout, but with some help from the landlord. In all humility, I must say, with the guidance of an interior designer, we did a commendable job and came up with yet another highly "creative" space that was fun to work in...and admired by clients and vendors.

A significant amount of work was required to make a decent amount of money in the record business. Every album had its own P&L. The wholesale cost of an album was approximately nine dollars, so a gold album (five hundred thousand copies, which only a very small percentage reached) generated about $4,500,000, out of which came a slew of expenses including production, artist, songwriter, and producer royalties, plus sales, advertising, and marketing. The road to riches had a few potholes.

However, we had a policy that, no matter the size of the label or the project, we always busted our asses to do the best job we could. Our service policy did not change with the size of the client or the budget. This was best exemplified in a specific situation.

A fellow I knew and liked, Randy Miller, was hired to run Sire Records, a brand with a proud heritage but not much going for it at the time. Randy's job was to change that.

JUST ANOTHER DICK

He had a small staff and someone, maybe the receptionist, would be delegated to call us wanting, for example, to do cable advertising in fifteen markets for a budget of $15,000 for a hopefully up-and-coming artist. We'd give them a proposal, but then the budget might go up or down, so then we'd give them alternate proposals based on the new budget. Or, sometimes, the whole thing went away and there was no budget. But we always respected and treated Randy like he came in the front door.

A year or two later, he left Sire to head up marketing for Jive Records, a white-hot label whose artist roster then included Britney Spears, 'N Sync, the Backstreet Boys, and others. We were getting calls with budgets of $1,000,000 and more. It became our hottest label. None of that would have happened if not for our philosophy of equality.

One of the dangers in our business was credit, especially with new and independent labels. It's very easy—and stupid—to be so insecure that you wouldn't turn down business or sully a new relationship by asking for cash in advance for any advertising being placed by a new label. The reality is that our media buying revenue was solely based on commission from the media on the business we placed with them, and their credit terms were generally loose, especially if the agency had a track record. But, if we didn't get paid by the client, we still owed the money to the media, and we'd have about as much chance of collecting it as we would powder skiing in Arizona in August. Not getting the money in front is a good way to go out of business quickly. We had been burned a couple of times, learned from it, and instituted some strict cash in advance policies for new independent labels to avoid that in the future.

Then one day, I got a call from Death Row Records. At the time, hip-hop was very hot and, due to its controversial nature, it seemed many of its artists were being used for target practice. Regardless of their status, both wannabes and major artists were being gunned down. I don't know how Suge Knight, Death Row's owner, chose the name, but at the time, he was serving time, I forget for what. I got the call, not from him, but from his label. I doubt he'd use the one call he was allowed on me.

So, there I was with a dilemma. Death Row wanted to get on the air in a hurry and we had a cash-in-advance policy for all new labels. I was nervous to say the least. Given what was going on, I didn't know what would happen if the spots didn't sell. Ultimately, I decided I'd rather be shot than stiffed, so I told the caller about our policy. He said, "So how fast can I get on the air?" I replied, "As soon as the check clears. If speed is of the essence, give us a cashier's check." And that's what they did. We did more work for Death Row, and we never had a problem. One funny thing was that we had to buy spots in a totally irrelevant market because that's where Suge was imprisoned, and he wanted to be able to see his advertising. I don't know how that works in prison, but I doubt he had a television in his cell.

Meanwhile, being very busy and armed with all our successes, we forgot to renew our lease, but very graciously, our landlord reminded us. They gave us a renewal that confused us. I called and said we didn't want to buy the building; we were only renting a small space. They advised me that they were aware of that and did we want the deal or not. We didn't, and I told them that. But we didn't want to move either, as we had a ton of money invested in the improvements and renovation and the space worked well for us. Nevertheless, we reluctantly started looking and they started showing it.

I decided to take one more shot. I had heard that the woman managing the building made Mata Hari look like Helen Keller, but charging ahead, I set up an appointment at their offices and showed up for the meeting. She had her lieutenants with her.

I directed my remarks to her and opened with, "Your company is a good landlord. You maintain the place well. We are an excellent tenant; we respect your property; we have upgraded it; and we always pay our rent promptly. But I hear you are a very difficult person to deal with, and I'm sure a lot of people probably think I'm an asshole. So here we are, both of us about to make bad decisions for our companies."

"Well," she said, recovering nicely from my compliment, "We'd like you to stay." "

"And we want to," I quickly replied. "What kind of a deal can we make?"

She looked a bit surprised and countered, "You have the deal...in writing."

"OK," I replied, "If that's the deal, I have just one more question." With that, I got up and got my parking ticket out and asked, "Do you validate?"

She looked pissed but said, "Sit down. Let's make a deal." And we did, for less than she wanted and more than we wanted to pay. I wonder what would happen if Congress ever tried this.

In the early days when I'd be on the road constantly, selling, selling, selling, Elsa would basically be running the company. We'd collaborate on creative, coming up with innovative ways to present and promote the clients, but Elsa was clearly the media expert.

Much of our success can be attributed to her knowledge and creativity in media usage, her communication and credibility with clients, and her unwavering integrity. While we also did creative work, the far greater percentage of our revenue came from media buying, but she was also good at creative.

Basically, as the agency continued to grow, Elsa's importance eclipsed mine. She was the brain, and I was the brawn. At the time, we were more occupied doing the business we had than trying to get more of it, and I felt she should be recognized for her abilities and assume my title of President. Another great characteristic of Elsa's is that the word "ego" is not in her vocabulary. I had to work hard to sell her on the idea. Thus, she replaced me as President, and I assumed the less operational but far from honorary role of Co-Chairman. I morphed into servicing many of our out-of-town clients, especially my friends in Nashville, overseeing the creative area and working with Elsa on new concepts.

Most of the creative involved writing and producing television spots for our record label clients and, while it became my territory, it was not a highly "creative" challenge. The labels gave us videos of the songs being promoted, and from a copy standpoint, the less said the better because we didn't want to step on the music any more than necessary.

I likened it to buying a car. The copy was the salesman's patter and the music itself was the test drive. Which would you rather do? Listen to the salesman or drive the car?

But, despite the success, sometimes there were challenges of another sort that got our attention...all our attention. One night at home, Elsa and I were watching television when we decided to rent a movie on VOD (Video On Demand). We were refused. I called the cable company for an explanation and was informed we hadn't paid our bill. Since we felt television was a legitimate business expense, the company paid for it. The next day, we asked our Controller for a copy of both the Accounts Payable and Receivable, two reports Elsa and I previously, and wrongly, had little interest in. Hey, the company was kicking ass; who needs to stop to count the dough? Talk about a little rain on our parade? We found a tsunami.

Apparently, our Controller, a person who had been with us for several years and done a good job, had decided to take a sabbatical and spend it in the office. A huge amount of our payables were over ninety days past due, and from the receivables, it was obvious that we hadn't been billing for the media we'd been buying. So, we basically owed everybody, paid nobody, and had nothing coming in. Now there's a formula for long-term success. We were stunned. A healthy and ostensibly quite profitable company could go out of business because our rapid success and the work it entailed became too much for our Controller and her support staff. And, of course, she didn't think it important enough to share with us.

Our first move was to have a meeting with her, at which we gave her directions to the unemployment office where she would now be picking up her future checks. She had sensed we were on to the problem and brought her husband to the meeting. He was surly and abusive, and it looked like he and I would come to blows, to the point that someone in the office called the police. He, having no desire to share a cell with a stranger, left before they arrived. Another day at the office. But when they split, they left the problem behind.

Elsa and I literally spent the next few months of our lives trying to solve this grungy, depressing problem. She supervised getting the billing out and deciding whom to pay as the money dribbled in. I spent my entire days on the phone with our creditors. I was totally upfront with them, told them what had happened and what we were doing about it, and asked for their patience. We had a long history of being financially responsible clients and most understood. We finally got through it, collected the money, paid the bills, and were later told by our vendors that our candor, rather than giving them a bogus line of bullshit, was appreciated and probably the reason no legal actions were taken.

Not too long after that, another issue arose. The performance of one of our senior buyers, a guy who we had also put in charge of the independent labels, seemed to be flagging. This was most evident when he opted not to attend SXSW, the biggest, most important gathering of independent labels that takes place annually in Austin, Texas. It also seems that about that time, a new website was introduced called *Rate My Cop*, and who owned that site and was being interviewed on television at the same time SXSW was taking place? You guessed it. Our guy!

He immediately became free to create other websites, but not on our time. He chose to go into business as our competitor. He respected us so much, he decided to use a close derivative of our URL, *www.thegarygroup.com* as his own. What a coincidence! Our official, legal name is The Gary Group, but for computer simplification we chose to drop "the" in our company URL, *www.garygroup.com*. Quick, call the attorneys! We sued and won a cash settlement.

Despite the obstacles, business was good. We kept a low profile in the industry, but given our success, we felt it was time to share it with some who might need the benefits of that success, as in personal charitable contributions. We had been very happy with the education Amanda got at Middlebury, and when the college asked for scholarship support, we readily and willingly agreed to subsidize a four-year scholarship for a student, but with one stipulation. It had to be a Native American.

Business As Unusual

Middlebury was highly responsible in acceding to this request. They did a thorough search and came up with a qualified candidate, a young woman from an Alaskan Island. Her family was very poor, and we included some extra money in our donation so that she could go home a few times a year. The upshot was that she did well, and we were invited to her graduation. In fact, one of the department heads gave her a party the day before the main event, which we attended and got to meet her family. They were highly appreciative and gave us some native art in thanks.

After the ceremony, we drove through the exquisite Vermont countryside to Boston, the departure city for our flight back to Los Angeles. I was seated next to Elsa on an aisle. Shortly before takeoff, a lady led a blind gentleman up the aisle and they were seated across from us, with him also being on the aisle. A couple of hours after takeoff, I noticed the fellow, a young guy in his mid-late thirties, was getting restive. The lady had fallen asleep, so I asked him if he needed to go to the restroom, and he did. I led him to it, waited until he was done, and then escorted him back to his seat.

We got talking and finally got around to "What do you do?" I started explaining our advertising agency and the work we did for labels. He then said, "That sounds a lot like what The Gary Group does."

I told him, "We are very similar. In fact, I'm Dick Gary." It turned out he owned a small label, and they became clients on the spot. I was ecstatic, not so much about the new business, but that after years of laboring in obscurity, his comment acknowledged that we did indeed have visibility in the industry.

TWENTY-FIVE
The New Music Biz Izn't

They say nothing lasts forever. How I wish they were wrong!

The Gary Group had been sailing along, the clear choice of most major and some independent labels. Life was very good...until those rats Sean Parker and Sean Fanning showed up with Napster. Just kidding. They're not rats, more like visionaries who saw an opportunity that became the end of the music business as many of us knew it.

Napster, the free music downloading site burst onto the scene in a huge way. Now anyone, especially music's prime audience, the tech-savvy young people, could download their favorite music. Illegally, but free. The RIAA, a music industry organization composed primarily of major labels, was frothing at the mouth.

While all this was wending its way through the courts, a guy named Steve Jobs, yes that Steve Jobs, stepped in and made the music industry Costco instead of Nordstrom. His creation: iTunes. Its impact on the industry: devastating. He made it possible to download singles legally for ninety-nine cents a song. And with that, the world of music changed dramatically forever and, with it, so did our business.

Before iTunes, there were no singles for sale. If you liked the song, you had to buy the album. Labels wholesaled CDs for about nine dollars each. With iTunes, they got sixty-five to seventy cents per downloaded tune. People stopped buying albums in stores and stared buying only the hits online. Virtually all record stores closed. Tower Records now exists only as an answer in a trivia game.

Now, downloading has been eclipsed by streaming. When it started, for a songwriter to make any money, virtually everyone in the country would have to be streaming his or her song twenty-four seven. A good friend of mine, a successful songwriter, told me one of his songs had two million streams and he got a check for twelve dollars. Songwriters used to get about eleven cents for every song on every album sold. So, if a songwriter had one song (they usually had more) on an album that went gold (five hundred thousand copies), he or she would make $55,000 for each song on the album regardless of whether or not it was a single, $110,000 on a platinum album. It ain't what it used to be. All the talk in the industry soon became digital...and I didn't speak that language.

When I found music, I knew I had found a lasting industry, and I rode that pony from the vinyl LP to the 8-track, then to the cassette, and on to the CD. And then Jobs showed up. I know and understand as much about technology as I do about astrophysics and have about the same level of interest and curiosity. I was now a stranger in a strange land. In fact, at some meetings I attended, the interns were the most knowledgeable people in the room.

Even without that development, I think Elsa and I weren't enjoying the business nearly as much as we had before our company became successful. We wound up having to delegate the fun stuff so we could do the shit, like HR and accounting, for which I had conclusively proven in my abbreviated college career that I had no interest or aptitude. Today, I doubt if I could land a job at a label as an intern.

Nevertheless, it's not a helluva lot of fun to see the company you built with your sweat and blood shrinking. But, in our case, it was slow and not yet fatal. We were still growing as the business was dying, but that couldn't last forever. If we hoped to stay in business, we'd better get with the program.

Elsa and I had been delegating much of the business as we prepared for retirement. We also became more active in the T.J. Martell Foundation and, when we created *Artworks For The Cure,* we wound up spending virtually all our time on it.

Enter Rick Rogers. We met Rick when he was selling for *Time Magazine*, and we were working with Sunkyong/SKC, a Korean manufacturer of blank audio tape. We were trying to put a deal together with our client and *Time* for the 1988 Seoul Olympics. It never came to fruition, but we liked and respected Rick. One day, I was in New York for a meeting I had set up with the marketing person at Polygram Records. The receptionist told me he was not available, but that I would be meeting with someone else. That someone was Rick Rogers. It turned out he also had a music background. We bonded again and he became a valued client.

From there, Rick got into the digital business in a big way as VP/Marketing for Kabang, one of the early dot-com commercial entries. He hired us as his agency. In those days, dot-coms were falling faster than George Bush's ratings. I googled the meaning of Kabang and found it was a hero dog but, unfortunately, the dot-com version of that dog didn't hunt. After short spurts in which they blew their angel funding in advance of finding markets that didn't yet exist, Kabang ceased to exist.

We liked and respected Rick. He was smart, creative, hardworking, and honest. We hired him as President, and he put his Internet knowledge to work. He created an online division for the company that he ran quite successfully. He introduced some very popular and successful digital applications to our labels and that soon was another significant revenue stream for us, which was fortunate, as the whole freaking world was going digital, and what had been our primary source of revenue, CDs, was disappearing. I really wasn't a part of that new revolution. Nobody wanted to hear about my definition of Facebook being a podium for people with nothing to say. Yes, I know it's changed since then.

Rick's primary job: keep what there was of our music business and re-invent the agency to have a broader spectrum of clients. He made major inroads for a short time in a new business sector, boxing, and the MMA. So, I guess you could say we were still promoting the hits.

As I said in the beginning of the chapter, nothing lasts forever, and from the state of the industry and our shrinking revenues, it became obvious we were destined to be a part of that shrinkage. We weren't losing business; our clients simply stopped doing what we were doing for them. In December 2019, the doctor declared the patient dead. We'd had a forty-plus-year run. It had been challenging, exciting, and fun. Now we were ready for the next phase of our lives...retirement and freedom.

As you read on, you'll find we haven't yet reached that mecca.

TWENTY-SIX
Did Someone Mention Brooklyn?

Back before the undertaker, gaily festooned as a CPA, put the final lid on The Gary Group, Elsa and I had seen the writing on the wall and started thinking of retirement.

We had named Rick as president, and he was pretty much running the show. We were spending more time in Park City. Elsa had become a highly creative and proficient photographer, and I was slogging away at this book.

I loved Malibu when I moved there and I used it: running on the beach, riding the waves, surfing them in my Hobie cat and playing tennis. But unfortunately, sun is not the recommended cure for skin cancer, and I got it. I thought it was well deserved and honestly earned, but also, after six skin cancer operations, I thought maybe it was a good idea for the sun and I to part ways.

When I got there in 1975, Malibu was a quiet little town, but it always had a glamor reputation because it was on the ocean and probably the third home to some celebrated actors. Unfortunately, at least for me, Malibu had become what everybody always thought it was. The former lumberyard is now a row of fancy, upscale international boutiques and a lot of the store owners who provided residents with essentials have been driven out by rent increases. Some of the new restaurants should have bankers on the premises so you could apply for a second mortgage to pay for dinner. The way I describe it is if you want a pair of $400 jeans, you've got a great selection. If you want to get a haircut, good luck finding a parking space.

Did Someone Mention Brooklyn?

We wanted a lifestyle change. We loved Park City in the summer, winter, and early fall, but that left a few months to fill. We had been going to New York on business, perhaps a little more than necessary, because we liked it. I think real New Yorkers never quite get that needle out of their arms...or their minds.

One night in New York, as we were heading to meet Dylan for a movie in Greenwich Village, the air was pungent with the fragrant and disgusting aroma of cigarette smoke. I said to Elsa, "Can you imagine actually living here?" And we began to imagine actually living there. It probably has more theatre, film, and art than can be found in the rest of the country combined, and you can get to it all on subways. No need for a goddamn car.

Speaking of theatre, let me digress to share the story of Elsa's and my Broadway investments. As it turned out, investment was not a highly appropriate word. Since our cash flow was good and we had about as much interest in the stock market as we did in farming, we wanted to find something that interested us in which to put some minimal spare cash. Enter the fantastic world of Broadway show backing. We ultimately learned that the definition of major success in show investment is getting *some* of your money back, with exceptions. We saw and liked most of the shows we invested in. However, when considering the amount invested versus the return, you might say the ticket price was high.

One of our Broadway investments was a sure smash, *High Fidelity*. It was a successful book and an excellent, well-received film. On Broadway, it became a magic show...now you see it and now you don't. It closed after about ten performances.

Another show we really liked, in fact loved, but did not put us in a higher tax bracket was *In The Heights,* with book and music by Lin-Manuel Miranda. Name familiar? Right! He also did *Hamilton*. Fortunately, we avoided tax problems by staying away from that one, not that we were asked. Had we been, I expect we would have politely declined. Imagine someone asking you to invest in a hip hop version of Alexander

Hamilton's life! **NO**, would have been the polite answer, but the wrong one given its unparalleled success.

Meanwhile, here's another digression to the flow of the story. As I got older and some of my parts went out of warranty, I began to experience the thrilling adventures of aging, meaning fun things like colonoscopies. I also saw a urologist a couple times a year for a PSA test, considered a necessity for men above a certain age (so long ago I forget the age) because the prostate gland really is not man's best friend.

Prostate cancer is to men what breast cancer is to women, and the older a man gets, the more likely he is to get it. A doctor friend of mine said that in older men, the percentage having it was equal to their age. If that was so, it would be harder to get an appointment with a urologist than it would be to get Springsteen tickets on opening night.

In any event, there aren't symptoms, so there are probably a lot of men walking around who don't know they have it. In that case, ignorance IS bliss.

But I got it! The doctor said it was a very mild case and I would most likely die of old age. I said, "I'm already seventy-six (at that time). How much time do you think I have?" He looked at me and then he looked at his watch.

That's not true, but he and I did have one other non-medical exchange. The urologist knew I was in the music business. When Napster was flying high, he told me he felt there was nothing wrong with taking music, created by others as a means of making a living, and not paying for it. I reciprocated by telling him that was fine, and it would also be fair if I gave his name and number to the Grammy people and offered, on his behalf, that he would treat songwriters at no charge as a quid pro quo. He looked at me like perhaps I should change urologists, which I did. Back to the story line.

While we loved Park City in the winter and summer, there's no sense in being there in the spring when the snow is dirty and melting and the trails are muddy, or in late fall when it gets cold as a preview of the coming winter. There's nothing quite like freezing while breaking the ice to go kayaking. So how about New York for spring and fall, a total change and a way to vent our love of art, not to mention being close to Dylan?

We decided to look around and see if a New York move made sense. We didn't always do what made sense. This was a huge decision...to totally uproot our lives after almost forty years in Malibu, leave all our friends and the spectacular weather and try to build a whole new life, or a partial one with Park City still occupying the other part.

The stark reality was that we were priced out of Manhattan, at least to get more than a bench in the park in a bad neighborhood. But, if we moved to the city, we would want access to a park. It's very true that living in New York you do a lot of walking in your everyday activities, but it's also nice to see an occasional tree.

Dylan was, and is, the President of the Brooklyn Fan Club. He has lived there for several years, and he graciously showed us around. We knew Brooklyn was hot but hadn't really considered living there, probably a subconscious throwback to our recollection of when it was a mecca for gangbangers and deadbeats, and the primary form of entertainment was street fights. But, as we saw more of it, we really liked it because, while only a few subway stops away, Brooklyn was less dense and frantic than Manhattan. We began to seriously consider it. In a way I couldn't believe it; if anyone ever told me I might move to Brooklyn for culture, I would have recommended psychiatric care.

Dylan had bought a studio in a co-op building in the Prospect Heights section and we really liked the neighborhood. He was on Eastern Parkway, a broad avenue without bumper-to-bumper traffic. On one side is the Brooklyn Museum, a stately old building housing some very cool contemporary exhibits. Next to that is the Brooklyn Botanic Gardens, a beautiful place to stroll through with a colorful variety of constantly changing fauna and flora that I know absolutely nothing about but enjoyed seeing. Adjacent is Prospect Park, Brooklyn's answer to Central Park...and it's a great answer. A magnificent arch stands at the entrance to the park, reminiscent of Paris' Arc de Triomphe, but with a Brooklyn accent.

Down the street on Flatbush Avenue are BAM (the Brooklyn Academy of Music) and the Barclay Center. BAM has four screens that show independent and classic films. There is also a theatre for stage productions and another for music and dance. It's walkable.

We also found you could dine like a prince for the price of a pauper. For instance, we found a Thai restaurant where at lunchtime you get an appetizer and entrée for $6.75. Or if you're feeling wealthy and want to show off, hit the Italian place and get a salad and pasta entrée for eleven dollars. And both are really good. We recently dined at a Park City restaurant where we could get a bowl of spaghetti and meatballs for only thirty-eight dollars.

So, we spent a month renting a couple of places in the area via Airbnb and VRBO, excellent services despite municipalities across the globe hating them for the transient tax revenue they're losing. The purpose of our mission was to find out if we wanted to live there, and if so, where. It came down to yes, we do, and it should be in Prospect Heights.

We found a realtor who sent us to open houses. The market was tilted strongly in favor of the seller. It seemed the drill was that when a broker got a listing, they would quickly do a few open houses. Immediately after that, they would ask for a "last and best" offer from all interested parties. It was like a bidding war with many properties selling over their asking prices. And, if you were serious, a cash offer was expected.

We soon learned our perception of Brooklyn was mistaken. It was EXPENSIVE! As we knew, New York apartments are much smaller than California houses, but acceptable to the owners or tenants because there is so much to do that people don't spend as much time at home. Despite the prices, we were still convinced we wanted a place there.

In October, we returned to New York for three weeks during which we intended to learn all we needed to know about the market and, hopefully, find a place. The plan was then to return to Malibu, remodel our twenty-five-year-old kitchen, a bathroom, and everything else that showed the difficulties of living with us for a quarter century. Then we would put the house on the market, sell it, and return to Brooklyn with money in our pockets to make the deal of the year. Sound good?

Well, a couple of days before we left, we got an email from the Brooklyn real estate agent saying there was a place we should see. It was an old building, and she knew we wanted contemporary, but this three-bedroom co-op had been renovated in a contemporary style and it was exactly where we wanted to be. To be sure! It was at 135 Eastern Parkway and Dylan was at 55 Eastern Parkway. The building itself is called Turner Towers, and it is directly across the street from the Brooklyn Museum. It was built around 1925 and has 190 units on sixteen floors. Someone recently told us that it was the tallest building in Brooklyn at that time and was built by New York Jews who were finding the same level of acceptance that Black people enjoyed almost wherever they went if it wasn't a ghetto.

We decided to go to the open house. When we arrived, we entered the lobby, and it was huge, beautiful by many standards with marble floors and other handsome accouterments, but not really our style because, again, we favor the clean, simple, minimal lines of contemporary design. But we were there so what the hell. We headed for 3A.

When we got off the elevator, we almost left. The walls, maybe in the style of the day, looked like they had cement thrown at them and then were painted a dull, nondescript beige. Oh well, the door to the apartment was open and we went in. In the setting of the building, 3A was like the errant child of a dull, conservative family. It was bright and open. The renovation had been done with exquisite taste, at least for us. Walls had been knocked down and the appliances were all top-of-the-line and stainless steel. It was a front apartment, so rather than looking out the windows in the living room and master bedroom and seeing a wall of bricks across the street, we saw only the Brooklyn Museum and the Botanic Gardens. Additionally, there was a subway stop immediately in front of the building (a big deal in New York unless your uncle owns Uber and you've got the time to sit in traffic).

Despite ourselves, we really liked the place and felt it could work well for us. But we weren't there to buy...were we? Nevertheless, we went back to another open house to look at the place again a few days later...and twice more after that. By then, we had seen a bunch of places, and this one topped them all.

We were in a quandary. We were afraid we might not find another place we liked as much, but we didn't think we were ready to buy, at least not yet. We still had to do the renovations to the Malibu house, put it on the market, and sell it before we'd have the money to buy anything. The whole process could take six to eight months...or more.

You know the old saying that figures don't lie but liars figure...and that's what we started to do. Fortunately, we owned the Malibu house outright after twenty-five years of mortgage payments, and the value of the house exceeded the cost of the apartment. We intended to buy whatever we finally settled on with the cash from the sale of our house, so this seemed premature. If we bought this place then, we'd still have to pay for the renovations on the Malibu house, and then get an equity loan and pay that until the house was sold and the escrow closed. Not too smart financially, but...what the hell. We weren't going to live forever, so we made an offer...and it was ACCEPTED. Was that the good news or, possibly, the bad? We didn't care.

But then Lady Luck gave us a big shit-eating grin. As I mentioned earlier (I hope), our Malibu house was directly across the street from Pepperdine University. A friend of ours, Dennis Torres, was Pepperdine's Vice President for real estate, in charge of their many holdings in that area. Before we left for Brooklyn, he and I were having breakfast together, and I told him what we were doing. He said that at one time, Pepperdine had been interested in acquiring some of the homes contiguous to the University. He said he'd check with the President, and I thought nothing more of it.

So, a couple of days after our offer was accepted, as we were contemplating our sanity or lack of it, we were having lunch with Dylan when my phone rang. It was our friend. He said, "I talked with Andy (the President) and we want to buy it."

My first question was, "Are you a bottom feeder?" He laughed and said we would be very satisfied with whatever deal we worked out. And he was a man of his word.

When we got back to Malibu, we spoke with a couple of realtors and got a clear estimate of the house's value. We made a deal with Pepperdine that was very fair for both parties. Nobody got rich; nobody got screwed. And the best part was that it closed quickly. They bought it "as is" and we didn't have to do any renovations; we didn't have to take out the home equity loan; we had the money to close the Brooklyn sale, plus, since it was a direct sale, there was no real estate agent commission to pay.

When we told our friends, the initial reaction was, "You're moving from Malibu to Brooklyn? You're trading the Pacific Ocean for the Gowanus Canal, the filthiest body of water in the fifty states? What were you thinking?" Our response, "We WERE thinking!"

When buying a co-op, you are really only purchasing shares in the building rather than the actual apartment you would occupy. So, the other owners are interested in meeting all newcomers and rolling out their blackballs when they see someone they feel could create a nuisance. In fact, many luxury co-ops in Manhattan want no part of celebrities, but that certainly would not be a problem with us. A meeting was arranged for us with the Board of Directors.

We were briefed on the meeting by the seller's real estate agent. He said WE WERE NOT to ask any questions of the Board and he actually presented us with a written Code of Conduct, clearly describing our dos and don'ts at the meeting. This pissed us off. We didn't just have a chip on our shoulders, it was more like a redwood tree.

Included was the necessity for six letters of recommendation from business associates and friends. I was going to submit one extolling our virtues as pillars of the community, humanitarians, and activists, then sign it with a fictitious name and insert the title "Parole Officer" under it. Elsa talked me out of it.

Nevertheless, we wanted to find out who our prospective neighbors might be, so we showed up early for the meeting and sat in the lobby observing the interaction between the residents, the doorman, etc. If it looked like a convocation of the very privileged, we would try to piss the Board off to the extent we failed the interview; they blackballed us; and we got our money back. That was not the case. There seemed to be genuine good rapport and respect on both sides. And there was also diversity on the Board, which pleased us.

They seemed friendly and helpful. They asked what had drawn us to the neighborhood and the building. We answered and they asked if we had any questions. You just can't let that pass by, so I said, "We're not allowed to ask any questions." They looked at us like we had just said the earth is oblong. "What are you talking about?" asked the President. So, we told him in a humorous way, and they all got a kick out of it and emphasized they'd be happy to answer any questions we had. We really didn't have any.

Then they asked if we were familiar with the plumbing "issue." We weren't. It seems that in buildings of that vintage, shit happens, and Turner Towers was no exception. In that building's case, shit was an accurate description. There was an $11 million plumbing repair job in process, and we could count on numerous water service disruptions for a prolonged period.

So, the reason for the Code of Conduct seemed clear. Caveat emptor, buyer beware. And we were now very aware, so the next day, after some conversations about remediation with the agents, we were able to get a slightly reduced price. We also then heard that, in a massive case of poor judgment, the Board had approved us. We were in!

We headed back to Malibu for the highly rewarding task of packing. We had only been in the house for twenty-five years and how much junk can you really collect in that time? Boring work and equally boring to write about. I'm only spending so much time on this because it's so fresh in my mind, and at my age, when something is fresh, you water it.

Back in Malibu, we had also fallen in love with the work of a Santa Fe sculptor, Frederick Prescott. Frederick likes big things, very big things, and gracing our front yard were four life-sized, metal, powder-coated animal sculptures: a mother giraffe with baby, a tiger, and a baby elephant. In back, by the pool, was an alligator. They each weighed about one thousand pounds and we were pretty sure they wouldn't find a home in the Brooklyn jungle. But they did find a home at the Exceptional Children's Foundation, a very worthwhile organization that works with kids who have challenges.

So we became official residents of Utah where the tax rate is less than half of New York and California's. The downside is the political climate but you're about to read how we intend to change all that.

The combo of city and country seems like a good one for us. People with places in Park City say that you come for the winter and stay for the summer. While considered predominately a ski area, there's a helluva lot of fun outdoor activities in summer. Plus, there are ten movie screens (versus two in Malibu), the Sundance Film Festival, a legitimate theatre, a Performing Arts Center, a band shell at the Deer Valley ski area where lots of name acts perform during the summer, and more. But it ain't New York!

This bears no relationship to the above, but before I end this confessional, I must share with you two of the biggest and most sensational surprises that I have ever had, both on birthdays, and both compliments of Elsa.

For my fiftieth, we planned to have dinner with Stan Moress in Santa Monica. At the time, he owned a small limo company (one car) and, as a gift, had the driver pick us up. As we got into Santa Monica, the driver stopped at the Santa Monica Bowl, a bowling alley (or lanes per the terminology introduced by AMF to rid the sport of the unsavory connotation that "alleys" gave). There were klieg lights in front lighting up the sky. You usually only saw these things at major events and I, being slightly unconscious and not knowing why we were stopping, said, "Wow, some-body's got a big deal going on here."

"Yes, it's you. Happy Birthday, Dick." This was from Elsa, who had organized a big party for all my friends, including VIP guests Dylan and Amanda. She sent the invitations out on a cassette (the operative recording device at the time) and my favorite announcer, the late Ernie Anderson, had recorded it for free. It was a total surprise, and we had a great night.

For my seventy-fifth, Elsa decided to play "*Can You Top This*." We were in Miami for Art Basel, and I anticipated a nice, quiet dinner for the two of us. After seventy-four prior birthdays, the expectations were low. Elsa made dinner reservations at a nice restaurant in South Beach, near where we were staying. We got to the place and gave our name to the Maître D, who led us to the patio. We walked past several empty tables for two until there were no more. We seemed headed for a table of four where there were already two people sitting with their backs to us. I was confused until the two occupants of the table turned around and it was Dylan and Amanda, both in from Buenos Aires. I was so surprised I literally could not speak, something Dylan rather enjoyed and a first for me. There's no describing the joy I felt. We hadn't seen either of them for months, and to preserve the element of surprise, Elsa booked them at a different hotel from us so there couldn't be an accidental encounter. So, if you're looking to create a genuine, innovative, creative, and memorable surprise for someone you love, give Elsa a call.

TWENTY-SEVEN
The Last Hurrah(S)

Politically, I had pretty much been sitting on the bench since my Ed Koch days, simply a spectator. That lasted until our nation became blessed with George Bush in 2000 and the follies began with the stupidest and most costly war in terms of life and money, Iraq. However, George apparently viewed it through a different lens. I felt that after his MISSION ACCOMPLISHED speech, he forgot the rest of it, which was, "I've fucked up the entire Mideast for decades to come."

In the 2004 national elections, we did wake up. As maniacally progressive Democrats, Elsa and I were very anxious to see George Bush come in a distant second, but it was not to be. We had given sporadically to John Kerry but, to our thinking, not a lot of dough. However, it seemed that the Democrats keep better track of their donors than the reigning lords of the crap tables in Vegas. When the time came for the 2006 mid-term election, Elsa got a call from Blanche Lincoln, then the Democratic Senator from Nebraska, on behalf of the DSCC, the Democratic Senatorial Campaign Committee, looking for a donation. Unfortunately for Blanche, there was an earthquake during the call and Elsa had to get off the line.

Chuck Schumer had better luck with his call to me. Unfortunately, there was no earthquake, but Elsa was in my office when the call came in and we silently agreed to what we felt was a substantial contribution, the biggest we'd ever made. In our opinion, the Senator had been generously rewarded for his call. He apparently agreed and, as a gesture of thanks, invited us to a small luncheon with him and Dick Durbin that

Saturday at Shutters, a cool hotel on the sand in Santa Monica. It was free but Elsa had a good line, "It doesn't cost anything to get in, but it could be expensive to leave."

At the luncheon, Chuck and Dick, note my instant familiarity, explained their strategy for the upcoming Senatorial elections. Fight only the fights you can win. They listed Tennessee as a key state for a possible Democratic win.

As soon as the lunch and their speeches were over, Elsa and I approached them and explained that, while we were nobody in Los Angeles, we knew a lot of somebodies in Tennessee, particularly in the music business in Nashville. That hit a high note and we were off on another adventure that more than made up for my boredom at The Gary Group.

Harold Ford Jr. was then a sitting Congressman in Memphis and the Democratic candidate for the Senate from Tennessee. If he won, Harold would be the first African American from the South elected to the Senate since Reconstruction (I don't know what that is, but it was a long time ago). We began communicating with his staff in Nashville and his fundraising people in LA. We had never met Harold, but we were invited to a fundraiser for him in LA, hosted by his Finance Committee Chairman, Lindsay Gardner, at his place of employment, Fox Studios. Yes, I said that. Fox Studios was the site of a fundraiser for a Democratic candidate. I was afraid to eat anything.

Immediately before he went up to speak, we were introduced to Harold and spent a couple of very brief moments talking with him. He then opened his speech with, "Thanks for coming, everybody. As you know, I'm from Tennessee and many of you may not be as familiar with the politics in Tennessee as are my good friends, Elsa and Dick Gary." Thankfully, we were not tested.

We hooked Harold up with some key people, like our friend and fellow Democrat, Frances Preston, and we ultimately arranged for a fundraiser to be held at the home of Luke Lewis, then the CEO of Universal Records in Nashville. We had a terrific turnout; virtually every major label head and lots more influential people in the industry were in attendance. Of course, being a Democratic soiree, there were virtually no artists there, Republican being the favored brand of country acts. The Republicans seem to be better at keeping those necks red.

We later attended another fundraiser for Harold at the home of billionaire entrepreneur and philanthropist Haim Saban in Beverly Hills. Al Gore was a featured speaker. Those opportunities tend to come up when you're the former Vice President. We got to talk with him before the event started and that was cool. We didn't get to speak with Harold before his talk, but we approached him after to say hello and he said, "Oh man, I didn't know you were here, or I would have called you out." Fame can be bought.

One of Harold's most active LA volunteers was Nicole Avant, the daughter of legendary music industry entrepreneur, Clarence Avant, who is known as Godfather to innumerable urban music artists. Clarence was also on the Clintons' speed dial. Unfortunately, and partly because of an absolutely disgusting, scurrilous, and racist commercial on behalf of Harold's Republican opponent, Bob Corker, he lost the election by a few points. He took the defeat gracefully.

I didn't know Clarence at the time, but I was aware of his standing in the music community. The CEO of T.J. Martell wanted me to meet him, so he set up a lunch.

When he introduced us, Clarence said, "I'm glad to meet you."

I replied, "We've met before."

"Really? Where?"

"At your house," I smilingly answered. After the election, in a very classy move, Clarence and Nicole had hosted a party for Harold's supporters even though he lost, and Elsa and I were there. Clarence and I became friends and there are very few people I enjoyed spending time with more. He passed in 2023 and I miss him.

Those fundraisers had an unexpected positive and indirect benefit for me. When an event was over and we were waiting for our car at the valet stand with our environmentally concerned fellow Dems, they'd bring our car around and it was a gas guzzling Ford Explorer. I think Elsa and I, both committed environmentalists, were a little embarrassed to be hopping into our planet polluter. So, for my seventieth birthday, Elsa said, "Get in the car. I'm going to drive you to your present." I had absolutely no idea what she was talking about, but we left Malibu and drove over the canyon into the San Fernando Valley and headed north. I couldn't figure where the hell we were going...until we pulled into the Toyota dealership in Thousand Oaks and I soon drove out in my ecologically correct new Toyota Prius, a car that I loved and kept for almost ten years. I guess you could say those fundraisers were very expensive in slightly unrelated ways...but well worth it.

In 2007, we shifted from the Senatorial to Presidential races. We had both fully embraced Obama from the start. I liked Hillary but thought she might be too divisive.

Rufus Gifford, whom we had gotten to know when he was working for the Harold Ford Jr. campaign, was now in charge of Obama's LA fundraising. Rufus contacted us and we attended the first big Los Angeles event held for Obama. It was hosted by David Geffen, Stephen Spielberg, and Jeffrey Katzenberg at the Beverly Hilton Hotel. Our friend and client, Steve McKeever, a native Chicagoan and friend of the Obamas, briefly introduced us to the future president before he took the stage. Barack's speech was OK. They had dragged his ass all over LA that day and he was exhausted. However, Michelle stole the show with her talk. It was strong, self-deprecating, and humorous. She humanized Barack. We were hooked.

The following night, we were in Park City attending a fundraiser for the Park City Performing Arts Foundation, of which we were Board members. Park City is a blue town in what has been a scarlet red state for a half century. Elsa wondered if it might make sense to do something there for Barack. If you are a Democrat in Utah, voting is considered by many to be a waste of time. The state had an extremely low national rating for voter turnout. The one way in which your donations might have any impact is at the Presidential level.

The Last Hurrah(S)

We spoke with the Executive Director of the foundation and some other key folks and got resounding support for the idea of a Park City fundraiser. I brought it to Rufus. He expressed great interest and took it to the national people.

They also had interest from Mark Gilbert, who worked for an investment house and had a second home in Park City. He was also on Obama's National Finance Committee and had also approached the national headquarters with the same idea of a Park City fundraiser. We got in touch with each other, decided to work together, and got a commitment from Barack to attend. Elsa and I managed to secure a venue for the event, the home of John and Kristi Cumming, then the owners of the major local ski area, Park City Mountain Resort. It was a magnificent home and they put an enormous tent up in back where guests would gather and Barack would speak.

It was a beautiful August day and we had a terrific turnout. Elsa and I were extremely pleased that we could make a tangible contribution to Obama's Presidential campaign. Plus, we got to spend a few minutes alone with him. We're not so blasé as to not be proud to have supported, met, and talked with the future President of the United States; although, that outcome was not assured, as he had not yet gotten the nomination.

There were a couple of interesting side notes to the occasion. We had met the McKeevers, Steve and Candace, an African American couple, when they worked at Motown Records, a Gary Group client. Steve had also worked for Harold Ford Jr. His sister played tennis regularly with Michelle, and their kids were buddies. Steve and Candace both received degrees from Harvard as, of course, did Barack and Michelle. Candace is Julian Bond's niece and, thus, they were both very invested in politics and Obama's campaign, so we invited them up for the weekend and told them that we had extra room if they knew anyone else who might enjoy (and donate to) the experience. Their friend, Donald Walton, another African American Harvard graduate, came and brought his seven-year-old daughter, Sarah.

We were all in a room in the Cumming's house awaiting Barack's arrival when the first guy in his entourage, an African American named Bryan, arrived. Steve, Candace, and Donald all knew him.

I asked where they all met and Steve said, "Harvard."

I commented, "Wow! I didn't know Harvard was a Black school." That got a laugh.

After the Harold Ford, Jr. campaign, Nicole then transferred her considerable energies from Harold to Barack Obama and, after his victory, she was named Ambassador to the Bahamas, the first African American ever to represent the United States in that area.

Another instance of political namedropping was with Bill Clinton. Elsa and I were at Stanford for our niece Stephanie's graduation. She was in the same class as Chelsea and shared the same major. After Carly Fiorina, then CEO of Hewlett-Packard, gave the commencement address, there was a separate ceremony for each major at the university.

Bill and Hillary arrived for Chelsea's, and as they took their seats, they graciously shook every hand that got in the way of their sitting down, including Elsa's and mine. Stephanie, a very bright student, had won an award, and when her name was called, she went up and received her honor.

Later, when the ceremony had concluded and nature called, Stephanie was walking across the lawn to the restroom as Bill was returning from it. He saw her and commented, "Congratulations, STEPHANIE. Good work!" It seems the one area in which all politicians excel is name recall. No, he didn't ask for her number.

As long as I'm bragging about my political "connections," I met a future President and a Vice President at a charity fundraiser, the Senators' Ski Cup, held at the Park City Mountain Ski Area and benefitting the Primary Children's Medical Center in Salt Lake City. We had gotten BMI involved, as the event drew fifteen to twenty Senators. It was a great lobbying opportunity for them, and they brought major talent to perform. The event featured competitive slalom races with each team having a Senator as its captain. I was on Joe Biden's team and got to sit with him at the closing dinner.

The second instance concerned the then current Vice President, Dan Quayle. At the finish line of the racecourse, a huge tent was set up mid-mountain to serve lunch and keep everyone lubricated during what were not Olympic-caliber races. One afternoon, I felt the call of nature and was relieving myself in one of the port-a-johns whose lock was not functioning when the door opened, and there, face to face with me, was the Vice President of the United States. I wouldn't say we became close friends, but it certainly was up close and personal.

The eight years of Obama's presidency had brought about some real progress. He saved the nation from financial ruin and re-energized the stock market; he dramatically reduced unemployment; his Affordable Care Act, that I refer to as "Obamacares," gave over twenty million people health care; he appointed women to the Supreme Court; and scored many other less publicized victories despite the stone wall erected by Republicans.

Moving to Park City was a political revelation for us. After basking in Democratic regions our entire lives, we were now prisoners in a Republican stronghold. We both still had the political needle in our arm. The Supreme Court's Citizens United decision was proving a disaster. With the tsunami of money it created, billions of dollars, flooding in from those with vested interests and the wherewithal to protect, preserve, and perpetuate them, our elections were becoming auctions with the highest donors winning. After all, too much is never enough for the advantaged. But if something wasn't done, they'd have it their way and the rest of us would pay for it in one way or another.

We were also concerned—horrified being a better word—about the results of a 2008 study that showed only thirty-six percent of those surveyed could identify which party controlled the House and the Senate. So, apparently two-thirds of Americans didn't know shit about what was happening in or to their country.

By now, you must have a clear idea of Elsa and my politics. So, armed with good intentions and little else, we decided to stop bitching and try to do something about it. But what? We figured that if most of the existing potential voters knew so little about what was going on, and apparently cared less, we'd better get some new prospects into the voting booths.

A little research clearly showed that the most under-represented demographic at the polls were the eighteen-to-twenty-nine-year-olds, a group larger than the baby boomers, but one that is Missing In Action (inaction could be one word in this case) on Election Day. They have, by far, the worst registration and voting records of any age group. Case in point, in the 2014 mid-terms, only 8.9% of Utah's 18-29 year olds voted. Why? They are cynical, disgusted, distrustful of our government, have grown to hate politics, and they feel their vote doesn't count.

Yet, this was also a group whose lives would be dramatically impacted by future legislation on issues vital to them...the environment, women's rights, jobs and wages, education, student loans, LGBTQ, and more. They have a lot of skin in the game, and it was time they stepped up and made their voices heard. But, to do that, they must first be registered, so that's what we decided to do. We also felt that our music marketing experience with this demographic would be an asset.

Meanwhile, the Republican party was hard at work selecting a nominee to run our country...into the ground...for the next four years. There seemed to be agreement among the cast of characters running that their first priority would be to repeal Obamacare (or Obamacares as I prefer) and strip over twenty million Americans of their healthcare, causing thousands to die before their time. With that done, they could get on with reversing Roe v. Wade, shutting down Planned Parenthood, shredding the rights of women to make decisions for their own bodies, and gutting Social Security. Sound familiar?

Global warming, of course, was not an issue, as most Republicans knew it was simply a hoax. And they did not waste their time discussing education where the United States falls somewhere behind Somalia in the ratings. Or minimum wages, so that our fellow citizens might actually be able to support a family. Or the college loans that seem to allow our bright young men and women to graduate with a diploma that's like a future bankruptcy statement. Or the current issue that has the United States leading the world, gun violence.

So, to correct these potential disasters, Elsa and I created a nonprofit, nonpartisan 501(C)(3) called *No Vote IS A Vote,* the idea being that when you don't vote, you're giving your vote and your voice to someone who does vote and who might have a far different agenda from yours. We later changed it to *Voterise* because some felt the original name could be interpreted as "don't vote." Our mission was to get eighteen-to-twenty-nine-year-olds to register and vote. Research showed that when millennials registered, they also voted, and did so predominantly for progressive, rather than conservative, candidates, and they continue to vote for the rest of their lives. We also added underrepresented groups to our mission, primarily Hispanics, LGBTQ, etc. African Americans comprise only about one percent of Utah's population and they are spread wide, so there is no effective way to reach them. We chose Utah as our battleground.

UTAH??? I know! Your first question is, "Are you shitting me? That place is redder than a matador's cape." That is the national perception, but upon closer examination, there is an interesting dynamic happening in Utah that is little known outside the state.

It is true that on a national basis, Utah is a very red state, but Salt Lake City and County have voted Democratic for decades. In fact, Salt Lake City, on a per-capita basis, has the second largest gay population of any city in the country and, at that time, had elected a lesbian for Mayor. That ain't conservative! It has also become a tech hub that attracts a great number of new businesses to the area and has made Utah the second or third fastest growing state in the nation as well as the youngest. It figures. There is a very favorable business climate; living is cheaper than in many other states; and, with its mountains, deserts, and national parks, it is arguably the most varied and most beautiful state in the country. Outside Salt Lake County, in the rural areas, the Mormon religion predominates and historically breeds more conservative thinkers. However, there is evidence that the younger Mormons do not necessarily have such conservative views as do their elders.

The major obstacle to success was the Utah Legislature and its impressive skills at totally turning a deaf ear to the people's desires and gerrymandering to an absurd degree.

In fact, Utah has four representatives in the U.S. House and there is one intersection in Salt Lake City that is now represented by four different congressmen, thus muzzling any non-conservative voice the city might have. Case in point! In the 2020 election, we informed the Democratic candidate, Ben McAdams, that we had registered four thousand residents in his district. "That's the difference," he responded. He won by 684 votes. In the 2022 election, after the gerrymandering, he was soundly defeated. I considered doing a fundraiser and, with the proceeds, buying hearing aids for the Legislature.

Voterise launched in mid-July 2016 with a multi-faceted program, registering young men and women at schools, concerts, other events, and businesses, as well as creating affiliations with other nonprofits for whom we provided fast and easy registration tools.

In 2018, Elsa and I became State Democratic delegates...after a bitter and divisive campaign that was totally comprised of our showing up at the Democratic convention and being asked if we'd agree to be delegates.

In 2018, *Voterise* accounted for thirty percent of new Utah registrations. In 2019, we introduced a resolution, created by that Elsa, into the Legislature, proclaiming February 14th annually as Utah Women's Voter Registration Day. It miraculously passed unanimously in both the House and the Senate, making it the first day of its kind in the nation. The year 2020 was the centennial anniversary of women getting the right to vote, and we created the 2020 CHALLENGE, a massive promotion where we enlisted over eight hundred female Ambassadors, each agreeing to register twenty women.

The Last Hurrah(S)

In 2022, to raise some much-needed funds, we searched through our old bag of tricks and came up with an oldie but goodie, a charity art show, Art Works 4 Action, a three-day art extravaganza held at the Utah Film Studios, courtesy of the kind and generous owners, the Crandalls. It was highly praised, financially successful, and totally exhausting for Elsa and me.

Later in 2022, having completely and successfully embedded the "tired" into "retired," we folded *Voterise* into the Utah League of Women Voters, a highly respected organization with virtually the same mission as ours, but with greater resources and reach. Overall, we had registered over thirty thousand Utahns.

Voterise was a great experience that heavily involved us in Utah politics and allowed us to meet some highly interesting people, many of whom have become friends. Elsa claims the original *Voterise* idea was mine, but she was the source of virtually all the ideas that brought success. I was fortunate in developing a brand-new skill...licking stamps.

Subsequent to that, to prove to any doubters that we are truly slow learners, we repeated the experience in 2023 with another successful art show, this one to benefit the Intermountain Primary Children's Hospital, an amazing institution that treats about ten thousand kids a year regardless of financial capability. This one felt very good personally and was highly appreciated by the hospital.

Finally, we are now working on a Neuroburro Project. It started with our daughter Amanda, who fell in love with donkeys while working in Ireland, subsequently had neurosurgery and, while in recuperation, took up knitting with donkeys as the subject. She wanted them donated to sick kids in hospitals. We introduced them at the art show above. For a fifty-dollar donation, a neuroburro is given to a child in treatment in the hospital. They were a smash and we are continuing the project.

TWENTY-EIGHT
Good News! I'm Done.

I'm out of stories and I'm out of paper. As I re-read this, I realized what a fortunate life I've had, but as I said previously, nothing lasts forever, so I want to end this while I'm still breathing. Thanks for hanging in. I'm grateful for your time.

I want to leave you with some words from *THE PILGRIM,* a great Kris Kristofferson song.

> *"From the rockin' of the cradle to the rollin' of the hearse*
> *The goin' up was worth the comin' down."*

Please close the casket...I mean the book.

About the Author

As you may tell from the title, this book is not by the book, but it has a definite arc. Dick, our hero, had given little thought to his future and it shows. The book opens with him getting kicked out of college, having a rollicking two-year career in the military in Germany, finding a future in radio, operating a car and motorcycle racetrack, working closely with Ed Koch in his successful run for congress, moving to LA and starting a business with his wife Elsa, that became the premier ad agency for the music business.

He also has an interest in politics and art and has raised a bunch of money in those fields for good causes.

He moved from New York to Malibu and now lives in Park City where he can satisfy his skiing mania.

His has been an interesting, highly diversified life and he tells the story in a highly humorous and self-deprecating way.